Praise for *Rooted, Resilient,*

"As a mom of three children quickly beco.
to prepare them for the inevitable changes and pressures they will face as they grow up. Lindsay's book is not only perfect timing but refreshingly positive."

TAMARA TAGGART former CTV News broadcaster

"While not shying away from even the trickiest of subjects, Lindsay's knowledge, caring, and passion comes through on every page. Drawing from experts, personal vignettes, and Lindsay's wealth of experience, *Rooted, Resilient, and Ready* offers practical, thoughtful advice. A must-read for every parent, teacher, coach, and therapist who has the privilege of helping girls navigate into adulthood."

DR. AARON LAUTZENHISER R. Psych.

"Lindsay shows parents how to understand their teens and guide them to a positive self-image where they truly believe they can be anything."

ALLISON CEPLER co-founder and president of Girl Expo Canada

"A wonderful and empowering work, essential not only for mothers, but also for grandmothers, aunts, teachers, and mentors of young women. Filled with beautiful imagery as well as case studies threaded throughout, this book teaches us how to instill teenage girls with roots for becoming resilient in an ever-changing, often quaking, society."

KATE BARRETT, MD

"I know how important it is for myself and girls to be strong and know their worth. This book is a perfect guide for girls, young women, and parents to learn the tools of self-confidence and empowerment. I know I'll use it as I become stronger and continue to grow."

SPENCER LITZINGER host of YTV's "The Zone"

"Lindsay's heart for girls shines through in this book, as does her desire to spur girls on as they are 'becoming.' She encourages parents to cultivate connections with their daughter in new and creative ways, taking on the role of observer, listener, and 'eternal learner.' It is a wonderful resource for parents and adults who are longing for the girls in their lives to be rooted, resilient, and ready for all that awaits them now and in the future!"

LAURA D'ANGELO author of *A Month of Mindful Moments*

"In *Rooted, Resilient, and Ready* Lindsay inspires with terrific anecdotes and suggestions to help our daughters feel grounded in a fast-changing world. Affirming yet challenging, this book is an important resource for anyone who wants to see our daughters and students grow into strong, successful, and happy young women."

JASON BORKOWSKI elementary school principal and father of four daughters

"This book is full of insight and advice that can actually be put to use! As a parent of a teenage daughter myself, I found this book to be instrumental in empowering me to be a better mother!"

DELIA PERRY creator and host of the podcast *Girls 4 Greatness*

"Lindsay's practical tips on how to better communicate to teenage daughters to support them during these challenging years assure me that I can take this on!"

DR. ADRIENNE CHAN, DR. TCM

"A moving, powerful book about all the issues that our young women face. This brilliant book is a wonderful guide and support for professionals, families, and young girls navigating this crazy world."

JEN EAYRS youth and family worker, TAP (Tupper Alternative Program)

"As a healthcare practitioner working with teens, *Rooted, Resilient, and Ready* is now the 'textbook' I refer to. It serves me as a guide for talking to and connecting to teens, especially in today's world."

DR. ERIN TEWINKEL, ND

"Lindsay's insights shine an empowering light on young girls and parenting. I truly wish *Rooted, Resilient, and Ready* was published when I was a young girl."

ROBYN LIECHTI author of *The Making of a Grateful Heart*

"As a mom who wants to raise her daughter with a strong sense of self, *Rooted, Resilient, and Ready* has given me the tools to step into these teenage years alongside my daughter with confidence."

SUSAN ELSTOB mom and founder of islapearl.com

"Lindsay Sealey shows her mastery of emotional intelligence and deep experience working with girls and parents in this work of great importance. *Rooted, Resilient, and Ready* is heartfelt, devastatingly honest, reassuringly hopeful, and an essential tool for every mom and dad."

PETER SALVADOR Director of Education & Events, Factors Group of Nutritional Companies Inc.

ROOTED, RESILIENT, AND READY

Empowering Teen Girls
as They Grow

LINDSAY SEALEY, MA ED

FOREWORD BY SHELBY ROWLAND,
founder and head coach of *gracie's gals*

A LifeTree Media Book

To Kelvin
Adventuring through life with you,
step by step, is a profound privilege.

20 21 22 23 24   5 4 3 2 1

Cataloguing data available from Library and
Archives Canada

ISBN 978-1-928055-44-0 (paperback)
ISBN 978-1-928055-45-7 (EPUB)
ISBN 978-1-928055-46-4 (PDF)

For bulk orders, email info@boldnewgirls.com

For speaking inquiries and bookings, and community col-
laborations, email info@boldnewgirls.com

Cover and interior design: Setareh Ashrafologhalai
Author photo: Lindsay Faber
Front cover photograph: iStock.com/martin-dm
Back cover photograph: Shutterstock.com/Waseef Akhtar
Girls' photos taken by Lexa Bergen with the exception
of Emily's photo (Amanda Chan) and Misha's photo
(Edward Chang)

Published by LifeTree Media Ltd.
LifeTreeMedia.com

Distributed in the U.S. by Publishers Group West
and in Canada by Publishers Group Canada

Printed and bound in Canada

CONTENTS

FOREWORD

ONE SATURDAY AFTERNOON I went to my neighbourhood bookstore to purchase additional copies of Lindsay Sealey's *Growing Strong Girls*. After reading my copy in just a day, I knew two things: I loved it and I had to share it with the other parents I know. Suddenly a thought popped into my mind: I should send Lindsay a message and see if she would sign a copy for me. Standing in the middle of the bookstore—a stack of books under my arm, chai latte in one hand, and my phone in the other—I messaged her via Instagram. She answered right away, and said yes.

It was in this moment, and then over the course of the years to come, that I learned about Lindsay's character. She says "yes" a lot—to making time for people, to listening and offering ideas and insights, and to investing her time in growing strong girls and strong parents.

In my work with *gracie's gals*, I hear again and again that girls are anxious and worried about becoming teenagers. "Why do I feel this way?" they ask themselves. "What's wrong with me?" They tell me, "I should feel that way instead. I am not enough. I will never be enough. I can't keep up. I don't fit in." Girls are sometimes feeling lost, and as their self-belief dwindles, so too does their security. At *gracie's gals*, we focus on building girls up. We show them that they can turn their perceived weaknesses into triumphs, and teach them to view their experiences as successes and strengths, no matter what. We support them on their way to finding that everything they need is already within them and there's nothing wrong with who they are. However, many young girls feel overwhelmed by the need to "keep up." As adults, many of us struggle with the same feelings of not being enough. We don't expect to handle those uncomfortable feelings without anxiety or fear. Why would we expect girls to do so?

That's where Lindsay steps in. She reminds us that it's all right to be unsure, and she helps us take the necessary steps to feel certain and strong in our coaching and parenting skills. She reassures us that we are doing our best, and that most days, our best is more than enough.

Lindsay understands teen girls deeply. In *Rooted, Resilient, and Ready*, she shares her experiences—what works best and what doesn't work as well—and shows us how to help girls navigate those "not enough" feelings. Imagine if you woke up every morning and told your daughters, "You are rooted. You are resilient. You are ready." Lindsay encourages us to remind them of this. We must let girls know that there is no step-by-step guide to growing up, just as we know that there is no concrete guide to parenting, coaching, or being a role model. That being said, there are steps you can take to guide girls along the way. As they grow, their journeys are unique and varied. Books like Lindsay's—with tools, tips, ideas, strategies, and a healthy dose of hope—offer tremendous support along the way. In fact, *Rooted, Resilient, and Ready* may just be your game changer.

Lindsay is a great listener and empath. She gives her time and her creative ideas. She is authentic. She is certainly one of the most curious people I know. All of these wonderful qualities are on display here. She isn't afraid to ask questions that might seem uncomfortable; she knows that in a world where our girls are bombarded by the false, the fake, and the manufactured, honesty and authenticity are appreciated. Lindsay always comes from a place of love, care, and compassion for our girls and the adults in their lives—a place free from judgment coupled with an obvious desire to help. Through Lindsay's writing, I have come to understand my own journey through the teen years, and how my lessons learned help me in my work with young girls. Recently, I even found myself affirming, "I am rooted. I am resilient. I am ready!" I feel free to take up space knowing this; I don't feel small and I know that everything I need is within me.

Lindsay's insights, patience, and passion for empowering teen girls shine through every sentence in this book. Here, readers will find the support and confidence they need to authentically connect with the girls in their lives. What a difference it has made in my own work with girls entering their teens. What a difference I trust her book will make for you, too.

SHELBY ROWLAND
Founder and head coach, *gracie's gals*
August 2019

INTRODUCTION

IT'S 5 A.M. and I am sitting at my local coffee shop. Nobody is here yet and I am relishing the quiet. My pencils are sharpened, my brightly coloured Crayola felts are fanned out around me, and I am opened to a fresh, blank page in my notebook. I am a little afraid, a little nervous, but mostly, I feel excited and energized to begin writing this book. I am ready—ready to ask questions, to delve into tough topics, to learn and grow, and to empower you to be ready for the teen years as well. I am ready to be real and raw, ready to work hard and keep focused, and ready to inspire change. Even still, I have a problem.

I have so much to say when it comes to growing our teenage girls that I don't know where to begin. Maybe you feel this way too sometimes: you want to support your daughter so much but you don't know where to start. Don't you just wish you could ask Alexa, or maybe Siri: "How do I help my teenage daughter?"

Suddenly, I become aware of three questions swirling through my mind like a merry-go-round: What do I wonder about young girls? What do I worry about when it comes to teen girls? And what do I wish for every girl? This is where I will begin.

I wonder all the time about teenage girls today. I wonder how they are feeling and what they avoid feeling. I wonder what they are thinking about and what they have yet to consider. I wonder if they have learned that it's okay to be themselves—whether that means being focused and serious, silly or a little crazy, spontaneous or predictable, boisterous or demure, adventurous or safe. I wonder how they are navigating the newness of the teen years and all the changes this stage of life brings. I wonder who they are becoming and how they are being influenced and shaped. I wonder how they see our world. I wonder if they feel they belong in this world.

At the same time, I worry about today's girls. I worry about how quickly they are growing up, and the pressure I know they feel to be "perfect." I worry about their busy schedules, their push for more, and the stress they are forced to deal with every day—to keep up, to fit in, to look like they know what they are doing, to achieve, and to succeed. I worry about the pressures they feel specifically when it comes to relationships, sex, and social media. I worry they are becoming who others want them to be rather than investing the time needed to figure out who *they* want to be.

I also spend a lot of time wishing. I wish adolescent girls could see what we see. I wish they could see their potential for power, strength, and confidence. I wish for them to grow up strong, with self-belief, dogged determination, and the ability to work hard—with grit, perseverance, and unwavering resilience. I wish that every single teenage girl could love and value herself, do all that she loves to do, know her greatness, see her beauty, feel confident, take risks, show her boldness and audacity, voice her opinion, and absolutely not care what people think. Ultimately, I wish for teen girls to feel rooted, resilient, and ready for this world—for both what it has to offer them and for all they have to contribute.

That's why I wrote this book—to help you guide her to be rooted in her identity, resilient to the changes and challenges she will face as she grows up, and ready to become her best self as she steps into her future. One parent I spoke to said it best: "We want our girls to be strong, happy, and healthy, filled with love and hope, and purpose." Yes, we do. The question is "How?" I hear often from parents with variations on this simple question. "How do we nurture relationships with our teen girls when they push us away?" "How do we get close when we feel so far removed?" "How do we understand what they are going through when they don't tell us any details?" "How do we support teen girls as they grow up, guiding them in the right direction while also giving them the space they want and need to make their own mistakes and figure things out for themselves?" I know you wonder and worry too. And I want to address your concerns, offer suggestions, and answer those questions.

The things that I wonder about, worry about, and wish for girls have changed and intensified as the world has advanced rapidly. Twenty years ago, the world was a different place. Over a decade ago we didn't have smartphones, Facebook, Instagram, or Snapchat. We shopped in real stores, not virtual ones. We had in-person conversations and caught up over coffee. We may be getting used to this version of living—this is all girls know to be true—but there's no doubt that many of these recent changes have increased the pressure for teen girls to grow up. There is pressure to be beautiful and talented, equipped and empowered, and involved in the community. There is pressure to keep up with social media and trends, fit in with friends (while also discovering her uniqueness), and make it all look effortless.

Girls today are part of the iGeneration, a cohort born between 1995 and 2012. They are known to be super-comfortable with technology and constantly "connected" to social media and their devices.[1] This is how they relate to one another, how they survive; in fact, it is the only way they know. They prefer software to hardware (an e-book or audio version as opposed to an actual book), and they live in a fast-paced, always changing, digital world, with access to anything they want 24/7. Occasionally, they will step out of their online world (BRB, or "be right back") to spend brief moments in the real world—perhaps for a breath of fresh air or a snack—before heading back to the familiarity and comfort of the internet. She will typically be wearing jeans, a topknot, and ear buds, and she's likely involved in several "textlationships" (a relationship primarily based on texting).

There's no doubt that this ubiquitous digital world shapes and influences a girl, exposing her to thousands of digital images as she scrolls and swipes her device for up to nine hours each day.[2] I am convinced that this constant stream of info and imagery is having a profound impact on the pressure she feels to be all things to all people. Research[3] shows that this generation of girls is growing up sooner and faster than any other generation, physically, emotionally, socially, and, yes, sexually.[4] There is the pressure to be herself but also to conform; to have a voice but refrain from being too loud or too strong; to be a leader but not overly ambitious or threatening; to do her part in the home while creating her own life outside of its comforts; to think for herself but to ask for help when she needs it; to maintain her social media profile yet withstand the pressures to be pretty and sexy; to focus on being her best self without joining the chase for perfection. These are the pressures girls talk openly about.

Less often mentioned, but arguably applying even more pressure, are the silent struggles teen girls often hide: struggles with gender identity, sex and sexualization, and mental health concerns such as anxiety and depression. And then there is the brewing conflict between yearning for independence and feeling stuck in a state of dependence, between wanting to face the world alone and prepared, and knowing (but perhaps not admitting) that she's just not ready—yet.

Your teenage daughter is changing in every way imaginable. Her body is changing as she goes through puberty. Her brain is changing as it sprouts, prunes, and reorganizes neuronal circuits.[5] Her language is shifting to become more self-deprecating and comparative. And her social circles are evolving as she tries to figure out who she is and where she belongs. These are the years when her inner circle of friends becomes so important. Not only do they benefit from her time and attention, but they also become the holders of her secrets, the ones she trusts with the inner workings of her mind. It is a time of great change for you as well, as you must learn to let go of her hand and let her grow up.

Imagine a circle. When your daughter was a little girl, the two of you stood together in that circle. Now that she is a teen, she is standing in the circle on her own. Using a hula hoop as a prop, I tell girls: "You are the centre of your own circle. Two feet planted firmly on the ground. You are the one who gets to make your own choices and decisions and decide who and what you want in or out of your circle." Her circle is her boundary; her circle is her power; her circle is the life she is creating for herself. And it truly is *her* circle. You are no longer in the centre with her, and this is a healthy indicator of her growth.

Although you are her chef, chauffeur, cheerleader, tutor, coach, counsellor, and— let's face it—bank machine, you are no longer her everything. But you *are* her someone. As she grows, you experience the tacit process of letting go of who she once was and watching her grow into someone new. This can be difficult. At the same time, though, it is incredibly rewarding. As teens grow, they are yearning for independence, freedom, and the chance to show you that they can do it, that they don't need you quite as much as they used to. The hand that reaches out to hold yours every once in a while is just as likely to be raised in the classic gesture that says "stop." It's her way of telling you, "I got this. I don't need your help!"

Parenting from the Periphery

Popular culture has some stereotypical boxes for parents, including tiger parents (strict and demanding parents who push and pressure their children); helicopter parents (who pay extremely close attention to their child's experiences and problems); lawnmower or snowplow parents (who attempt to save their children from any obstacle, pain, or inconvenience they may face); outsourcers (parents who choose to pay professionals to do the work of parenting for them); and jellyfish parents (who let their kids do anything they want).[6] In *The Dolphin Way*, Dr. Shimi Kang suggests that the ideal parent is authoritative in nature but firm and flexible.[7]

The parenting style that is best for you and your daughter will depend on your unique relationship. Sometimes parenting will require tough love: reinforcing the rules you have set out for her when she needs to be held accountable for her actions (or inactions), or when she has to be called out on rudeness, disrespect, and disobedience. Other times, you'll need to offer her soft love: when she is being hard on herself, when she has royally screwed up and she knows it, or when she is going through hardships or a season of loss. You know best how she ticks, and what is needed depending on the situation at hand.

The style of parenting I recommend is that of the periphery parent. You are not her friend or in her circle. You are her parent—far enough away so she has the space and freedom to make her own choices, to feel free to be herself, and, yes, to make her own mistakes, but close enough to offer your encouragement and guidance and provide strength and security as she needs. She will show you she is ready to be her own person, but remember this: she still needs you, just in new and different ways.

Parenting from the periphery requires a new way of relating and a new approach. Periphery parenting means getting comfortable with being the observer on the outskirts, the silent supporter, ready when she needs you or when absolutely necessary but avoiding interfering or intervening when she is doing all right on her own. As we all know, teen girls can be moody, unpredictable, rebellious, truculent, and confusing. But they can also be strong, brave, confident, courageous, loving, enthusiastic, surprising, and amazing. This is why how we speak to them and also about them matters so much, as does how we treat them. Treading carefully and intentionally through these unchartered waters is not easy (we may fall into power struggles, arguments, and use of "colourful language"). Nevertheless, I encourage you to keep at it with patience and practice, to acquire some knowledge of the development of the teenage brain, and to accept that from time to time you will make mistakes too. Because that is what she wants from you!

Begin parenting on the periphery with listening: listen to what your teen girl has to say, and feel for the emotions behind her words. Listen without judgment. Wait in the silence and allow her to pause and consider before speaking. Hold space for her to simply be in the moment or in the feeling with you. Let your daughter make choices and help her predict the consequences. Choose truth-telling without sugar-coating or lies. Carefully monitor her emotions and decide when a situation is serious enough to get involved. Be ready to talk and "lean in" when she signals that she is open for it, and be willing to back away and commit to trying again another day when you feel her shut down. Opt for asking open questions such as "Can you tell me more about your weekend?" instead of "Did you have fun?" Let her speak and don't rush to change topics, especially if you feel uncomfortable. Give advice if it is warranted, but ask her if she wants it first. Choose guidelines over rules and, where possible, create these together.

On days when you feel you are screwing up—such as when you make assumptions about her, lose your patience, pick a fight, correct her, take over to show her how it's done, or jump in to solve her problem—accept that you are not perfect, and neither is your daughter. What you can be is an "eternal learner," a parent committed to learning every day and never giving up.

So much can get in your way when you parent your teen girl. You may feel you are inadequate, archaic, or irrelevant (teen girls are adept at making you feel this way!). You may be consumed or overwhelmed with your own history or past mistakes. Your daughter needs you to let go of and move through those feelings so you can keep providing her with a safe space to be her true self, to unburden, and to lean on you. This will take self-belief and confidence, time, effort, and so much patience on your part. And then, just when you figure it out, she will change and need you in a new way. This is precisely what makes parenting both interesting (and surprising) and unending.

Connecting with Your Teen

Your connection with your teen girl, and how you connect with her, is everything. As a parent on the periphery you'll be challenged to cultivate connection in new and possibly creative ways. Research in the 1960s and 1970s conducted by attachment theorists such as John Bowlby and Mary Ainsworth[8] and the most recent neuroscientific studies support the concept that there is great power and vitality in relational connection. Attachment is the innate biological mechanism that bonds humans together and underlies love. When you create a safe and trusting relationship with time, presence, understanding, and emotional attunement, your teen learns she can rely on you. She feels seen, heard, validated, and valued; she feels that you "get" her. This kind of connection—whether with you or someone else who is close to her—helps a girl feel secure and calm.

When you connect in any way with your teen girl, you contribute to her brain's neural connectivity and its physical structure. Neuropsychologist Donald Hebb coined the phrase "neurons that fire together, wire together" to describe the process of neurons in her brain firing with each experience. Over time and with repetition, this firing creates stronger and faster neural connections, particularly in the limbic system, where the attachment circuitry lies and where her emotions are regulated.

The "right" kind of connection transpires when her experiences are met with kindness, empathy, and reassurance: words, for example, such as "I am here for you" or "I understand how you are feeling." This stands in contrast to the connections that are forged out of criticism and judgment or shame and blame. These negative connections activate a girl's stress response system. They alert her to danger by flooding her body with adrenaline and cortisol (the stress hormones) and propelling her into the automatic "flight, fight, and freeze" mode. They also wire her brain's circuitry to be hyper-aware for and anxious about the next instance of perceived danger. She will flounder and feel uprooted.

If you are feeling concerned because your daughter has already experienced anxiety-provoking situations or trauma, please hear this: There is hope. The plasticity of the brain allows for change. Wherever she is at and whatever she has experienced, her brain has the capacity to create new neural pathways. You can help to rewire her brain by exposing her to new experiences and connecting with her via empathy, compassion, and care, all of which allow her to feel safe and cared for, decrease her stress levels, and increase feelings of security. In order to feel competent, teen girls need one relationship that engages heart and mind. This relationship may be with you as her parent, or another adult with whom she can be herself and share and feel safe.

Researchers and scientists work hard at proposing hypotheses, experimenting, and reporting their findings. We glean the benefits of such diligence. But beyond all of the research, and beyond all of the things that you instinctively know, is one vital thing: love. Despite the teen rebellion, despite the eye rolling, the hand-on-hip mannerisms, and the sarcastic wit she has now mastered, you love your teen daughter unconditionally, relentlessly, fervently, deeply, and unequivocally. You love her because that is the most important thing you have to offer her as her parent. Your love promotes connection.

Disconnection happens when your daughter feels unable to speak freely. She may feel blocked by fear of being judged, criticized, or misunderstood, and she will hold back and hang on to the accompanying frustration of her missed opportunity to disclose. Disconnection sounds like "Really? You decided to wear that today?" or "Are you still working on your homework? What's taking so long?" We disconnect from teens any time we judge, criticize, assume, and throw doubt or disbelief their way; when we tell them how they are feeling, give advice too readily, or try to fix or solve problems without involving them. Disconnection is not what you or your teen girl wants, but it can happen in the blink of an eye, and afterward, you may catch yourself wondering why you said what you said or did what you did. No one is immune. This happens often with my teen clients, especially when I say the wrong thing, make the wrong suggestion, or forget something she has told me countless times. The imaginary brick wall comes down—she will not say a thing—and I am stonewalled. But these moments of disconnect can be remedied if you work to become aware of when they are happening and seek to turn that around. I wrote this book to help you do just that.

The insights in these pages are based on my experience with teen girls and those supporting them. I have gained a plethora of ideas from girls who have told me what helps their growth, and what hinders it. I've also learned from their parents, who have expressed their concerns and let me know where they have most succeeded. *Rooted, Resilient, and Ready* is designed to help you parent your "becoming" teen daughter in this changing world. It offers an exploration of the eight most important concerns when it comes to raising teenage girls today: identity, body image, mental health, social media, relationships, peer pressure, sex, and the future. Throughout, I will offer my own revelations about teen girls and the practical tools I have tried; what parents are experiencing with their daughters; and what girls themselves have to say. Each chapter includes conversation starters, and ends with concrete steps you can take to help her growth, along with a list of corresponding countersteps that can hinder it. For printable PDFs of key concepts, visit www.LindsaySealey.com. There is also a resource section at the end of this book with recommended websites, apps, and TED Talks.

Teenage girls have always interested and fascinated me as much as they have baffled and bewildered me. At times, girls offer viewpoints that I find so refreshing and creative. Other times, I too experience the brick wall—the one constructed to keep us out and block us from reaching her. Like you, I sometimes don't know how to get in. What I do know is that I never give up. I keep trying and, eventually, I find my way. I am asking you to do the same. Some days, I celebrate my triumphs (even the small ones, like getting her to smile). Other days I wallow in my failings (I know I came across as critical and harsh). What works one day may not work the next. What works with one girl might never work with another. We all have to remember that we are doing our best, and as life changes and she changes, we can change too. And please be assured that not all of the changes I discuss in this book are going to happen all at once!

You decide what works best for you and your daughter—there is no perfect blueprint. You will have to find your own way as well. Take one step and one day at a time. As she establishes her circle and feels your support from the periphery, she is likely to invite you in—but in her time and her way. If we want girls to step into the best version of themselves, we need to step out of their way while we continue to reassure them that we'll be there for them. Step by step, we can help girls be more rooted, resilient, and ready for whatever their future may bring.

NOTE TO READERS ON INCLUSION

Rooted, Resilient, and Ready has been written to nurture and support those raising teenage girls. Its aim is to provide the necessary and relevant research, information, experiences, and ideas and, at the same time, be as inclusive, expansive, and collaborative as possible.

With this goal comes the consideration of a diversity of teenage girls with respect to size, shape, and body type; ages and abilities; family, cultural, ethnic, and religious backgrounds; levels of education, social economic status, and external influencing factors; psychological dispositions, personality types, and maturity levels. Some content will be more relevant for your thirteen-year-old; other content will be more suitable for your seventeen-year-old.

That said, *Rooted, Resilient, and Ready* has its limitations. First, there is the limit of the author's worldview. How we make sense of the world is shaped by personal life experiences, cognitive capacity, and perceptions and interpretations. Even with an open mind and good intentions, one can not consider all possibilities or all perspectives. This is also true when considering different beliefs and value systems. Different parents will have different "hard lines" when it comes to various topics, especially with relationships, substance use, and sex.

Second, *Rooted, Resilient, and Ready* seeks to proffer advice and guidance to readers. But a book can never replace professional medical attention. Those with serious concerns need customized advice from the most appropriate experts. If you feel that a young person is in danger or is endangering someone else, please take immediate action and seek professional assistance.

Third, this book is bound to the societal constructs of gender and non-traditional gender identities. For constancy, the pronouns "she" and "her" are used throughout, even when individuals have identified as non-binary. However, it is the hope that as societal changes are further embraced and accepted, the language will become more inclusive and new language will emerge.

Finally, the true stories and experiences of girls and their supporters are presented. To protect the privacy of individuals and their families, names and identifying details have been changed and thus individual stories have become compilation stories. This is with the exception of the photos throughout the book, where the girls have permitted the use of their real names.

PART ONE

ROOTED

Girls who are rooted have two feet firmly planted on the ground. They are certain and secure; fierce and fearless; unapologetic about who they are.

A rooted girl believes she is valuable and worthy. She accepts her strengths and areas of growth, knows her values. Society may pressure her to look a certain way, but she sets her own identity. She sees through the illusions of social media and chooses not to measure her self-worth through likes and followers. She knows her time is better invested in knowing herself.

Rooted girls use their voices to ask for what they need and to speak up for what matters most to them. They can clarify who they are and what they are becoming, their dreams and goals.

Rootedness is the solid foundation on which teen girls can stand. The deeper their roots, the stronger they will be. That is why we must help girls to be grounded and strong. When we see her as she is and "get" her by actively listening to her, she becomes more rooted, more confident, and more likely to grow into a strong and powerful woman.

I

WHO SHE IS BECOMING

ELFIES. NETFLIX. MUSIC. Spotify. YouTube. Hanging out with friends. Ripped jeans and sneakers. Scrolling through her social media feeds: this is your teen girl's world. Pleasing, performing, and perfecting: these are her challenges.

Undoubtedly, by the time she turns thirteen and is officially entering adolescence, she has already been doing more on her own, wanting to spend her time with friends, and showing early signs of "teenager rebellion," such as boundary pushing, especially when it comes to household rules around curfew, clothing, and screen time. Yes, she is likely doing some eye rolling and offering up a little sass, telling you that you "just don't get her" while her strategically positioned hand rests on her hip.

And yet, "getting" a young, impressionable teenage girl is no easy task. It's difficult to determine who she is *becoming* because she is in a state of constant flux amid chaotic societal influences. Some girls seem to be clear on who they are and are confident enough to tell me what makes them unique, like fourteen-year-old Ayisha: "I think my voice makes me unique," she said. "Many people say that I'm too loud, but I think they are too quiet." Other girls showed more doubt—like Morgan, who shyly responded with typical teen upspeak, "I think I am nice and caring?" When I interviewed eighteen-year-old Laurel, a girl with an incredibly calm demeanour and a light sprinkle of freckles dusted across her face, she quietly reflected, "It's funny when you look at pictures of your younger self, thinking that you knew it all." Girls often feel more grown up than they are and feeling that way is part of growing up.

Psychologists tell us that the two most fundamental milestones of adolescent development include understanding identity and gaining social acceptance—knowing who she is and feeling she belongs. As girls are figuring out what roles they play, such as daughter, sister, friend, student, and teammate, they are also figuring out themselves: their interests, hobbies, qualities, likes, dislikes, and beliefs. During this dynamic time, teenage girls are perpetually changing, developing, and learning, and are deeply engaged in the maturation process. According to David G. Myers and C. Nathan DeWall, "adolescence is a time of vitality without the cares of adulthood, a time of rewarding friendships, heightened idealism, and a growing sense of life's exciting possibilities."[1] Adolescents don't know everything, but they are beginning to know something, especially that their lives are filled with a combination of exhilaration and angst.

A growing teen girl's identity is shaped by many factors and is the culmination of her values, interests, beliefs, personality, and "place in life." She is becoming herself through the interactions she has with others and the feedback she receives. Keep in mind that her brain is developing. Teen girls experience the most dramatic brain growth in adolescence, during which there is an increase in brain matter and the brain is becoming more interconnected and gaining processing power. In her early teen years, her brain relies more heavily on the limbic system (the emotional centre) than the prefrontal cortex (the rational centre). As your teen girl grows, other parts of her brain are able to process emotion and she is more able to be calm, rational, and reasonable.[2] Eventually, the sometimes-exaggerated emotions of middle adolescence will become less intense and more balanced as she considers who she is and absorbs the broader perspective of who she is becoming.

Parents have the privileged position of watching as their teen girls grow into increasingly independent and mature young women. Many a parent has shared with me their wonder over this transition. ("I felt so proud watching her positive energy with her friends on their way to the concert," for example.) But parents also tell me how, at times, watching the growth process can be difficult. So many changes are happening all at once, and there are changes they didn't anticipate. The toughest part for parents seems to be dealing with disappointment around who their teen daughter is becoming. You may have hoped she would be an athlete, but she would rather draw and work on her art. You may have wanted her to be social, like you, and enjoy a large and eclectic circle of friends, yet all she wants is alone time in her room, where she can be absorbed with her imagination or her smartphone. You may have imagined her wearing skirts and dresses, but her style is pants and her older brother's hoodies.

When parents feel that their expectations are not being met or that their daughter is not living up to her potential, they typically try to help. Unfortunately, that "help" often comes via limiting language, which can cause frustration. A discussion about career choices could include a statement such as "You really don't want to pursue hair and makeup; there's no money in that." Or a chat about an extracurricular passion might end with "Honey, you're just not the musical type," or "Perhaps you should let someone else take the lead in the school musical." Your intention may be to help her "be her best," and even to protect her from any hint of disappointment, but what she's hearing you say is this: "You are not good enough as you are."

You want the best for her. You may even want her to have a better life than yours. But she needs to choose a life of her own. One of the most important things I hear from teen girls—and I hear it often—is that they need you to accept their choices as they figure out their uniqueness.

Helping your teen girl explore her identity begins with letting go of any preconceived expectations of who you want her to be. In doing so, you can give her the space she needs to step into who she truly wants to be. In the quest to be supportive, parents may inadvertently tell girls who they should be, especially when applying labels or offering guidance or limitations: "You are quirky," or "You have a dancer's body," or "You need to put more time into science so you can get a good job in that field." This may cause confusion. Labels can feel like boundaries, but she may nevertheless sacrifice herself to fit them. From a brain-development perspective, her connection to you is her lifeline.[3] Most girls will do anything to keep that lifeline of attachment open, even if it means bending to meet parental expectations. Essentially, she will be who she thinks you need her to be in order to alleviate fears of separation and disconnection.

What if you don't like who she is becoming and your knee-jerk reaction is to steer her in the opposite direction? This is when you need to be calm, centre yourself, and change your approach. Remember, periphery parent. Be ready to guide her, not control her, by asking questions about how she's changing and if she is happy with the person she's becoming. Try asking, "What do you like best about yourself, or least?" Consider offering her this compliment: "I love how (kind/confident/competent) you are becoming." When we tell girls who we want them to be and place them in categories, we hinder their quest for authentic identity. Instead of being in denial about who she is becoming ("My daughter would never be bisexual"—despite the fact that she's mentioned having both boy and girl crushes) or being dismissive ("Her interest in playing the drums is just a phase"—even though she's been practising for years), we help girls tremendously when we accept what they show us. Ultimately, when we accept her, she learns to accept herself.

SAMI

I actually don't like it when people over-identify with any one aspect of their identity. It bothers me. Even with people who are part of the LGBTQ spectrum and only identify with that part of them and I know there has to be more to them. There is so much more to them. That's one of my pet peeves. I try not to over-identify with any one part of me because I know there are so many aspects of me. All of our different parts fit into a puzzle, and I acknowledge that all those pieces are there and they make up a picture that is me. To take any one of those pieces and focus too hard on it is not really respecting all the other pieces and allowing myself to be the entire puzzle.

I am light-skinned but I am half black and I am treated as the acceptable token black person. I am "ethnically ambiguous." When people ask me, "What are you?" I know it's such an inappropriate question. I am not denying myself but I know how to pull on different aspects of my identity when they serve me best. It's similar to code-switching, which a lot of people of colour have to do. They have to know how to talk to different groups in a different way to be taken seriously. Women have to do this as well. They can talk to their friends a certain way. But when they talk to their bosses or men, they have to speak differently to get their point across.

Her Centre and Circles of Influence

Identity is a tricky concept to unpack, as these teen years are all about growth, movement, and expansion. I view a teen girl as surrounded by a series of concentric circles representing her genetics, family, peers, and her culture and society. Your daughter is standing in the centre of her own circle surrounded by these circles of influence, all of which may exert pressure and constantly reflect back to her a version of "who she is." As she learns to stand strong and rooted in her own circle, she feels the competing interests and allegiances between these circles. At best, she will deal with the pressures by setting firm boundaries and becoming more secure and certain in her own choices and decisions. At worst, she will give in, give up, and yield to the pressures around her. This may result in her feeling deflated, disappointed, and, most likely, lost in her identity.

We need her to feel shaped positively by surrounding circles of influence but still free to discover who she is, in her own way and in her own time. For when she stands inside her circle, she is rooted in her strengths and capabilities, and she is strong and secure. She will not be pushed out of her own circle. She knows she has the right to be standing there. She owns her space.

As described in the introduction, you are standing in a supportive role as a "parent on the periphery" (p. 6), but you are also closest to her centre. Now is the time to view her identity on a broad spectrum of possibilities rather than through a specific definition or role. Nothing will feel better to her than knowing you are there—with an open mind—if she needs you, and that she has your full support and space to grow. The world will try to tell her who she ought to be. Your message to her must be louder and stronger: "You do you." The knowledge that you have her back will safeguard her against any insult or pushback she receives from others. Your assurance that she is the centre of her own circle will serve as a defence against other circles that have the potential to distort her true identity.

Therapist Tiffani Van Buckley told me that when it comes to teen girls figuring out who they are, the greatest challenges she witnesses are judgment from others and self-judgment. When I asked her to offer one piece of advice to parents who notice teen girls struggling to accept themselves, she said this: "Practise acceptance of who they are rather than impose ideas of who they should be." Teens girls are tough enough on themselves. Let's just see them for all they are in this moment. Let's validate the good stuff and suspend all judgment.

Genetics—How She is Born

Identity is an ongoing and multi-faceted aspect of a teen girl's journey; how she is born is simply the beginning of that journey. The influence of genetics unfolds in the womb in that DNA will determine her gender, eye colour, height and body type, and potentially her behaviour and personality. DNA also dictates the health of her genes, her genetic predispositions, and her cognitive functioning, including possible brain-based disorders (such as attention deficit hyperactive disorder, attention deficit disorder, sensory processing disorder, or autism spectrum disorder), anxiety levels and responsiveness to stress, and physical disabilities. Some girls will be born with a genetic advantage such as intellectual giftedness, artistic or athletic prowess, or some other kind of talent. A few girls will win what Cameron Russell, in her TEDx Talk, called the "genetic lottery."[4]

Some girls don't feel like girls at all. New research on transgender or transfluid individuals now shows that there are differences in hormone levels in the brains and bodies of those who feel they don't match their DNA. In an interesting article in *The Atlantic*, Jesse Singal explores the complications that can arise when teens identify as transgender. For parents, this identification often results in great uncertainty. Is it the result of an intensified search for identity in the uncertain years of adolescence, or of exposure to internet articles and YouTube videos? Or is the identification an indicator of an actual conflict between their child's gender identity and the sex assigned at birth?[5]

Whatever your child's genetic makeup, you have the most influence when it comes to helping your teen to accept what she was born with, without shame or blame, and then move forward. You can do this by telling them, "How you are born is out of your control, never your fault, and what you have to accept." Then reassure them that "what you *can* control is what you do with your genetics," and that this begins with embracing the fact that we are all unique. Girls can get stuck on labels (such as being anxious or ADD), and their fixation inevitably limits their growth and damages their self-esteem. Encourage girls to expand their view of themselves and their circle by first acknowledging what holds them back. Meet them where they are in their struggle. Connect before you redirect the conversation. Then you can ask, "What else you got?" This will prompt them to consider themselves beyond their genetic fate. You can acknowledge that she may feel she is simply "not a writer," but you can also help her see that where she puts her focus, time, and effort is where she will develop her skill set, whether we are talking about mathematics or socializing. This is what matters most when it comes to her growth and progress. The approach is all about widening the circle of her self-perception.

Family and Life Circumstances

Teen girls live inside all kinds of families: biological, adopted, foster, blended, single-parent, double-parent, two moms, two dads, and as many differences within families as between them. Some families have greater financial means; others struggle to make ends meet. Some families are dealing with addiction, health concerns, and even extreme circumstances such as abuse and incarceration. Some girls are born into order and peace, while others are born into chaos and drama.

All families function differently, depending on family values such as integrity, curiosity, loyalty, respect, and kindness, as well as family traditions and rituals. Communication styles vary too. Some family members speak about feelings and concerns in an open and honest way. Others tend to avoid or deny feelings and important conversations. All families also have ancestral history, behavioural patterns established long ago that a teen girl is often not privy to until she is older.

No matter what circumstances she is born into, family can have a profound effect on a growing girl's identity. Family can push her with the encouragement she needs to take a chance when scared. It can also pull at her with demands and responsibilities for which she is not ready: "As the oldest, I expect you to be in charge." Yet a girl can reciprocate by doing some pushing and pulling of her own: simultaneously pushing family members away so she can go it alone and pulling them close for comfort and familiarity. Parents often speak to me about this confusing "I need you but I don't want to need you" experience. Believe me, she feels as confused as you do! Some girls tell me that their parents "just don't get" them or "are so overprotective and ask way too many questions." But other girls surprise me with comments like "My family will be there for me in a way friends can't be," or "Even when I totally mess up, my parents still love me."

What's happening here is that your teen is testing your boundaries to see what she can get away with and if your strength and security can keep her safe. She is also learning to fact-check you—more to prove she can think for herself than to prove you wrong—and to cross-check family beliefs and values with her own. Family can be her rock, a place where she feels most like herself and where she can unburden her stressors. But family can also be a source of stress, forcing her to be someone she is not. The conflict between wanting to be independent and yet needing to feel dependent on family is deeply felt by many teen girls, whether they are fourteen or nineteen. It will take some balance from you to show her how to balance that conflict in herself.

Choice and Voice

The teen years are tricky to navigate when it comes to family. You may want to continue with family time and the "way things were," while she is eager to break free from "jail." You'll need to find compromise and balance. Living in your home, she's still expected to have chores, duties, and responsibilities. A teen girl trying to figure out who she is as a separate entity from her family will need more choice to use her voice. Choice and voice in the family home will build up her self-confidence and her self-worth, both of which will serve her well outside of the home. Here are some ways to provide opportunities for her to practise using her voice:

- Ask her opinion about dinner and weekend plans, and delve deeper into current events and social issues. She may instinctively say, "I don't know," but give her time to consider and ask what she does know.

- Encourage her to examine her opinions and state why she thinks what she does. Listen and stay open-minded. Say things like "I want to understand where you are coming from. Tell me more."

- Avoid assuming that she is unaware of various topics or dismissing what she says as uninformed.

- Assure your teen that she can tell you anything—and mean it. Show her you are available and ask questions out of curiosity, not judgment.

- Be inquisitive about what's below the surface. Ask, "How was the party last night? Was it what you expected?" Or "I notice you're putting in a lot of time on social media. What kinds of posts are you seeing?" Or "You seem quiet lately. I'd love to hear what's on your mind." When you ask creative and open-ended questions— questions she may not expect from you—you invite her to share.

- Respond with understanding and encouragement when she offers you an insight into her world. Even if you are shocked by what she says, remain calm in your response.

- Refrain from assuming she doesn't want to talk; she may not know how to get her words out. Giving her choice instead can help: "Does your 'I'm fine' mean you are, in fact, fine, or do you need more time to consider how you are doing?" (Sometimes "I'm fine" actually means "I really want to share with you but I am afraid you will react or overreact.")

She'll talk when she's ready, and you need to be ready and available for these occasionally rare moments. Conversations can be had around the dinner table, or during rituals parents commit to, such as Saturday morning breakfast at her favourite cafe. But more likely these conversations will happen spontaneously: in the car on the drive home from soccer, just before bed when you say a quick good night, or when you find her lounging across your bed with her iPad. Remember: your frustrations about her choice of clothing or friends, or undone chores and homework, or myriad other things you fight about are not the conversations she wants to have—they distract from the real stuff, the good stuff. She wants to tell you how afraid she feels to go to PE class and about the rejection she sometimes feels in her peer group. But she can't get there until she feels safe and ready. Most of all, a girl needs to know that her decision to create a life better than the one she was born into is a positive step forward. She need not feel guilty or ashamed. Family circumstances do not—should not—hold her back from who and all she wants to become. We can tell her this!

The Effect of Peers on a Teen Girl's Identity

I'll talk more about the influence of peers, for good and bad, in chapter 6. Here, though, I want to explore the effects of peers on a teen girl's identity, as these are formative influences. There comes a point in every teen girl's life when she likes spending time with her family a little less and time with her friends a little more. This transition period from the comfort of home to the new and unfamiliar social world can be easy for parents who choose to let go and more difficult for those who choose to cling tighter, filled with worry and trepidation that pressures from peers are too much for their little girls.

Without a doubt, her friends are now influencing her far more than you can. You may not like her friends or even know them. Gone are the days of scheduling play dates and chatting with other parents to confirm (and vet) them beforehand. She's making her own choices now and it's tough to watch, especially when those choices are not healthy, when she gives up who she is in order to be accepted, and when she is so worried about fitting in that she forgets about herself. The truth is that her identity, her values, her interests, her habits, and her self-worth work in close connection. She is learning important social mores, such as letting her friend finish her story before offering her own opinion, and the unwritten social rules of girlhood, like sharing exciting news with confidence but not conceit. Other girls will call her out on unacceptable social behaviours, and she will learn quickly. But right now, she needs others to understand both her own identity and how to behave.

She will start sorting out whom she wants to spend time with: Someone like her, with shared values and interests? Or someone not like her at all, so she can learn to step outside of her comfort zone? She is figuring out who she is in relationships, what kinds of friends she wants in her circle, and what kind of friend she wants to be. And she's wondering where she belongs: Is it with the cool girls, the girly girls, the sporty girls, the creatively artistic girls, or the girls who have formed a group because none of them belong anywhere else? Fourteen-year-old Sierra, with tight blond curls and a bouncy personality to match, told me, "Trust is one of the most important parts of friendship. You need to know who you can count on and who will keep your secrets, no matter what." Finally, your teen girl will have to figure out who she is amidst confusing friendship tactics like exclusion, boast posts on social media designed to activate her fear of missing out, or the silent treatment. As twenty-two-year-old Mila, who is now pursuing her college degree, shared, "Friends can be the best and worst. They can come into your life at your worst times, but also leave you at your best."

Girls I speak with love having a group of friends that they feel build them up and embolden them to be brave. Friends help them to feel "normal" when they share common interests, hobbies, opinions, and worries as well as an emotional connection. But girls also feel deeply the pressures that come with friendships: to dress like other girls, to talk like them, to be interested in the same things, and to even share the same tastes in music and celebrities, even if that means not being true to themselves (see chapter 6 for more on peer pressure). Although there is safety and normalcy in sameness and conformity, girls also often reveal how much they wish they could "do whatever I want and not be judged."

I met Emma when her mother reached out to me for help with Emma's social skills. Emma had no real friendships at school and was labelled "weird" in the worst sense of the word, as in "weirdo." Emma had slowly separated from the other girls in her class, with whom she felt she had nothing in common. Instead, she began to solidify what she loved to do: she biked to school instead of getting a ride, like the other girls; she brought her lunch to school in recyclable containers instead of buying one; and in class she would speak up about feminist issues, while avoiding chats with girls about boys and weekend plans.

I was challenged because I did not want to confuse Emma with a mixed message: be yourself but change to fit in. As we got to know each other better, I affirmed all the times she used positive social skills, such as asking questions, listening and responding to some of my comments, and complimenting me. Emma was less strong in social skills such as showing empathy, connecting with others' feelings, and taking the time to understand or even learn from an opinion different than her own. I loved that Emma was herself, and I told her so frequently. At the same time, I helped her develop her social skills so that she could have "the best of both worlds." I'll never forget the joy that spread across her face when she told me how the other girls were starting to ask her questions about riding her bike to school and some of her passion projects around social issues.

Girls do know that their identities are being shaped by people they spend a lot of time with, and they do struggle to find their unique identity within the group culture. Just like Emma, they want the best of both worlds: enough conformity to feel "normal" and enough authenticity to feel "special." Girls long for this kind of balance. Yet research shows us that despite their best intentions to be independent thinkers and have unique personalities, when the choice is between staying true to their voice or giving in to the group, most girls choose the latter because the fear of social rejection is debilitating. A teen girl often feels she does not have a choice between these two poles—she either agrees and gives in or is ostracized, also known as social disaster. The desire for belonging is so great that a teen girl will do anything—and I mean anything—to belong, even if she knows the danger of surrender means losing herself in favour of pleasing others. In other words, she will shape-shift, or be defined by and shaped by other people. I will talk more about how to help your teen girl avoid this pitfall later (p. 42).

Your daughter's experiences in friendship are where you will see the most experimentation with her personality. Depending on the group she is hanging out with, she may be mean or bossy, sweet or quiet, hyper or crazy, quirky or calm. You may drop her off at school in the morning sporting one personality only to pick her up in the afternoon trying out a new one, complete with its own vernacular and attitude: "Mom, you totally don't, like, get it, but you need to take me for sushi. I'm staaaaaaarving." This imposter may not be the daughter you waved goodbye to in the morning, but never fear: she will be back, once she figures out how to sound more like herself.

What you can do is keep an eye on her, be curious about her friends, and check in with her about how she's feeling after spending time with different people. Ask her what qualities are important to her in friendship and remind her that you trust her. Tell her to listen to her gut and trust her feelings about which friends are best suited to her. For instance, you can ask, "What do you like best about Zoe?" Or "I notice you giving up a lot to do what Sophie wants. What does Sophie give up for you?" We can help girls pay attention to their friend experiences in order to gain a better understanding of some fundamentals of friendship—namely, respect, reciprocity, loyalty, and care. If a friend doesn't fit her standard, then empower her to let go and move on to new friends.

The worst thing you can do here is project your fears onto her. Tell a teenage girl who she can't hang out with and she will often purposefully defy you by making her casual acquaintance her new best friend forever (BFF). She will see you as a controlling helicopter parent (yes, she knows exactly what this is), and she will hate you hovering over her when she is trying to figure out who is in her circle. I beg you, don't be a helicopter. At the end of the day, most girls do find their way through the "spring cleaning" season of friends, and they understand that those who surround them are shaping them. Again, this is her choice, not yours.

Culture and Society

The final ring in the series of circles surrounding your teen daughter's centre is culture and society. The world—society in general, but social media specifically—is constantly telling your daughter who to be and how she should be defined. She is categorized by gender, sexual orientation, race, religion, clothing and style, body type, lifestyle choices, socio-economic status, education, and achievement. Concurrently, she is influenced through music, music videos, video games, movies, social media sites, television, magazines, books, billboards, celebrities, online sensations, and advertising. Marketing companies target youth by sending them a mixed message: "Be anything you want to be," but "Be this kind of beautiful and this kind of successful." These companies are also selling brands and products to "help" improve our impressionable girls, while simultaneously teaching them that more is better (you can never have too much) and you gotta have it now (why wait?). This is smart from a business perspective—it plants the seeds of consumerism for future buyers—but it is damaging to teen girls' self-worth. How influential is media and social media on your teen daughter? Research tells us: very.[6]

Everywhere girls turn—whether to the online world or a concert featuring their favourite indie band—the message is loud and clear: be what the world tells you to be. Girls absorb the societal pressures to be good at everything, which results in the "supergirl syndrome" of trying to be super-powerful, super-strong, and super-talented—and making it look effortless. What girls may not know is that in striving for perfection they are undermining their own self-confidence as their stress skyrockets. Girls feel the demands of social stereotypes acutely as they find themselves trapped in a box that, all too often, they did not choose.

Societal messages are noisy, incessant, and often unrealistic and unhealthy, especially when it comes to body image (see chapter 2).[7] The often-competing messages teen girls receive are cause for parental concern. She needs time and space to hear the quieter voice within, guiding her to follow her own path. You do not want her voice to be dimmed or silenced. So how can you help to protect your teen girl from warped societal and cultural messages? Can we undo what she's already been brainwashed to believe and reteach her more positive messages? Yes. What I know is that girls need to be both positively inspired and positively influenced. Here are some ways to do this:

- Maintain ongoing conversations with her about limiting her screen time, as what she views is what she will see as "truth."

- Provide competition for screen time by planning activities with her. You won't get her to give up her phone entirely, but you may be able to entice her to go to a movie or the newest clothing store.

- Explore your own social circles for healthy role models. Look for a family friend, an older cousin, or an aunt willing to spend time with her and provide a powerful example.

The Masks of Her Identity

When adolescent girls feel they need to shield their authentic feelings and identity, they often reach quickly for a mask. A mask can serve them well when they are feeling vulnerable or deciding whom to trust. However, masks also keep girls distant and disconnected not only from others but also from themselves. And, if masks are worn constantly, girls are at risk for mistaking the mask for who they really are. If you think your teen girl is hiding behind a mask, the best way to help her lower it is simply to notice it, and then to be curious and slowly encourage her to reveal her true self.

In *Growing Strong Girls*, I discussed both the mean girl and the good girl facades: the former excluding, degrading, and tormenting other girls to gain a sense of power and dominance; the latter acting as the obedient rule-follower, who is an expert at keeping up appearances and being, well, "good." Each persona serves as a disguise for the real girl who desperately wants to be included and accepted. In many ways, masks provide the perfect disguise for a teen girl seeking (even subconsciously) to protect her identity and safeguard herself from her ultimate fears of being known or misunderstood.

Let's explore three different yet equally common masks teen girls wear: the supergirl, the invisible girl, and the cool girl. It's important to note that girls can adopt all of these masks at various times, or none of them. Perhaps she wears an entirely different mask. In my experience, however, these three tend to be the most common.

The Supergirl Mask

The supergirl mask is conspicuous: she is the girl who does it all. She's active on sports teams, involved in school and community activities. Not only is she a member of clubs, but she is also a leader—and don't be surprised if her supergirl awesomeness extends to responsibilities in the home. Likely she is the eldest sibling (or appears to be) and agrees to cook dinner, babysit younger siblings, while still having time to do her homework and complete bonus projects. She's ambitious and driven, and her achievements are outstanding. Still, I can't help but wonder if the mask of achievement isn't covering a deeper drive to prove her worth instead of knowing her worth. The fear of being "nothing" is so great that she pushes beyond her boundaries to achieve, but she is frequently left feeling stressed out, exhausted, and empty. What she often fails to see is that even supergirls need to recharge, and that there is a difference between wanting to "do it all" and feeling she *has* to "do it all."

The demands on a supergirl are many—be productive, be ambitious, be competitive, keep up, stand out, and do something to make your life count. In her head she hears, *Don't be mediocre, average, or ordinary. Be everything.* These demands can lead girls to enter the cycle of perfection (p. 39). You can support the supergirl who is all things to all people by helping her to slowly remove her mask in two clear ways. First, acknowledge her efforts. See all she is doing and give her credit. Even better, ask her to reflect on her effort and give herself credit. When girls pause and look back, they begin to "get" all they are doing. Second, offer your support. Granted, she may not take it, but offer it anyway. I will ask a supergirl client if she wants to share what is on her mind, to offload her burdens. I write out every item she tells me is on her to-do list. Then we go through each item and come up with action steps to get the job done. In this way, she can see all that is on her plate. She can make the abstract stressors real and tangible while feeling more empowered to act and much less overwhelmed.

Supergirls are often happy being productive, and happy when accomplishing. My client Rose, for example, is gifted and excelling academically. She is also musical, the lead in her high school play, and athletic—she is on two track teams. Yet every so often she tells me, "I just have occasional meltdown moments where it all feels like too much to handle. I have a big cry and usually feel better and back to myself." My experience has taught me that regular check-ins and talks where Rose can share can provide a release. Sometimes it is that simple; she just needs a moment to find her way back to balance.

The Invisible Mask

If the supergirl believes she needs to be everything, the invisible girl is convinced she is nothing. She fades into the background of life and blends in easily. She will hide in her hoodie, slouch, and offer little eye contact. At the first hint of discomfort—when meeting new people, for example, or being called on in class—she wishes for the superpower of invisibility. She may speak, but she's apt to do so in a mere whisper and usually in a self-deprecating way: "Why bother going? Nobody will notice me anyway."

Rarely will these invisible "nobodies" share their voices or make choices. The more you demand of her, the more frustrated you may feel, and the smaller she will want to become. Invisible girls are wearing the mask of "nobody loves me and I don't love myself," and they are covering up not only low self-esteem but also fading self-belief. They prefer to hide and be overlooked unknowns than to draw any attention to themselves. Granted, some girls are more shy and sensitive than others, and choose to be under the radar. But their "I don't matter" mask is often covering up an internal scream: *I want to matter and I don't know how!* Since these girls protect themselves well with their masks, they are often dismissed and discounted, which leads them to conclude that they are not important.

The invisible mask is a challenging one to remove; the girl who is wearing it is the hardest to reach, guarded and scared. However, it is possible to reach her slowly and patiently. Girls who feel invisible often want to stay that way. You can gently encourage her out of her shell by helping her to see herself in a more positive light. Seek out moments where she reveals anything—whether via a witty comment, a cheeky smile, or a one-off insight—and bring it to her attention. "Wow, that was astute." Tell her repeatedly that when she reveals herself you really enjoy who she is, and encourage that girl to show up more often. Reassure her that she is most definitely a "somebody" and help her develop her self-belief by gathering evidence in her favour. Girls often do the opposite, building a case against themselves to prove how they "always screw up." Comments like "See! You thought you could never order your own food in a restaurant, but now you do it all the time" are the kind of evidence she needs to hear. With practice she will learn to be less uncomfortable showing up as who she really is.

The Cool Girl Mask

Is your daughter always "fine," indifferent, apathetic, often showing little interest? If so, she is likely masquerading as the cool girl—too cool to try, too cool to take risks, and too cool to take part in new activities. At the same time, she knows it all and has done it all. I often see this mask in place during my workshops. The girl wearing it is the participant who refuses to join in. She may opt for sketching instead of completing a handout. She may challenge a group activity by standing on the sidelines, offering up long sighs of exasperation coupled with dramatic eye rolling. If she eventually agrees to join in, she does so with an oh-so-dismissive "whatever" or the know-it-all phrase "I've done this before." It is difficult to convince her to try anything because she is set on her intentional indifference.

The cool girl mask serves a purpose: to hide the fear of not knowing how, not succeeding, and looking foolish. Taking a chance on something new, and sharing her real feelings, makes her feel too vulnerable, so she becomes the cool girl and a powerful influence on her peers.

To encourage the cool girl to show her true self, you must be on her side, saying things like "I know this may not be your thing." At the same time, you need to attune to her feelings: "You seem a little scared. Did I get that right?" Girls wearing the cool girl mask benefit from feeling understood and finding compromise. Link something she knows how to do, such as math, with something that is new to her and that she appears not to care about, like computer coding. Point out the connection—both require her trial-and-error learning skills—and be there with her as she tries. Cool girls need plenty of reminders to share who they are; they need to be shown, again and again, that people want to see the "real" them. Celebrate any time she steps out of her comfort zone and any steps of bravery she takes.

SONG-AH

For sure I wear the tough girl mask and definitely in sports because all my friends are in very competitive sports—like at the national level—in swimming, in soccer, and in softball. I feel like when I play sports with them, I try to be tough and pretend I know what I am doing because they are so good. I don't want them to see that I doubt myself and feel I am not yet good enough at sports. It's easier not to be vulnerable. When you are vulnerable you can get really hurt by people and they could make fun of you. If you act tough, people can't hurt you. I don't feel ready to lower this mask yet. I feel like it would be hard and I'd feel that people would treat me differently or exclude me. If I weren't wearing the tough girl mask, I think I'd be happy inside that I don't have to pretend anymore and also relieved—it's a lot of pressure to keep it on! Actually, I'd be okay with it. Maybe I am not as athletic as some of my friends. Talent only takes you so far and then it becomes all about hard work and whatever I put my mind to.

Perfectionism and Inadequacy

Not good enough—three powerful and crippling words. Teen girls everywhere are feeling the "not good enough" epidemic, and it comes in many forms: not pretty enough, not smart enough, not popular enough, not sexy or skinny enough, not racialized enough, not rich or poor enough, not "normal" enough. The categories may take different forms but the memo is loud and clear when it comes to her identity formation: "You are just not enough." The obsession with achievement and perfection is pervasive in our society—through advertising and online images, celebrity status, and even peer status—and this destroys a teen girl's sense of selfhood. In *Enough As She Is*, Rachel Simmons writes about the damage of perfectionism in this way: "It costs girls their courage, curbing their ability to figure out who they are and what really matters most to them, exactly at the moment when this developmental task must be undertaken."[8]

Feelings of inadequacy are pushing your teen daughter to be "better," often beyond her own limits; they are also preventing her from honouring her unique identity. No surprise, then, that the more girls try to be "good enough," the less worthy they feel and the more perfect they try to be—a vicious cycle.

All day, every day, girls see "perfect" in the carefully curated images on their social media feeds; they decide they need to be perfect too, believing this is their ticket to feeling happy, successful, and included. They strive for perfection: to be the perfect friend, to earn perfect grades, to attain the perfect look. And when they fail to reach these unrealistic ideals, they conclude there is something wrong with them—instead of realizing there is something wrong with the unhealthy societal standards that set them up in the first place. Unfortunately, a teen's perceived failure will convince her to try harder, to be even more perfect. This cycle never ends because it is fuelled by deeply rooted seeds of "not good enough." There is a direct correlation between the choice to be anything—or, for some girls, everything—and low self-worth. Perfectionism is an easy tool to grab to control the burden of inadequacy.

The cycle is damaging and destructive. You'll see her push and punish herself, trying so hard yet never feeling satisfied, and showing not a hint of kindness or self-compassion. Many girls I work with are perfectionists, and we often start by deconstructing perfection. I want to give every girl a T-shirt that declares *Perfect, just as I am* or *Good enough, as is*. I often ask, "If perfect wasn't an option, who would you be?" They pause and then come back with words like "free" or "happy." Free to practise and progress, free to make mistakes, free to feel good as they take steps toward improvement, and free to be brave and take risks. Happy, just as she is. Once girls "get" that letting go of perfect may be a healthy option—an option that will also relieve them of enormous stress and strain—they come to an amazing realization: they can still achieve, but from a place of "I am enough" and self-confidence rather than from a place of "I need to prove I am enough."

You can't prevent your teen girl from absorbing cultural messages that encourage her to be "more" or perfect. You can, however, be proactive in delivering your own message: you do not expect perfection of yourself, and she should not expect it of herself either. We need to tell girls every day that they are enough as they are. By focusing on inner qualities such as her kindness, her compassion, and her willingness to try, we help her to focus on what matters most—her core values, not her achievements. This is not to say she should not strive for excellence. Excellence and perfectionism are not the same thing. Excellence is a journey of better and better every day, a gentle nudge for ongoing improvement that feels like progress. Perfectionism is an elusive destination that nobody ever reaches.

There are simple ways you can help your perfectionist teen daughter recognize that she is good enough as is. Tell her that you love her, just as she is, with a tender touch, a simple hug, and by simply being there. Yes, being there and the power of your presence is something, even though you may feel it's not doing anything. Praise her while she's working on her homework or a project and ask if she needs help. Ensure she takes the time to talk or just to have fun, to take her mind off her stress. "Not good enough" can become "good enough as is and getting better every day" for every single one of our perfectionistic daughters. Perfection need not be an inevitable part of a teen girl's identity. In fact, we can liberate our girls from the quest for perfectionism by guiding them to let go.

All She Can Be

Five years ago, with clarity and intentionality, I named my company Bold New Girls. The "bold" stands for the confidence and bravery that we all want girls to feel. And "new" stands for the hope that every day is a new day—a new chance to embrace a fresh start and become all she can and wants to be, with neither the limits of the world nor the limitations she places on herself weighing her down. When a girl is "all she can be," she is letting go of the idea of who she *should* be. She is letting go of pleasing and impressing others, letting go of searching for validation and approval outside of herself and instead seeking self-acceptance and self-love. She is lowering any masks she might be wearing to hide her true self and releasing any pressure she puts on herself to be perfect.

To help your teen girl achieve all she can be, I recommend you begin with a question of playful curiosity that I often use in my practice: "What if?" This poignant question dares her to imagine: "What if you were a little braver every day? What if you weren't afraid of failure? What if you had that difficult conversation you needed to have, even though it was uncomfortable? What if you could be anything, and all possibilities were open for your taking? What if your identity and who you are are good enough—then who would you be?" When I ask these questions, the looks on girls' faces often move from confused (*good enough?*) to relief (*good enough!*). They pause. They think.

Planting seeds with the language of possibility is crucial. Your teen girl cannot become what she does not know is possible, and she cannot know what is possible if it is not talked about. Once you help her imagine the outcomes, she can work backwards and start taking small steps toward actualizing her goal. Girls need to know they can embrace their identities despite family circumstances, school, and cultural and societal expectations. Teen girls need to know they can be what they choose: lawyers, designers, teachers, engineers, investors, inventors, moms, entrepreneurs, artists, or musicians. Your message of "you can be anything" must be louder and stronger than any cultural message.

From the outside looking in, a teenage girl's world appears complex—and it is. But as you and she navigate it—you from the periphery and she from the inside—an amazing thing happens. With every step she takes, every stumble she overcomes, every choice and challenge she engages, she gains deeper insight and a broader understanding of herself. She is widening her circle; her identity is expanding beyond her initial expectations. She is taking time to listen to and then trust her inner voice, fine-tuning her intuition, living out her integrity and values, and showing the courage to own and share her story. She is learning to follow both her moral compass and her heart, as well as evaluating who and what is influencing her, how this affects her, what she knows to be right and true, and what she feels is best for her. This is what it means for a teenage girl to be rooted in her identity. And you can help her get there!

How Parents HELP Growth

- Showing support by parenting on the periphery of her circle
- Accepting who she is becoming
- Letting her choose who she wants to be
- Showing genuine curiosity about her interests
- Providing her with opportunities for choice and voice
- Listening and being curious about her choices

How Parents HINDER Growth

- Expecting her to be who you want her to be
- Limiting her with labels such as "social" or "shy"
- Deciding who her friends are
- Being a "helicopter parent"
- Believing the masks she wears are who she is
- Pushing her to be perfect

2

BEYOND APPEARANCES

I WAS A CONFIDENT teen. By the time I was sixteen, I had found my place in high school on sports teams, in band and choir, and with friends. I studied hard and earned good grades. Then it happened. One day, as I walked past a group of popular boys in the cafeteria, they called out, "Hey, Farms!" and followed it up with lots of snickering. At first, I had no idea that this unusual greeting had anything to do with me, but I became suspicious when this phrase kept popping up when I was around. I begged a friend to tell me what she knew. Reluctantly, she spilled the secret. "Farms" was a word they'd made up to merge "fat" and "arms"—and they were using it to refer to my arms.

Before this catastrophic moment, I felt beautiful in my body and was blissfully unaware of the normal weight gain teen girls often experience as they grow. I decided that my best weapon in fighting off these hurtful comments was retaliation—and this came in the form of self-neglect and, eventually, an eating disorder. I ate less; I ran more. I pushed, punished, and starved myself. Essentially, I developed an unhealthy coping tool to deal with life's stressors. I thought my body was the problem and that changing my body was the obvious solution. Less obvious to me at the time was the underlying issue: my inability to love myself exactly as I was.

My challenge with holding a healthy body image emerged out of a lack of positive role models for how to love my body. Today, I want to share my experience with girls as a message: your bodies are not the problem. The deeper concern is the capacity to accept who you are and feel good about yourselves at any shape and size, and regardless of other people's opinions. Looking back now, I feel incredibly sad for my teen self who didn't know what to do with uncomfortable criticism and who was incredibly beautiful and healthy just as she was. Still, I am grateful for this experience. It inspired my passion to empower girls to be more preventative when faced with stress and strife. This chapter is all about body image—how deeply it is felt as a defining part of a teen girl's overall image, and how it can be both a positive and negative influence. An adolescent's view of her body can become convoluted so quickly as she grows and becomes more aware of what a body "should" look like. Girls are born loving themselves wholly and completely. We need to remind them of this and guide them back from self-loathing to self-loving.

Body Love and Loathing

"It's a girl!"

Do you remember when she was born? Those chubby little thighs, round tummy, and teeny fingers and toes? What your daughter needed then was simple: your love and attention. She did not ponder if she should eat fast food for lunch. She wasn't wondering how many calories she could burn at the gym later in the afternoon so she could eat the muffin staring her down at the bakery. She wasn't stressing over every bite she ate, counting each calorie consumed. As a little girl, entrenched in the sensory experience of being and feeling, your daughter knew exactly how to love herself; it was natural and intuitive. At the age of ten, Alya told me this: "When I was younger, I felt as beautiful as a Disney princess." I somehow doubt she still feels this way. Alya lives in a world that convinces little girls there is one physically superior look, a world where fifteen-year-olds such as Emma-Jane routinely say things like "I hate all the fat on my body. I don't know why, but I do." Born in love, learning to hate. So, what happens as girls grow?

As her parent, you may notice your teen girl's emerging focus on the minutiae of her appearance, the drastic increase in her mirror time, the obsessing over hair, makeup, clothing style, and physique—more care, more conscientiousness, and more self-criticism. There are both biological and sociological reasons for this shift of focus to her appearance. According to Louann Brizendine, author of *The Female Brain*, when girls enter puberty, chemical changes to the brain facilitate this obsession with their looks. "The teen girl's brain is sprouting, reorganizing and pruning neuronal circuits that drive the way she thinks, feels, and acts—and obsesses over her looks," Brizendine says. "Her brain is unfolding ancient instructions on how to be a woman."[1] This speaks to the biological reasons why your teen girl may be obsessed with her appearance, but what else is going on? It's possible that she may be mistaking looking good for feeling good.

Ginny Jones, editor of More-Love.org—an online resource for parents of children with eating disorders—asserts that a teen girl's obsession with and criticism of her looks should not be looked on as normal or acceptable. She says:

We live in a culture that has normalized body hatred, and poor body image. This includes feelings of despair and anguish over the appearance of one's body. When we hate our bodies, we believe they are flawed. Believing that the body is flawed, especially when one is physically healthy and able-bodied, makes us vulnerable to body hate, disordered eating, and eating disorders. What is actually "normal" from a health standpoint is body acceptance. True health occurs not based on a number on the scale. Health is only possible when we believe our body is fundamentally good. We take better care of our bodies when we accept them.[2]

I love that girls want to look their best, and careful grooming is a form of self-care. Still, I worry that girls put too much emphasis on their looks and embrace too much maintenance (lash lifts, gel nails, lip fillers, and hair extensions, to name a few) as they strive for the "perfect look" at the cost of true self-worth and self-acceptance. When girls feel too fat, too ugly, too awkward, too disgusting, they want to sink inside themselves, turn on themselves, or protect themselves by rebelling against any beauty standard at all. In short, they want to alter themselves and conform. One girl told me she wants to change "all my fat into muscle so I wouldn't hate looking in the mirror so much."

Sadly, as girls grow up, and especially as they approach puberty, they learn to hate their appearance. Most body self-criticism takes root between birth and puberty. Although she was born loving herself as is, cultural, societal, and even familial pressures promote negative messaging such as "Be tall, skinny, and this kind of beautiful, with flawless skin and a bright smile." In other words, "Your body is not good enough as is." She didn't choose to internalize this way of thinking or to not love her body, but these messages are prevalent. In fact, we have become so accustomed to believing these directives that we also think self-criticism is necessary and important for self-development. In *Come as You Are*, Emily Nagoski discusses how women are reluctant to believe they are beautiful and to let go of self-criticism in order to nourish self-confidence and adopt healthy lifestyle habits. She says that body criticism is so entrenched in Western culture that most women hardly notice how ubiquitous and toxic it is. It's so ingrained, in fact, that "when women start to think concretely about it, they begin to discover a sense that they need their self-criticism in order to stay motivated. We believe it does us good to torture ourselves, at least a little bit."[3] That's right: self-criticism is seen as both necessary and beneficial.

When I look at girls, I see beauty in many different forms—unique ethnicities, abilities, personalities, and shapes and sizes. I'm sure you see divergent aesthetics in your daughter too. Girls are beautiful, but they are reluctant to believe us when we tell them. There are so many obstacles in her way when it comes to feeling beautiful: her own self-doubt, for example, and unfortunate cultural and societal messages that bombard her with images typically showing one body type and size and a single, narrow definition of physical attractiveness. I'll give you a hint: it's not voluptuous and curvy.

Girls learn that the body they have should be scrutinized, must be flawed, and most certainly needs to be altered. They also look outside of themselves for cultural standards around appearance. Kayla, now seventeen years old, told me she didn't think much about her body until she was older. "I believe it was in Grade 9 when I started comparing my body to my peers and thinking I should be critical, you know, because they were doing it."

At the same time as your teen is comparing her body to her peers, she's also sizing herself up against the digitally altered images she sees on her social media feed. She'll conclude that her body is not only different but wrong. She'll struggle to find anything that she appreciates about it, and she'll learn to talk like every other girl around her: "I am so fat!" "I ate way too much last night, so I'm not eating anything today." Or she'll ask others, "What do you eat every day? I'd do anything to be thin, like you!" Another girl I spoke with said, "I consciously and subconsciously compare myself to others via pictures and videos of people I see online. This can be for the worse because I will think to myself, *They are so fit and healthy. How can I be like them? What do I need to change about myself to become like that?*

So what about the girl who does feel beautiful? Who accepts her body? Strangely, she is often viewed as "abnormal," or even considered a social anomaly. I asked girls what would happen if another girl approached them and declared, "I feel amazing about my body today and love my healthy, glowing skin!" They laughed, thinking I was joking. "This would never happen," one of them told me. "Never." Find me a girl who is body confident and you will also find a girl labelled as conceited and "into herself."

Our competitive and comparative culture puts insane pressure on our girls. Exposure to social media; the obsession with selfies; the power and allure of crafted images that show idealized appearance standards; and myriad products that make empty promises of shinier hair, whiter teeth, and reduced cellulite—taken together, these influences are all too often overwhelming. And they leave teen girls emulating what they see and not what they feel, all the while believing that the perfect body and look can be attained through hard work, sacrifice, and sheer force of will. Girls as young as seven years old complain about frizzy hair, fat legs, and flat chests. I see girls who hide in their hoodies, slouching and turning their bodies inward in an attempt to diminish their developing breasts, and awkwardly carrying around their gangly bodies. One of my clients, Alexis, was mortified by the fact she got so tall, so quickly. Not only did she have to contend with being taller than every boy in her class, but she also had to put up with the constant annoying commentary—"You are so big!" "No kidding," she'd tell me. What all these girls share is a deep dissatisfaction with their bodies and confusion as to why they don't feel good. "My body is not enough," they conclude, "so I'll change it." What they long for is unconditional love for themselves. What they experience, whether it is self-imposed or coming from outside influences, is rejection.

Rejection is borne of the self-critical language that so many girls are convinced is the motivator for change (an idea society as a whole has bought into). "If I am harsh on myself," goes the rationale, "telling myself I am fat, ugly, lazy, and not beautiful enough, I will be driven to change and I will never become complacent or conceited." It's the perfect plan to guarantee transformation. Except, in the process, there is no self-love, self-kindness, or self-compassion. A teen girl who pushes herself to lose ten pounds so she feels better about herself may lose the weight, but she may feel awful still, and then confused as to why losing the weight didn't result in happiness or contentment. This is not the motivation she needs. She may punish herself, perhaps depriving herself of nutrition, exercising in the extreme, or using harsh, self-deprecating criticism. Often, she'll use the weight scale to measure her self-worth and social currency. Starving for self-love and acceptance, she may wish she were taller, thinner, and more beautiful, with clearer skin, whiter teeth, and curlier hair. Eventually she will disconnect from herself.

I had been working with Naomi for almost a year when she blurted out, "My boobs are too big." Caught off guard by the randomness of this comment, I asked her to tell me more. Naomi explained that when she was fitted for a new bra the week prior (Mom had vetoed her sports bra preference), the lady helping her figure out the proper size told her she was "small everywhere, except in your bust." Naomi was mortified. She decided right then and there her boobs were too big and she hated them. She asked me how she could lose weight to shrink her boobs.

I had to tread lightly for a few reasons, as you will have to as well when it comes to growing girls wanting to change their bodies. First, she will be super-sensitive when talking about these issues. Second, her body is still changing, and interrupting the natural process is not advisable. Third, and most importantly, her body is not the problem; the real problem is her *perception* of her body. What helped Naomi, over the course of our next four sessions, was a shift in focus: from body hating to finding ways to feel good about her whole self.

If your daughter comes to you and expresses a desire to change her body, empathize with her: "This is tough for you and I completely understand." Then segue from talking about changing her body to changing her habits, and away from losing weight toward gaining a positive relationship with her body. Let her know that there is always something she can do to feel better about herself as she is.

ASHA

A lot of my friends are super-skinny, not that they can control it, but they always say they look anorexic or how they don't have boobs and butts. This makes me feel so frustrated because I'd kill to have their bodies. I have never tried to change my body, but sometimes I'll trace imaginary lines on my body and pretend to cut the fat off like a plastic surgeon.

I think I just need to not be so obsessed with what I look like. I probably need more of my own self-confidence and fewer negative thoughts. I probably need less social media too. When you look at any Instagram "model," you notice how they are all skinny, all muscle, and so beautiful. I think girls compare themselves to other girls and then they obsess over wanting to look like so-and-so. This makes them obsess over what they look like instead of who they are as a person. I probably am the one person who has influenced my relationship with my body—I have a negative influence on my body. My mom always tells me I'm beautiful.

Body Image and the Family Dynamic

Like identity, body image is formed over time and with the feedback of others. For a teen girl, body image can be a positive, accurate, and healthy view. In this scenario, she accepts her shape, size, and body parts, wears clothes that flatter her figure, and feels relaxed and confident as she moves. But body image can also be negative, distorted, and unhealthy. In this scenario, a teen girl is dissatisfied with how she looks and fixated on the body parts she hates. She wears clothes that neither fit nor flatter her unique shape, and looks and feels uncomfortable in her own skin.

While girls worry about how they look, parents worry about how girls feel about their looks. One mom told me, "I think she has a level head on her now, but I worry with middle school that she will start to feel the pressure to look a certain way. I try to keep her focused on what she loves rather than buying into the notion that at this age you have to dress and act a specific way. We worry about her being teased because she doesn't fit the standard mould."

Even though cultural and media messages influence your teen girl powerfully, the messages that come from within the family are just as powerful, perhaps more so. I believe parents have an enormous opportunity to positively shape how girls see themselves, despite exponential exposure to media and advertisements. In this section, I want to have a direct conversation with "Mom" and "Dad" about the ways in which you can affect how your teen girl looks at herself through her individual relationship to her body.

Please know that I am using "Mom" and "Dad" loosely here to refer to different types of influence in a teen girl's life. The roles and responsibilities of parents are shifting from traditional and stereotypical to be much more fluid, expansive, and inclusive. At the same time, though, one parent is often the primary caregiver in the family—meaning their role is more hands-on than a parent who is less involved in the day to day. Here, I will look at the role of each parent separately, with a focus on how teen girls are affected. Regardless of family configuration (single-parent or blended, same-sex or hetero, traditional or non-traditional), your teen daughter benefits from different parenting styles and support. If you think she may need another positive figure in her life, by all means bring one in. You might consider a mentor, a family friend, a member of the neighbourhood, or someone in your faith community. This trusted individual should be someone who can provide her with a different perspective and a different kind of relationship than the one you are cultivating with her. Think of it this way: no one parent (or person) can fulfill all her needs. Thus, a more healthy and balanced approach is to widen her support circle. Add new and interesting people who will see her differently, have varied conversations with her, and have a novel connection to her.

The Mom Effect

Moms often ask me, "How do I teach my daughter to have a positive body image and compete with the unrealistic images she sees daily on her social media feeds and in advertisements?" The answer is to provide ample messages of your own that are healthier and more realistic as you encourage her toward body appreciation.

Start with you: Change begins first with how you speak about your own body and other women. By paying attention to what you do today, you can alter the trajectory of your teen's relationship with her body for the rest of her life. Complaining that you "look old and tired" or making a comment like "I can't believe she's wearing leggings out in public" is damaging. Your daughter hears you, and she will instantly reflect on her own look and clothing choice. Be patient. It may take some time for you to become more aware of your relationship with your body.

If you spend time looking in the mirror and critiquing your body, she will learn to copy you. If you push food around on your plate, pretending to eat, she'll push her food around too. If you overeat or undereat to deal with uncomfortable feelings like frustration, sadness, or rejection, she'll add this "coping" tool to her own toolkit. If you limit the types of foods you eat, talk about dieting, or are obsessive with fitness and exercise, guess what? She will follow your lead. By contrast, if you eat a well-balanced diet, focus on fitness, and emphasize feeling good about your body by actively practising self-care, she will learn that this is the path to follow.

Stand strong: I know this is a big ask, especially if you struggle with your own body image, but begin by nurturing her body confidence, which is all about how she stands: tall, head up and chin out, shoulders back, looking strong and poised. At first, this may feel foreign to her, but research on body language and high-power poses by social psychologist Amy Cuddy shows us that how we stand influences body chemistry—lowering cortisol (the stress hormone) and raising testosterone (the dominance hormone). Standing strong can translate into feeling strong. As Cuddy explains, standing like a superhero for only two minutes can create the belief that "I can do anything" and empower girls to feel assertive and brave enough to take risks. "Fake it 'til you become it."[4] Stand with her; practise together. Feel good about your bodies together.

Focus on feeling over appearance: It is all too easy to gain quick connection with our girls by complimenting their appearance: "I love your outfit," or "You look so pretty today." Well-intentioned, yes, but when we highlight the superficial, she comes to believe that this is her true value. In other words, she internalizes the idea that what she looks like matters most, and she may feel our attention and love are contingent on her appearance. Let's use our words wisely, commenting on her attitude, her work ethic, and the dreams she wants to create and step into. Instead of complimenting her physical beauty, try complimenting her competence: "I see how hard you have been working today," or "You're really showing focus and determination when you practise." Phrases like these help her embody her core qualities and prioritize her power over her prettiness. When she asks you, "How do I look?" you can answer, but don't leave it there. Ask her, "How do you feel?" Remind her to focus on personalities and not attire when she is with her friends, and let her know that she can influence her peer group with her meaningful compliments in place of the social norm of criticism.

Shatter the mirror: Girls can become trapped in the mirror, endlessly fussing. Let them know that although we do not want them to leave the house with clothes mismatched or makeup running under their eyes, they need not spend too much time glaring at their reflections and looking for body parts they feel are imperfect or need "shaming." When she looks in the mirror, help her to focus on the body parts she loves and use positive messaging when speaking about herself: "My legs are so toned and strong," for example, or "I love the colour of my hair." Encourage her to shift her focus from the mirror to real life, where there is so much more to think about than just body image—creating arts and crafts, photography, playing sports, skateboarding at the skate park, or meeting up with friends. Teach her to care less about looking good and more about truly living.

Dr. Marissa Bentham—clinic owner, chiropractor, and mom—is aware of her impact on her daughter's self-image. She offers this insight: "I've maintained a strong awareness that my daughter is always watching and listening to me when I get dressed, when I do my hair and makeup, and when I look at myself in the mirror, so I am very intentional about the messages I send her. I am very careful not to criticize myself or my body, both for my own healthy body image, and for hers. I do put time, care, and attention into my appearance and sometimes I am concerned that it may be influencing my daughter to put too much focus in this area. I try to always reiterate to her that who we are is so much more important than how we look, but that it's okay to want to look and feel our best." Dr. Bentham makes a great point: a healthy body image can include both looking and feeling good; it doesn't have to be one or the other but a balance of both.

Choose connection over disconnection: Girls turn against themselves when something goes wrong, whether that something is a poor grade, a fight with a friend, or simply not feeling good enough. They can choose to suffer in silence and disconnect not only from us but also from themselves. Unfortunately, their bodies are easy and accessible targets for their sadness, frustration, and even anger. As she becomes hyper-focused on her body—and buys into the logic of "if I were prettier, skinnier, or sexier, then I'll feel happier"—she can easily disconnect by ignoring her feelings and often negating physical signs such as hunger, thirst, or fatigue. Worse yet, she can punish herself by overdoing it with eating, sleeping, and exercising, or distract herself from discomfort with social media and screen time. As she disconnects, she can feel more lost than ever.

This is where moms have an important role to play: you can remind her how to connect. She may not want to talk to you and connect through conversation, but you can gently point out that she may need to amp up her self-care regime. Make suggestions: drinking enough water; taking time to prepare and then nourish her body with a wholesome meal; moving her body and doing something she loves to do (preferably outside); getting enough sleep (despite the changes in her circadian rhythm that will make her want to stay up late);[5] taking time to process her feelings by journalling or speaking with you. Remind her that whatever she is going through is just a moment, and that moments have a beginning and, yes, an end.

The Dad Effect

Throughout my years of working with young girls and their parents, I have seen a drastic and impressive shift from dad disengagement to dad involvement, especially when it comes to body image. In the early years of my practice, dads often appeared awkward and uncomfortable around their teenage daughters with their changing bodies, changing hormones, and emergent and strong opinions. I would hear their oft-repeated refrain, "I leave those conversations [about puberty] to her mom." Now I field questions from interested dads who want to know, "How can I connect with her? How can I support her, and what do you think she needs to hear from me?"

Dads worry about their daughters—about their self-confidence, clothing choices, attention-seeking behaviours, and sometimes-provocative social media feeds. They may feel frustrated by the emergent conflict between her and her mom. Most dads want to be involved in their daughter's life, and they seek to establish a healthy, loving, and fulfilling relationship. However, they often don't understand why their daughters may radically fluctuate from bright and bubbly to angry and explosive. They wonder what happened to their sweet little girl, who has seemingly and spontaneously been replaced with a door-slamming teenager. They want to help but they don't know how. Here are some ways to move past that bewilderment.

Love her unconditionally: According to Steve Biddulph, author of *10 Things Girls Need Most*, "the No. 1 factor that determines the level of confidence a woman carries into her adult life is the relationship that woman had with her father. That he loved spending time with her, listened to her and talked softly and respectfully around her and around her mom."[6] Fathers have a tremendous opportunity to help their daughters defy prevalent stereotypes and encourage them to be strong and independent, to know their value and not be afraid to be their unique selves. Your daughter will likely look to you for approval and appreciation. Feeling she is loved unconditionally, on good days and bad, increases the likelihood she will love herself unconditionally.

Engage and encourage: We want girls to seek out their dads. The more removed dads are or the more they push their daughters away, the more vulnerable girls become. Vulnerable girls search for attention and affection elsewhere, and they will find it in the form of unhealthy online attention or in unhealthy relationships entered into for the wrong reasons.

This is not the time to check out and wait until she's older. It's not the time to disengage or allow the awkward signs of maturity and growth to scare you away. It is not the time to be critical, as she is extremely self-conscious in these growing years. Neither should you shame her body by embarrassing her for her changing physique. Even unintentional hurtful comments—"Your stomach is so chubby and cute," for example, or "You are definitely not lacking in the booty department"—can become the catalyst for her to push herself to alter her body. It's also not the time to encourage her to be "tough" or to overemphasize sports and fitness.

Dads: You know she is longing for validation and approval, so give it to her. By providing the healthy attention she needs, you can help her shift from someone who constantly seeks out the approval of others—looking for "proof" that she is enough—to someone who doesn't need that stamp of approval because she knows, without any doubt or hesitation, that she defines her own self-worth.

Connect in your way: When I ask girls about spending time with their dads, there is often a palpable and resounding excitement, although some also say simply that they "don't get enough time" with their fathers. Make the time to create consistent and predictable routines and rituals with your daughter. There is great value in father-daughter dates, crafted by both of you. Your time together does not need to be filled with conversation. Most girls I know don't even want this. They want your time and undivided attention and the chance to be adventurous and explore. Conversations may come, but they are more likely once she is relaxed and feels ready to share.

You could go on nature walks and hikes, bike ride, zip line, or kick a soccer ball around. You could bake or cook together, play puzzles or games, conduct a science experiment, build something, play music, attend concerts, or go on mini-excursions. Time together could be spent teaching her valuable life skills such as how to drive, how to grocery shop, or how to budget her money. She may even be able to teach you a thing or two about social media. Get her to show you her favourite app or how she curates images before posting. Take a selfie together—the goofier the better. So much of an adolescent girl's life is focused on appearance, on whether others think she is attractive or popular. Give her a break from thinking about what she looks like. Encourage her to be messy, silly, wild, and free, even if just for a moment. Help her let go of the expectations she clings to, the ones that tell her she needs to be perfect and to do things right all the time. Together, you can live, laugh, and play.

Make your words valuable: Typically, teen girls don't spend a lot of time with their dads, so your words can take on more weight than you know. Every day, tell her "you are special," "you are valuable," "you matter to me," "you can tell me anything." Tell her that you see her and love her exactly as she is. She may laugh or brush your words away, but trust me when I tell you that she hears you and is soaking it all up. This kind of positive messaging will compete with the demanding social media messages telling her how to look and behave. When she feels frustrated with herself and thinks that she's not meeting society's impossibly high standards of success, your words will be there for her to fall back on. Your words are her safety net and a reminder of how remarkable she actually is.

Appreciate her individuality: Girls often tell me that when they are with their dads, they feel they can be themselves. Girls can feel so weird and abnormal in the awkward teen years. See her for who she is, notice her qualities and values, and look for emerging personality traits and quirks. Use phrases such as "Wow, your sarcasm and wit are giving me a run for my money," or rhetorically ask her when she got so smart. When a girl feels noticed and accepted, something interesting happens: she understands that she doesn't need to change herself to fit in, that there is nothing wrong with her, and that being different is a good thing, not something to hide. As your daughter grows, the memories of her time with you will be deeply ingrained, and she'll know that being herself will always be a better choice than conformity.

The Three "Fs"

"Eat well, stress less, move more, love more. That's it."[7] This simple message is found in the book *The Whole Foods Diet*, but it's not an easy one for teen girls, or their parents, to put into practice. We know that young and impressionable girls are highly influenced to change their bodies because of confusing and unrealistic societal and cultural body messaging—messaging they cannot control. To help her grow a healthy body image, show her how she can focus on what she can control: food, fitness, and fun.

Food

Food is an important aspect of our lives, satisfying our bodies' needs, encouraging social connection and celebration, and promoting health and happiness. To support a positive body image in your teen girl, guide her to be aware of nutritious foods and healthy eating practices. Girls need nourishing food to grow, to feel healthy and energized, and to balance their emotions and moods. Nutritious food enables girls to think more clearly and serves a critical function in healthy brain development. As Karen Jensen, author of *Three Brains*, tells us, "Foods and supplements that contain antioxidants, essential fatty acids (EFAs), complex carbohydrates, and proteins are particularly helpful in boosting brain health" and provide a "smart start."[8]

But teen girls are not thinking about how food is affecting their brain development when they cut out entire food groups, such as carbs, in an attempt to lose weight. And they often make their relationship with food more complex when they eat for reasons other than physical hunger. Although food can provide temporary relief from uncomfortable feelings or stress, the real work is for her to figure out why she feels the way she does and what she needs instead of food to help alleviate those feelings. Sometimes she does need more (nutritious) food to help her mood; other times more rest or a meaningful conversation will be the fix. One thing that definitely hinders a teen's exploration into what she needs is when we critique her food choices, tell her what to eat and how much, or project our own issues with food onto her. It's tough, but we need to show girls that body love is much more than food focus. Kim D'Eon, a holistic nutritionist and natural wellness media advocate, offers this top tip for teen girls: "Practise loving yourself," she says, keeping it real. "Start practising this now because it might be one of the healthiest habits you ever adopt."

I believe we should take Kim's advice straight to teen girls (and be honest). Guide her to identify what she needs and when. Although there is no one size or one way to be healthy, the strongest message you can take to your teen girl is this: You know your body better than anyone else does, and you are learning to take care of its needs.

When you listen to your body's internal signs of hunger and fullness (also known as intuitive eating), you can make healthy choices about foods that have nutritional value and will provide you with energy.

You will need to exercise patience as your teen practises getting to know and listening to her body. Acupuncturist Dr. Adrienne Chan told me she teaches her four-year-old and six-year-old daughters to pay attention to what each food provides. She refrains from categorizing foods as "good" and "bad" or even "healthy" and "unhealthy." Instead, she provides her daughters with the knowledge of what each food offers.

Once your teen starts discerning the difference between head hunger ("I can't stop thinking about that candy bar") and the actual feelings of her body, she will be even more empowered to make better food choices. Parents can model making good food choices at home by choosing to cook healthy meals over grabbing cheap and easy fast food. In 2018, *Time* magazine reported that "cooking gives us control over what we put in our bodies. Studies have found that when we whip up meals at home we tend to take in fewer carbohydrates, less sugar and less fat than people who cook less or not at all."[9] This may be enough to convince her.

You can also talk with your teen girl about how the food industry offers an abundance of information or, rather, misinformation about food, often convincing us to eat foods that are anything but nutritious (think potato chips made with "organic potatoes" or "real fruit" smoothies). Here are my quick suggestions for keeping food real for your teen girl:

- Role model good food choices.

- Encourage her to listen to her body and think about whether she feels hungry or if she needs something else, like more water or rest.

- Fill your cupboards and fridge with nutritious food, but let her make the choice about what she wants to eat.

- Create space for healthy family dinners, even if it's just once a week, and cook and eat that meal together so that she associates food with connection rather than body image.

Fitness

It doesn't matter if your girl is playing sports such as volleyball, basketball, or soccer; taking part in dancing, swimming, or gymnastics; or trying rock climbing, sailing, or fencing: If she is trying new activities and learning to push herself out of her comfort zone, she is also learning about her body. She is learning what feels good, and what doesn't.

Girls who are physically active are more likely to feel a boost in self-confidence and a positive body image than girls who are sedentary. While exercising, girls are learning to be in the moment and feel their bodies in motion. And exercise has so many physical benefits: Body movement can lower stress levels and increase mental clarity, energy levels, and performance. The release of endorphins and adrenaline can also contribute to positive emotions and balanced moods. Exercise also aids in digestion, contributes to disease prevention, and improves sleep.

One of the most convincing reasons to help your teen girl participate in whatever form of fitness she enjoys is that this helps to influence a positive body image. Empowerment comes with challenging her fitness level and realizing she can reach beyond her own expectations. Physical challenge can build up both the assertive and competitive "muscles" in a teen girl.

For some adolescent girls, fitness is already enjoyable and they are consistently active. For these girls, fitness is not necessarily about "working out" but participating in positive body movement, whether that comes through walking the dog, indoor rock climbing, gardening, paddleboarding, Ultimate Frisbee, or bouncing on a trampoline. They know what they like to do and also why they like to do it: "I feel so refreshed when I go outside," or "I love how strong I feel when I am mountain biking."

Admittedly, like adults, not all girls want to be active. Your daughter may prefer to lie on the couch and read or scroll. She may even argue that swiping her finger across her screen is "exercise." But she can always do something. She may not participate in a team sport at school, but she may enjoy golfing or badminton, a simple walk, or yoga, meditation, and stretching. Encourage her interests whenever you can.

Although I recognize that not every girl will be interested in this, I'm a big proponent of encouraging girls to get involved in a team sport they like. Research tells us that girls who play team sports are typically more confident and make healthier lifestyle choices (especially when it comes to drug use and early sex) than girls who do not. A *Psychology Today* article states that "involvement in team sports has been positively associated with social acceptance and a sense of belonging, especially where such involvement is character-ised by positive coaching, progressive skill development and peer support."[10] These results, in turn, are often conducive to a positive self-perception that prompts girls to broaden their horizons.

Playing on a sports team allows your teen girl to learn some key life lessons. She'll gain social interactions, peer support, and a sense of belonging. She'll experience healthy competition (against her opponents and herself), and will come to see the importance of dedication and stick-to-it-iveness, of encouraging and supporting others, and of working hard together, struggling through losses and celebrating victories. This is where I believe the phrase "stronger together" really manifests.

Here is how you can help to encourage your teen to be active:

- Ask her what she *wants* to do instead of suggesting what activities she should do or telling her what your fitness routine looks like—she will be more likely to buy in.

- Spend some time with her discovering what she might like to do. This may mean doing some research online or talking to others about what they enjoy doing.

- Encourage her to try new activities with her friends or with you in a playful and open-minded way—it could be hiking, stand-up paddleboarding, dancing, playing baseball, or yoga.

Ultimately, girls can use fitness to know their bodies, trust their bodies, and learn to love and accept all their bodies can do for them. As a result, they are also likely to feel a sense of personal effectiveness, self-worth, and body appreciation.

Fun

One final way to promote a body positive image among teen girls is to bring back one simple basic: play. Play is an essential part of child development because it contributes to the cognitive, physical, social, and emotional well-being of children. In *Rest, Play, Grow*, Deborah MacNamara tells us that "young children cannot thrive or flourish in a world without play; the very essence of who they will become is defined by it."[11]

We should encourage teen girls to play and have fun as well. Play is where the imagination expands and competence is developed with enhanced confidence and resilience. Play develops leadership skills and healthy, active bodies and can reduce obesity. Above all, play is a simple joy and a cherished part of being a young person. When we encourage teen girls to play, they realize taking a break from their worries offers the release they need. As parents, we should be telling our teen girls to play just as often as we are asking them about their burdens.

Every girl is different when it comes to fun. Some like to read or cook or play a sport; others like to hang out with family and friends and listen to music or watch a live performance. One huge benefit that occurs when parents "play" with their daughters—whatever that looks like—is that you compete with their devices and social media. Encouraging your teen to seek out more opportunities for humour and laughter can improve their emotional health, strengthen relationships, and lead to greater happiness. Science supports the fact that laughter has numerous health benefits, such as improving the immune system and mood, diminishing pain, and safeguarding against the damaging effects of stress.[12]

So how do we help girls cultivate fun in their lives?

- Find out what fun means to them. Most girls I spoke with about fun gave me pretty simple responses such as "watching funny videos on YouTube or Netflix." One girl told me that, to her, fun meant "taking a break from thinking and just doing an activity I love so I can restore."

- Encourage your teen to trade her seriousness in for goofing around. Watch comedy shows together, or seek out jokes and stories to share with her that you know she'll find funny.

- Aim for a little fun every day—it might just make your day, too!

- Remember that fun doesn't have to be scripted or planned. Stay alert for the moments when she is open to having fun with you.

Whatever your teen girl chooses to do for fun, remind her that fun is an essential part of her growth. Not only do girls want to have fun, they need to have fun!

Eating Disorders

This book is not intended to be a guide to managing eating disorders in your teen girl. However, because these disorders are clearly linked with body image—body dissatisfaction is the best known contributor to the development of an eating disorder[13]—it is important that you are aware of the danger signs so that you can step into her circle when it is absolutely needed. The following information is based on my research and experience, but it is in no way intended to serve as a replacement for professional assistance. If you suspect your daughter suffers from any kind of eating disorder, or if you feel she's on the verge of developing one, please trust your gut and get the help you need. Eating disorders are serious and complex—they are both physically and psychologically demanding. If you want to learn more, I recommend these three books that support parents going through this experience: *A Parent's Guide to Defeating Eating Disorders* by Ahmed Boachie and Karin Jasper, *The Body Image*

Workbook for Teens by Julia V. Taylor, and *When Your Teen Has An Eating Disorder* by Lauren Muhlheim.

As your teenage daughter grows, she may be more vocal about her food choices, dramatic with her declarations, or simply curious about her food consumption. "Mom, I am becoming a vegetarian," she may declare one night at dinner, as she sits in front of the chicken stir-fry you spent the last hour preparing. You may notice drastic shifts in her appetite or dietary requirements, or changes in her behaviour when it comes to dieting and exercise. Perhaps you'll catch her making a quiet comment about cutting out carbs, "like the other girls." Or you may simply notice a disruption in your family's dinner schedule as your daughter increasingly opts to eat "at a friend's house" or "grab something later" when she goes out.

These changes may simply be a signal that she is figuring out what foods work best for her. Or they may indicate the beginning of a less-than-healthy relationship with food. Her decision to become vegan or vegetarian, pescatarian, ketogenic, flexitarian, or gluten- or dairy- free could be driven by a desire to eat in a healthier way or keep up with the newest food trends. Alternatively, feelings of body dissatisfaction or body hatred could be lurking below the surface. If you notice any or many of the following signs, your teen girl may be struggling:

- overly focused or even obsessed with physical health, food, and exercise
- not taking care of herself
- weight loss
- erratic weight fluctuations
- excessive exercise
- food avoidance
- going to the bathroom after each meal

If obsessive habits are neither noticed nor addressed, they can become a life-threatening eating disorder such as anorexia nervosa, bulimia nervosa, or the less commonly known disorder called orthorexia. There is no single easy answer to the question of why eating disorders begin, but some typical reasons include:

- the emotional and physical changes that accompany puberty

- feelings of embarrassment about body changes

- body dissatisfaction

- stress and anxiety

- burying feelings

- feeling out of control when it comes to life changes, or feeling controlled

- not having choice or a voice (especially in the home)

- parental pressure to be thinner or "healthier," or negative role modelling when it comes to attitudes around food and eating

- peer pressure to look like other girls

- cultural and societal messages to conform to a single body type

It is important to note that while eating disorders are typically more common among white females living in the Western world, recent studies suggest that eating disorders are on the rise for other ethnicities and in other parts of the world.[14] One report suggests that the explanation for this shift is social pressure resulting from the standards of female beauty imposed by modern Western cultures. Our hyper-connected online existence has no doubt played a role as well. As one HuffPost contributor stated, "For individuals struggling with an eating disorder, the constant streams of body and food conscious posts may cause heightened levels of stress and anxiety surrounding the 'perfect body image.'"[15] Below are the simple definitions and potentials signs of the three disorders that I see in clients most regularly.

Anorexia Nervosa

Anorexia nervosa is defined by extremely restrictive eating habits in a person. Often the individual believes they need to lose weight because they think they are "fat," but there is much more to this disorder than refusing food to lose weight. Genetics, the environment, social, psychological, and emotional factors—all of these variables can play into anorexia nervosa. Disordered eating may be an attempt to gain control over what seems like a chaotic life. Studies show that a girl's brain adapts to food restriction, and the message "feed me" conflicts with her desire to lose weight. The anorexic solves this inner conflict by not eating, which in turn reduces her anxiety.[16]

Signs of anorexia may include:

- a hyper-focus on calorie counting and low-caloric foods
- barely eating and pushing food around on her plate
- meal skipping
- weight loss
- thinning hair
- sleep troubles
- increased moodiness and irritability
- fatigue

Bulimia Nervosa

Bulimia nervosa is characterized by overeating large amounts of food in one sitting even when not hungry (a loaf of bread and a jar of peanut butter, for example), followed by purging by inducing vomiting or taking laxatives. Bulimics often hide how much they are eating, and their binges are often accompanied by overwhelming feelings of guilt, which can lead to a continuance of the vicious cycle of binge and purge.

Signs of bulimia may include:

- eating in secret
- hiding food
- excessive wrappers and empty containers in the garbage
- complaints of feeling "too full" and excessive stomach pains

Orthorexia Nervosa

This last disorder is typified with an obsession with healthy or "pure" eating of the "right" foods. Orthorexia can easily be mistaken as "health consciousness." This can make it difficult to detect, as it can initially appear acceptable, creating a grey area where eating disorders are concerned. On the surface, a teen who is orthorexic may appear healthy, but her behaviour and attitude toward food is unhealthy in many ways. She will base her value and worth on her ability to eat "clean," and to be "perfect" in her food choices.

Signs of orthorexia may include:

- compulsive checking of ingredient lists and nutritional labels

- overwhelming concern about health ingredients

- elimination of various food groups (such as all carbohydrates or all fats)

- inability to eat anything outside of her healthy list of foods

- extreme amount of time (hours each day) thinking about and planning meals

- high levels of stress when healthy foods are not readily available

There is nothing wrong with your teen daughter wanting to maintain an ideal weight, though you may need to talk about what "ideal weight" means. But an obsessive approach to dieting—which may include falling into or even choosing an eating disorder—is not going to be conducive to body satisfaction or a general state of happiness. Parents who have watched their daughters spiral into the abyss of an eating disorder know the agony and fear it elicits. If your daughter shows any signs or symptoms of an eating disorder, please reach out to get professional and compassionate guidance.

Find Her Sparkle

Girls are more than what they look like—or what they think they look like. Many girls I know are talented artistically or athletically. They are adventurous and confident in social situations. They are fierce and fearless. Many do not have a negative view of their bodies. In fact, some have a downright positive view. Take Katie, for instance. "I love the strength of my body," she told me. "My body allows me to live an active lifestyle and challenge myself with difficult exercise. I appreciate my body—both what it can do and what it looks like."

To encourage this fearlessness and confidence in who they are (as opposed to focusing on how they look), I offer girls this piece of advice: "Find out what you love to do and what makes you the happiest, and make the time to do it every single day. This is your sparkle, your passion, and your purpose." When girls tap into their passions and focus on what they love to do, they learn a key lesson: there is so much more to life than how you look.

Not every girl knows what makes her sparkle. Perhaps she's been afraid to explore her options, or she's playing it safe with activities she already knows. Maybe she's participating, but only half-heartedly and devoid of enthusiasm and joy. How do we help teen girls discover and embrace their joie de vivre? The simplest way to find out about her spark is to ask her. With time, conversation, and curiosity, nurture her to continually expand her interests and activities, whether they are easy or challenging for her. Eventually she may come to understand and know for herself what truly makes her happy. Let her try anything and everything you can reasonably offer.

When girls find their sparkle, they feel their purpose. Sparkle yields focus, direction, and the knowledge that what they do matters and has meaning. These benefits help girls shift from being overly self-focused to becoming "other focused" and, arguably, more balanced and fulfilled. Encouraging her to discover her sparkle can turn her away from her mirrors and screens and body obsession and back to the self-love she was born with, and then outward, toward the world and the chance to have an impact on others with her true essence.

Shelby Rowland is the founder of *gracie's gals*, a six-week training club for young girls that focuses on movement and positive affirmations. "At *gracie's gals* we focus on talking about everything other than gals' bodies," she told me, "because if we continue to talk about bodies, even in a good way, the emphasis remains in the same place. Bodies don't make us who we are; it's what's inside that counts. That is what we need to teach our gals to focus on: moving forward. One of my favourite things to tell the gals is 'don't search for compliments, aim for accomplishments; that will give you the most confidence.'" I couldn't agree more.

How Parents HELP Growth

- Modelling self-care by focusing on nutrition, fitness, sleep, play, and a positive body image
- Teaching her body confidence: standing tall, head held high, chin up, shoulders back, strong and poised stance
- Limiting mirror time by suggesting more real time
- Complimenting her on her changing and growing body
- Encouraging her to pursue what makes her sparkle

How Parents HINDER Growth

- Critiquing your body or hers
- Using words like "fat" or "diet" and holding unhealthy or obsessive ideas around food and exercise
- Complimenting her on her appearance only
- Ignoring any difficult concern; deferring to the other parent
- Comparing her body to someone else's

3

HEALTHY MINDS

T HE BEST WORD to describe Carmen is "luminescent": there is an inner light that radiates from within her. As she sipped her iced tea and nibbled on her brownie, she seemed eager to talk about her experience with mental illness. "On a typical school day I would wake up super-early in fear of being late," she told me. "Once I arrived at my first class I would spend the majority of the class being anxious because I was nervous I'd be asked a question on the spot. If I had a test in one class there was no way I'd be productive in my other classes because I'd be anxious about the test all day. On the days I had dance after school, I would be so excited to go because it was a place where I could focus on one thing that required both my body and mind to be present."

Carmen knew she was experiencing anxiety when she would stress about small things that wouldn't even faze other people, or when she would constantly second-guess herself. She told me that her first step in dealing with her anxiety was talking to her parents, who she trusted, followed by weekly sessions with her school counsellor. But what's been most helpful, she added, is that "I only surround myself with those who are loving, supportive, and who understand me. I've learned to check in with myself, especially in difficult and stressful situations. I also have learned to separate things that are worthy of being anxious about and things that simply aren't worth wasting my energy on."

There is a plethora of information available on anxiety and other mental health concerns, accompanied by some bleak statistics. I know this topic is dark and heavy, which is why I wanted to open this chapter with Carmen's story. She offers us all the light and hope we need, shifting our perception from the problem of mental illness to the promotion of mental health and wellness or healthy minds.

Parents of teens who may be suffering from a mental illness are often at a loss as to how to help. One father I spoke with said wisely, "We were distraught that our child was feeling so low, and we wanted to ensure that she had every resource at her disposal to get through this experience and thrive. Navigating the education and health system can be quite challenging. It takes considerable time for the system to move forward once you are in the queue, and yet your child is suffering. I would have started with coaching right away if I knew how productive it would have been."

This chapter will explore why a healthy mind is important for your teen daughter, what it looks like when that healthy mind is compromised, and what you can do to promote and support her mental health by making it a priority. As well, it will offer some insight into when you may need to intervene.

Mental Health and Wellness

Much of the conversation and many of the action steps around mental wellness focus primarily on mental illness. The problem with that approach is that when we focus on the sickness—on what is "wrong" with someone—we often create stigma and alienate or isolate the individual. This moves us away from what we really want: optimal health and healthy minds. But what exactly is mental health? Mental health is an amalgamation of emotional, psychological, and social well-being. It affects how we think, feel, and act. Mental health corresponds with how we handle stress, how we relate to others, and how we make certain choices. It's a general sense of energy and competency to complete daily tasks, and an inner calm, sense of self-worth, and hope and optimism about the present and the future. Mental health concerns can happen concurrently. For example, one of my clients, Sydney, experienced attention deficit hyperactivity disorder (ADHD), an anxiety disorder, and bouts of depression. Is this fair for a teen girl? No. Is this a teen girl's reality? Yes, sometimes.

It helps to know what having a healthy mind looks and sounds like. Painting a picture of strong mental health for your teen daughter promotes her awareness and gives her a healthy ideal to strive for. The more you talk about healthy minds and ask essential questions—for example, "How is your stress level today?" or "What's on your mind?"—the more you will understand about your teen's mental health and how it is affecting her life. This knowledge and awareness puts you in a position of power to, if necessary, take action steps toward healing and helping any kind of mental health concern.

Adolescent girls with positive self-esteem and robust healthy minds are able to face adversity; they see it as a challenge that can be met with support they ask for as needed. Daily stressors like school presentations or dance recitals become manageable, not overwhelming. A teen with a healthy mindset might say, "I don't understand why my grade is so low, so I am going to talk to my teacher tomorrow." Or "I didn't make the gymnastics team this year, but I will spend the summer working on my skills so I can try again next year." When girls are healthy, they are happy; conversely, when they are happy, they are healthy.

Why Do Healthy Minds Matter?

Healthy minds matter. The healthier girls feel, the happier and more balanced they will be in all other areas of their lives: emotional, social, psychological, spiritual, and mental. When girls have mental clarity, they can experience enhanced positive feelings, increased confidence and resilience, improved body image, and the ability to focus and concentrate, along with a decrease in stress or feelings of incompetency.

When teen girls have healthy thoughts about themselves, along with the necessary coping skills to manage uncomfortable feelings and life challenges—academic failure, social rejection, family upset such as divorce or even death—they can respond intentionally to tough stuff and better take care of themselves. Girls who have cultivated positive mental health are able to work productively, connect with others, create and nurture a support circle, realize their full potential, and make meaningful contributions to their school, their communities, their cities, and beyond. Isn't this what we want for our girls?

Out in the Open

There's no question that we live in a fast-paced, busy, stressful world. Thankfully, we also have language and different platforms through which people can engage and speak about mental wellness. Mental health concerns are being normalized in ways they never have been.

Unfortunately, teenage girls are twice as likely to experience mental health concerns as teenage boys, and the most common mental health challenge among teens is an eating disorder.[1] A study conducted by the National Institutes of Health found that media portrayals of body image and "ideal" lives created unrealistic expectations for teenagers, regardless of gender, disrupting normal identity development and often leading to depression.[2]

There are multiple factors behind mental health concerns, both biological and environmental, and they are not always easily discerned. Most importantly, mental illness does not discriminate—anyone can be affected, regardless of gender, age, race, religion, or educational or financial status. Research states that by the age of forty, about 50 percent of the population will have or have had a mental illness. One in five people directly experience a mental health problem or illness, and almost 49 percent of those who feel they have suffered from depression or anxiety have never gone to see a doctor or sought professional help.[3]

Everyone knows someone who has struggled with a mental health issue, and yet the continued stigma around mental illness often prevents those suffering from accessing diagnosis and treatment. How many girls, consumed by their need to look as though they are just fine and holding their lives together, desperately need support but feel too afraid, embarrassed, or ashamed to ask for it? And how many parents are struggling to understand their teens and how to help them?

Campaigns promoting mental health awareness do help. My student Lisa struggles with high anxiety and depression. I asked her to what extent social media sites have helped her tell her story, and also helped her to feel validated by the stories of others. "I couldn't believe when I read a girl's story that she had to leave school because she was getting panic attacks about even thinking about attending her math class," she told me. "I finally felt that I was not alone."

Before I recommend some ways you can support your teen daughter and protect her mental wellness, I'd like to take some time to deconstruct one of the most important contributors to mental health issues among teen girls—stress.

The Stress Cycle

Without doubt, girls are under stress. I see it in their faces and the strain around their eyes. It is why their shoulders are sometimes a mile high, and it often explains their sometimes truculent moods. To some degree, stress is pervasive and prevalent in all mental health disorders. Sometimes it's the starting point, as unaddressed stress builds up and, over time, can become an anxiety disorder. Or perhaps a mental health disorder already exists, and stress is entangled in the disorder itself (for example, obsessive-compulsive disorder).

A school counsellor I spoke with about the rise in mental health concerns among teens agreed that girls are under pressure to excel at everything, and in turn they place immense pressure on themselves. She also shared a fascinating insight. Girls seem to fall into one of two categories: they are either stressed all the time and know why but don't consider making any changes toward stronger mental health, or they are so used to their stress that they don't notice how it is affecting their lives. "Every day a girl comes into my office telling me she was told to come here by one of her teachers but she doesn't know why—she feels 'fine.' After talking for only a few minutes, we slowly start to unpack all that is on her plate. And once we unload her burdens, she starts to understand that she has a lot going on and this could be causing her some stress."

This is not to say that all stress is bad. In fact, stress may be necessary to help girls face new challenges and build new competencies. According to Lisa Damour, author of *Under Pressure*, "Stress gets a bad rap. Though people don't always enjoy being stretched to new limits, both common sense and scientific research tell us that stress operating beyond our comfort zones helps us grow."[4] Stress only becomes unhealthy when it exceeds what a girl can handle, and this tipping point varies from girl to girl and from situation to situation.

When stress permeates a teen's daily life, dominating her brain space, she has little time or energy to focus on much else. After all, we can't expect her to think about her future when she is surviving a tough day complete with too many deadlines, distressing texts from a friend, and not enough time for goofiness or creative joyfulness. These are the kinds of stresses girls face daily, and when they are unaddressed and unprocessed they have the potential to cause mental health concerns and lead to unhealthy minds. This is why it's vital to assist girls in recognizing their own stress and to support them in processing stress with healthy coping tools.

What's to Stress About?

Stress begins with stressors. For teens, some stressors are obvious and often uncontrollable: quizzes and tests at school, a busy schedule, an upcoming race, play, or game. But she may also be contending with many less obvious stressors: facing new and scary social situations, worrying about the subtext of a "we have to talk" text message, being called on by a teacher when she doesn't have an answer, and her own self-criticism. Whatever type of stress your teen may be dealing with, it's important to remember that stress causes discomfort and a surge of cortisol in her body; all she wants to do is rid herself of this discomfort.

If your daughter is not willing to share the stressors or triggers she is facing, you still have a role to play. You can talk about the things that might be contributing to her skyrocketing stress levels and educate her on her body's response to stress. Self-awareness is essential. Every girl is different and will respond to stress in her own unique way. It's paramount that girls pay attention to the signs of stress, including but not limited to: headache, stomach ache, tight jaw, change in body temperature (too hot, too cold), sweating, muscle soreness, or fatigue. When girls know their individual signs of stress, they are more self-aware and, therefore, more in control. Olivia said it best: "Even if I can pause and say, 'I am stressed,' I start to feel better," she told me. "I guess it's the acknowledgement that something's up for me." She is right: with awareness comes the potential for action.

Girls also need to know that their bodies have a built-in stress-response system that is activated in the face of danger—whether that takes the form of perceived threat of failure, rejection, or uncertainty, or a real danger like a stranger in the school. To protect itself, her body will respond in one of three ways: fight, flight, or freeze. For a teen girl, fight mode typically manifests as aggression or passive-aggressiveness. She may become snarky, for example, challenging you on established routines ("You take out the trash! Why do I have to always do it!?"). Flight is often about escape—to her device or into her bedroom. Freeze is a total shutdown. She will not let you near, and will block you with her body language (arms folded across her chest) and words ("I'm fine!"). It's important to be aware of these responses. Doing so allows you to understand her behaviours (and possibly take them less personally) and, consequently, help her better understand herself. When girls "get" why they fled the party or the classroom, or why they said something so hurtful but didn't mean it, they can get closer to an acceptance of "I am stressed."

By the time girls reach adolescence they have undoubtedly learned some coping skills for their stressors. In fact, they've learned them so well they are instinctual. Teen girls often cope with stress by binge-watching shows like *Pretty Little Liars*, *Riverdale*, or *Friends*, or spending hours aimlessly scrolling through their social media feeds. Some girls become overly perfectionistic, trying to get every last detail of a project just right, or they procrastinate by promising you that they'll "do it later." These coping skills serve one purpose: to help her relieve her stress. Unfortunately, they do not process the stress; they simply ameliorate it.

More disturbing is the growing trend—it might even be called a subculture—around girls and self-harm in response to overwhelming stress. When her stress is unbearable and she feels she has no other options, a young and desperate teenage girl may turn to self-harm in the form of cutting, burning, scratching, binge drinking or doing drugs, an eating disorder, emotional eating, social isolation, self-criticism, or self-neglect. She either wants to numb herself so she feels nothing, or she's seeking to validate her inner turmoil by harming herself to feel something. Both are attempts to deal with uncontrollable pain and anguish.

During my research for this book, I discovered that self-injury (SI) is a means to express emotional distress—what she is unable to express in words—and it may easily become a habit.[5] The injury actually makes a teen girl feel better, at least until the shame and guilt flood in. Her behaviour becomes her best-kept secret, the one part of life she feels she can control, and she will do anything to hide her external scars and wounds, from wearing long sleeves (even in hot weather) to washing her own bedding to hide signs of bleeding wounds. Whether she's hurting her wrists, arms, chest, or thighs, one thing is clear: she is struggling and feels she deserves the punishment. She needs healthier options for expressing herself and more time with you or another safe person, even if it seems like she is pushing you away. Self-harm is a devastating cry for love and attention. We need to intervene and understand why she is hurting herself. If you suspect your daughter of self-harming, seek professional help immediately.

Calm Down and...?

How can you best help your daughter when she is in stress mode? Offer and share with her healthy alternative coping tools such as yoga and meditation, physical activity, listening to or playing music, making art, baking, cooking, singing, dancing, journalling, crying, or punching a pillow. Other techniques include talking out her feelings with you or a trusted adviser, and fundamental "grounding techniques" such as lying on the ground while taking deep breaths, self-soothing with a warm bath, or focusing on the five senses of sight, smell, sound, touch, and taste. All of these tools can encourage her to calm down.

Once she learns to self-regulate and is better able to express herself, she needs to share her experiences, how she is feeling, and what she is thinking about. At the same time, you can nurture her fragile self-esteem. When a girl is in stress mode, she is often unable to see her own strengths and skills and is likely to feel isolated. She needs to know she is absolutely not hopeless. You can teach her to trust herself, see stress as an opportunity to better know and care for herself, and acknowledge her own efforts to work through the stressor.

Talking through a stressful situation can help her to truly process stress (not just avoid it) and bring a particular cycle of stress to a halt. This kind of talking takes time, effort, and practice. Yelling at her to pick her clothes up off the floor when she's at the high point of the stress cycle will only escalate her stress levels. And taking over in an attempt to protect her may not only further agitate her, but it may also rob her of the opportunity to manage the stress herself.

Instead, try to become aware of her individual signs of stress, noticing her shoulders rising or an edginess in her voice that wasn't there in the morning. Experiment with different communication tricks to nurture her through her pressure-filled moments. This may mean lowering your voice to bring her back to calm or asking questions of curiosity over criticism. It may even mean taking time for yourself in heated moments of frustration. Don't be afraid to walk out of the room, take a few deep breaths, and regain your composure before resuming the conversation. We can unknowingly add to a girl's stress with our own, be it the result of conflict with a partner or uncertainty about finances. Sometimes we can't avoid these stressors in our own lives, but how we become aware of them and cope with them is what matters most.

With awareness and a lot of practice, you can walk her through her stress and help her feel equipped for the next challenge. Doing so will pay off in so many wonderful ways. Most importantly, it will teach her an important life lesson: She can get through any stress that comes her way. Any stress. She may need your help at first, but eventually, she will be able to manage on her own.

CAILIN

When I play back conversations in my head— *I could have said that* or *Why did I say that?*— I wake up suddenly during the night and feel jolted by these thoughts. I didn't think I had anxiety; I was just having more meltdowns and I definitely felt more angry. My mom was "done with me," so she took me to see our family doctor. I chose to do online school instead of public school; I had a psycho-educational assessment done to better understand my learning profile; I started going to therapy; and I began medication but have slowly decreased the dosage. Today, I have better awareness of my moods and understanding of myself and my anxiety. I am also starting to take more positive risks, such as taking public transit downtown, walking places by myself, getting a part-time job at a coffee shop, and socializing more.

Signs of Trouble

Left unchecked, the stress cycle can create cracks in your daughter's mental health. Over the years, I've had many parents admit, with hindsight, that they didn't see the early signs. If you feel you may have missed something with your own teen, please don't be hard on yourself. Instead, shift to supportive action steps in moving forward, starting today. Many parents may feel that their daughter is exhibiting certain behaviours, such as moodiness, precisely because she is a teen. Right you are. The key can be found in the intensity of these exhibited behaviours or a change in your daughter's typical routines. If your daughter is a light or inconsistent sleeper, for example, insomnia may not be unusual or particularly troubling. But if she's always been a deep sleeper and suddenly starts to experience sleep troubles, there's your warning sign.

Early warning signs for mental health challenges are mostly associated with:

- changes in eating or sleeping patterns
- withdrawal from people or activities that once brought pleasure
- low or no energy
- unexplained aches and pains
- excessive smoking, drinking, or drug use
- feeling helpless, hopeless, confused, forgetful, angry, upset, worried, or scared
- frequent relational conflict
- severe mood swings
- negative ruminating thoughts
- talk of self-harming or actual self-harm
- an inability to do daily tasks and care for oneself

Mental Health Disorders: What to Look For

Undoubtedly, mental health disorders in adolescence are a significant problem. There are also many ways to support her back to health and wholeness. Your ability to notice the early signs and symptoms will play a big part in her intervention and recovery. Here, we'll look at the four most common mental health concerns among teenage girls—ADD/ADHD, anxiety disorder, depression, and bipolar disorder—along with ways to identify the early warning signs.

ADD/ADHD

Raising a girl is tough. Raising a girl with attention deficit hyperactivity disorder is *really* tough. ADHD can manifest as inattentiveness, hyperactivity and impulsiveness, or a combination thereof. Each girl is unique, even under the big umbrella of an ADHD diagnosis. Genetics are a key contributing factor, which means a girl with ADHD has a structurally different brain. She has reduced activity in the frontal regions—responsible for executive functioning skills—and may thus have difficulty focusing, paying attention, and exhibiting self-control.

While an increasing number of girls are being diagnosed with ADHD every year,[6] the diagnoses are often delayed because girls can hide difficulties well by being rule followers and people pleasers. On the outside, she may look like she's following the conversation, but on the inside, she may be clueless as to what's being discussed. Girls are often more likely to show inattention than the hyperactivity or impulsivity of their male counterparts, and as a result, they receive the unhappy and undeserved distinction of being scatterbrained or ditzy.

When I work with fourteen-year-old Elliot, I feel as if I'm sitting next to a firecracker that is popping and crackling constantly. She's fidgety and talkative, her stories go off in every direction, and she is both easily distracted and stimulated. She's also smart, a master negotiator—"Can we just do ten questions in math, not twenty?"—and when I find something she's really interested in doing, such as a puzzle, she can be shockingly focused and almost in a world of her own. Elliot has the hyperactive-impulsive form of ADHD, and after a diagnosis from the doctor, her parents decided to go with medication. It has worked for her.

By contrast, Amelia is calm and demure. She takes her time telling me about the intricacies of life as a sixteen-year-old, and she often pauses to ask if I have anything to interject. She'll notice every eye flicker or slight smile I offer her, and she will intuit when I am either confused or pleased. This intuition guides her, and she will inquire every time. Amelia will often tell me how she "pays attention" in class as long as she can, but she finds the teachers and lessons so boring that she eventually "zones out" and daydreams about her after-school plans. Amelia and I work on bringing her brain back to the present, and mindfulness is really helping. This begins with her awareness of her breath, her thoughts, and her feelings, and the action step of noticing her thoughts (not judging) and gently encouraging herself (again, without judgment) to be in the moment and ready to listen and learn.

What you may notice:

- difficulty focusing and paying attention; daydreaming or in a world of her own
- inability to listen when spoken to directly
- excessive fidgeting and talking
- blurting out comments that are off-topic or irrelevant
- lowered self-esteem
- school or task refusal
- avoidance strategies such as procrastination
- inability to follow through on instructions
- difficulties regulating emotions and/or overreactions
- challenges with social interactions such as reading social cues, facial expressions, and body language
- frequent forgetfulness, especially with dates and times
- messy, scattered, forgetful, disorganized; often misplaces items
- frequent interruptions in conversation

If you are looking for additional resources about ADD or ADHD, I recommend *Raising Girls with ADHD* by James W. Forgan and Mary Anne Richey and *The Gift of Failure* by Jessica Lahey.

Anxiety Disorder

"What if I don't make friends and fit in?" "What if I fail my test and never get into university?" "What if I forget my words and everyone laughs at me?" "What if my teacher doesn't understand my question?" "What if I'm late?" "What if I don't have enough time to get everything done?" This is what a teen girl's anxiety can sound like.

Anxiety, or the general feeling of unease about an immediate or future event or an uncertain outcome, can, at best, be alleviated by some calming techniques to regain balance and a sense of normalcy; at worst, it can become an anxiety attack or, if prolonged, develop into an anxiety disorder. These mental illnesses can be categorized as either generalized anxiety disorder or more specific disorders such as panic disorder, social anxiety disorder, obsessive-compulsive disorder, post-traumatic stress disorder, and a host of phobias.

If your daughter has an anxiety disorder of *any kind*, she may be like my client Bella. At first, Bella's parents assumed their daughter's nervousness—made obvious by both her constant hair twirling and nail biting—was simply because she was born a "worrier." Even as a child, Bella had asked frequent questions before an event, using a plethora of "what if" and "oh no" phrases. Her recent push for perfection at school—spending hours on projects to make them "just right" and staying up into the wee hours to rewrite her notes for the next day's class—was not only consuming all of her time but also likely the reason for her sleep disruption. Without doubt, teen girls can be very anxious, but you can support them.

What you may notice:

- restlessness and concentration difficulties

- prolonged moodiness and irritability

- changes or difficulties with eating and sleep patterns

- physical complaints such as fatigue, aches and pains, nausea, sweatiness, indigestion

- excessive worry or irrational fears (being late, failing, forgetting appointments)

- trouble making decisions, and being overly concerned with outcome

- frequent meltdowns or exaggerated responses to seemingly small situations

- thinking traps such as fortune-telling (predicting outcome), catastrophizing (imagining the worst-case scenario), black-and-white thinking, filtering, labelling (using single negative words to describe herself), or "should" statements (telling herself how she must feel or behave)

Some of my favourite resources for anxiety are *The Anxiety Workbook for Teens* by Lisa M. Schab and *Generation Stressed* by Michele Kambolis.

Depression

Depression is not the same thing as a bad day or a season of apathy. It's not a lack of motivation or laziness. Although depression may result in these qualities, it's so much more. It's deeper. Depression goes beyond her anxious thoughts, although anxiety can be a precursor for symptoms of depression. Depression is a mood disorder and a prolonged state of low energy and fatigue. A girl will be sadder and unhappier than usual, and this can be the result of a response to a stressful event or trauma, changes in brain chemistry, or genetics.

One of my clients, Taylor, articulated her experience with depression in this way: "You are trapped in darkness, unable to even conceive of any notion of light or happiness." Sage told me how she, too, was living in this darkness. Her depression emerged in her Grade 12 year. This was not a sudden condition but rather a slow and gradual shift in her mood and demeanour. Her decline into an abyss became obvious in her school attendance and performance. She no longer wanted to show up or try, and eventually she was failing her courses and isolating herself from friends. Sage didn't feel like doing anything. A simple act such as getting out of bed to shower felt like a mountain to climb and often didn't get accomplished. If your daughter is depressed, you will notice. She won't seem like herself, and she'll need your support.

By far, Beatrice has been my most "down" client—low-energy, despondent, lifeless. If her slight frame and unkempt hair weren't signs enough of depression, her sleeping patterns and desire to spend hours on end on her computer surely were. Despite Mom's very best efforts to get her up, nudge her to school, and guide her back to her formerly happy, social self, Beatrice was neither ready for nor capable of change. Girls like Beatrice, who are showing apathy and struggling with mental health, need to take tiny steps toward mental wellness. They are in an abyss they don't understand. They are scared and alone.

My sessions with Beatrice are only a half-hour long; I do not push for more. If she can do only one activity with me, that's what we do—and we celebrate it. If your daughter is like Beatrice and can't get out of bed in the morning, accept this (for now). If she wants to eat mac and cheese every single day at noon, make it together. If she chooses to watch a particular YouTube channel, watch it with her. It is only when you jump into her world that you'll be able to understand it. Eventually, you'll be able to suggest small changes such as a new lunch option or an alternative to screen time.

What you may notice:

- troubles sleeping and concentrating
- increased moodiness and irritability
- changes or difficulties with eating and sleep patterns
- physical symptoms like fatigue, aches and pains, nausea, sweatiness, indigestion
- loss of interest and withdrawal from activities she once enjoyed
- social isolation
- mood changes; more intensely negative, unhappy, and anxious
- persistent sadness
- lethargy
- language revealing self-loathing and low self-esteem
- risky or reckless behaviour
- hints or mentions of suicide or a preoccupation with death

If you do hear suicidal language, please consult a professional immediately. For more support when it comes to depression, check out *Beyond the Blues* by Lisa M. Schab and *Depression: A Teen's Guide to Survive and Thrive* by Jacqueline B. Toner and Claire A. B. Freeland.

Bipolar Disorder

Bipolar disorder, affecting less than 2 percent of teenage girls, is marked by opposite extremes: depression, sadness, and withdrawal on the one hand, and mania, elation, and overactivity on the other.[7] I've worked with only a few clients with bipolar, and this definition describes *exactly* how they feel. Mostly, they have been older girls, and they have all opted for medication to find better life balance and adjustment. I see how deep an impact bipolar disorder has on their lives, from having severe difficulty sleeping to experiencing frequent, unpredictable mood changes.

Bipolar is difficult to diagnose because it can resemble expected teen behaviour such as moodiness: the "ups" of elation, euphoria, and excessive happiness, and the "downs" of irritation, annoyance, and intense anger. Furthermore, there can be an eight-year lag between a first episode of feeling on top of the world and her feeling withdrawn and suicidal and receiving an actual diagnosis. Bipolar episodes sometimes last for days and sometimes for months.

My clients have taught me that being diagnosed with bipolar disorder can be something of a relief; they can now understand their own "crazy behaviours." After diagnosis, they feel a sense of control and comfort in the knowledge that there is help, that there are ways they can take care of their own mental health. One client articulated her experience in this way: "When I first found out I am bipolar I was ecstatic. I know that this is not the normal response, but I was happy because I knew that what I was feeling could be fixed and it wasn't something I was doing wrong. To this day I have worked to make sure I am in a good state of mind and that things have gone better for me since being diagnosed."

What you may notice:

- extreme high and low moods
- fast, racing thoughts
- unlimited energy
- increasingly risky or erratic behaviour
- problematic periods (such as longer cycles or long absences)
- suicidal ideation (thinking about or planning suicide)

Two books I recommend for better understanding bipolar disorder are *The Bipolar Disorder Survival Guide* by David J. Miklowitz and *The Bipolar Workbook for Teens* by Sheri Van Dijk and Karma Guindon.

HANNAH

Social media has definitely had a significant effect on mental health in teen girls. Most of what social media displays is perfection, whether that be a "perfect life" or a "perfect body." Constantly seeing perfection has made me feel bad about myself at times. Being in touch with myself and knowing myself has been the biggest tool for me, and I've learned so much by just getting to know myself and my boundaries. I feel very grateful to have become in touch with myself at a young age because I think, for some people, it can take a long time. Growing up in today's world, I think knowing your limits and boundaries is extremely important. Everyone is different. Find tools that work for you and make you feel stronger; it doesn't matter how unique they are.

Make Healthy Minds a Priority

My hope is that knowing the facts about mental health will not just educate parents and their supporters but will also empower you to take the requisite steps toward supporting teen girls in the ways they need. Let's rethink how we perceive, talk about, and approach mental health and the promotion of healthy minds. For example, we can start by talking about moods and emotions more than we talk about mental illness and mental health concerns.

As a society and culture, we are speaking more about and becoming more comfortable with mental illness and wellness. We are also learning to pay attention to early warning signs and becoming more aware of the myriad treatment options available, from individual and group therapies to medications. Mental health disorders are impossible to overcome without support. And in the end, support comes down to choosing the best fit for your daughter. Girls need to know that while you don't have all the answers, you can be present and ready and willing to talk and take the necessary steps to help them. Here are some ways to do that.

Make Sure She Knows She is Not Alone

What helps most, according to the teen girls I spoke with, is presence and company—someone to talk to or simply to be present when she wants to abstain from talking. Even a small attempt to understand and imagine what it's like to be her is of huge comfort. Girls need reassurance, not "it will be okay" platitudes. They view expressions like this as empty promises, and often mistrust the words. What girls want instead is validation: for example, "I will be here for you, and we will keep trying different ideas until we find you the support you need." They also appreciate phrases such as "You are not alone," "I am right here with you," "How can I help you take care of yourself?" and, of course, "I love you."

Take the Time to Listen

Straight up, what hinders girls the most from speaking out and getting the help they so desperately need is when we use phrases like "Mental health isn't real"; "You're just so sensitive"; "Snap out of it"; "I just don't understand what's wrong with you"; "Some people have it so much worse than you do; you should be grateful"; "You are being selfish"; "Get over it." All of these phrases give girls the same message: I do not understand you and I'm not taking the time to really listen. Without a doubt she will feel judged, misunderstood, and trapped in her pain. When girls feel dismissed and discounted, they can sink further into their own suffering or take matters into their own hands with actions such as self-hatred, self-harm, self-medicating with drugs or alcohol, or by trying not to feel their feelings of discomfort or feel anything at all. Even more damaging is when a teen girl's supporters don't take the time to find out how she is feeling, or when she feels their disapproval and disbelief even though they may not have said a word.

Focus on Wellness

Addressing your teen daughter's mental health begins with a paradigm shift: focus more on mental wellness and a healthy mind than on mental health concerns. When you sense an opening with her, check in about what's going on in every aspect of her life: her sleep, nutrition, and exercise habits; who she is spending time with and how she is using her time on her device; how she is managing herself; what she is thinking about; how she is taking care of herself; and how she is feeling. In doing so, you may be able to discover that she needs you in a specific way. Here is a checklist of questions I use with my clients:

- Are you eating enough wholesome foods?
- Are you getting at least eight to ten hours of quality sleep each night?
- How are you managing your stress to feel calm and centred?
- Are you feeling energized and positive?
- Are you practising at least one act of self-care each day?
- Are you seeking inspiration and creating joy?
- Are you following positive and healthy people on your social media feeds?

These check-in questions can serve as conversation starters between you and your daughter. I am often amazed how one simple question can encourage a girl to start talking. Once she starts, she often ends up telling me things I would never have guessed are on her mind. If your daughter is like so many adolescent girls, playing her cards close to her chest, don't push but rather affirm. Use her silence as an opportunity. Assure her that if anything is troubling her, you are there for her, and provide her with some creative ways she can take you up on that: for example, a shared journal or a blog just for the two of you, co-planning an event to look forward to and take her mind off what's bothering her, or giving her the options for who she needs you to be—sounding board, coach, cheerleader, lawyer, or referee.

Encouraging the Support Circle

We all need support. Girls need to create their own circles of support right now, to help them through high school, and into the future to help them with life. They can choose the people who best suit their needs at the time. Your teen girl may need a cheerleader, a coach, or an accountability partner, a lighthearted friend as well as a more serious companion. At other times she will look for someone who shares her opinions and someone who doesn't, someone who listens to and accepts her, and then challenges her to be better. Encourage your daughter to explore the answers to the following questions to gauge the level of support she currently has in her life and determine the types of support she can consider adding:

- Who is supporting you and how?
- Who is in your support circle? Do they listen to and understand you?
- Do you receive unending compassion from this support circle while also practising self-compassion?
- If not, who else can you invite into your circle?

Just thinking about these questions can help your daughter to become more self-aware of her healthy mind. They can bring her back to the centre of her own circle. From there, she can take any necessary steps toward change, with you supporting her on the periphery.

A FEW YEARS ago I was asked by an all-girls private school to give a fifteen-minute talk on mental health during the school's mental wellness week. After I said yes, I wondered how I was going to talk to an auditorium of curious girls about such a big topic in such a little amount of time. Then an idea came to me: What if I gave my talk first thing Monday morning, collaborated with the school to set up an online platform for the girls to ask any questions they wanted, and then came back on Friday to answer their questions? I gave my talk and shared part of my own struggle with stress and anxiety, offering the girls my best tried-and-true strategies for dealing with mental health concerns. When I received their questions later in the week, I was shocked.

I expected a few pretty typical questions: "How do you know if you have a mental health issue?" or "I am so worried about my friend who is struggling. How can I help her?" What I received were hundreds of deep and wide-ranging questions: "I feel like nobody will care about me if I tell them the truth. How do I share my true feelings?" "I've gotten used to wearing a mask and hiding my feelings from others because I don't think people expect I have problems. Can you please help me let people know what's really happening for me?" "Why doesn't our school do more to support our mental health?"

That Friday, I did my best to answer as many questions as possible, but I left the school feeling deflated, as though I had let the girls down. Had I set them up with a kind of false hope by telling them I could answer all their questions? Eventually I was comforted by the recognition that I had kick-started a process of thinking and talking about mental health. I also realized that girls wanted to discuss mental health, and they needed to tell their stories. Turns out, girls have a lot to say on the subject. I'd like to start a campaign called "Let's Listen."

How Parents HELP Growth

- Talking to her about her mental wellness and painting a picture of a healthy mind
- Staying alert to signs of stress
- Helping her with stress coping tools such as deep breathing, yoga, meditation, and self-expression
- Teaching her self-management tools such as using a calendar, preparing and planning, and creating to-do lists to minimize disorganization
- Helping her to balance her thinking—from "what ifs" to "what is"
- Assuring her that you are on her side and you will figure this out together

How Parents HINDER Growth

- Taking her stress personally and talking to her while she is in stress mode
- Expecting that she can talk about her feelings when you are ready to talk
- Choosing to solve her mental health "problems" or over-empathizing with her feelings
- Protecting her from setbacks, mistakes, and failures
- Dismissing her moods and changes, assuming she is just showing "typical teen behaviour"
- Using phrases such as "Snap out of it" or "You'll get over it"
- Delaying action to get her the help she needs

PART TWO

RESILIENT

Resilient girls bounce back from rejection, criticism, and condemnation. They may have fears about failing or doubts about their steps or missteps; they may be unsure whether they are making the right choices. They may feel frustrated, disappointed, depleted, or stuck. But they are not hesitating or holding back.

Girls will hear "no" a lot as they grow; they will battle naysayers who tell them they can't do it, and will have to silence their own inner critic. Their ideas may not pan out. Their inspiration may run out. Their desires may fizzle and fade. Their hearts may get broken. Yet they keep going.

Resilient girls will fall and get up and dust themselves off. With grit and determination, they will take another step forward, even if it's a small one. They will try a new way, take a different route, and start fresh. To build resilience in our teen girls, we need to help them realize just how strong they are, and be with them through difficulty rather than protecting them from it. Remind them they "got this" and they will learn to be resilient.

4

A GIRL AND HER PHONE

ORNING UNTIL NIGHT. All day, every day, except when teachers demand they put them away during class, or at meal times when the family rule favours real time over virtual time. This is how much a girl uses her phone. Think I'm exaggerating? I asked Kennedy, age fifteen, to describe a typical day in her social media life:

> I always check my phone the instant I wake up. Mostly to see who liked my Insta posts and also to see if I missed any chats. Then I scroll through my feeds to see what others are posting. Some days my phone blows up—mostly with the latest gossip. It's exciting news you don't want to miss. I might post a carefully curated mirror selfie, but it depends if I feel I look pretty enough when I get ready for school. I look at my phone as I'm walking to the bus stop, checking the bus schedule for updates. If I can't find anyone to sit with, I use it for something to do, look at people's VSCO or read some blogs. I'll constantly monitor my own post; if I don't hit my number (at least fifty likes in one hour), I'll delete it. At school, we are supposed to leave our phones in our lockers but nobody

does. We hide them under our desks and just text or snap when we can. School is so boring! At lunch, we eat together while we scroll, post, snap. After school, I usually go on YouTube and watch videos and stuff. If I have homework, I do it before dinner but I have my phone out too so I don't miss any conversations. Before bed, I watch Netflix and usually "talk" to friends at the same time so we can comment on the show—right now we are watching *Riverdale*.

What exactly is happening to a teenage girl's brain while she is spending innumerable hours each day on her phone? Know this: "Adolescence is a formative period of life, when neural pathways are malleable, and passion and creativity run high."[1] Her brain is bustling with change from her daily experiences. This means she is impressionable, vulnerable even. In *Turnaround Tools for the Teenage Brain*, authors Eric Jensen and Carole Snider explain that changes in the brain are both a challenge and an opportunity: "The brain's wild ride means that multiple systems and structures are undergoing massive changes—[but] it's just not done maturing."[2] Specifically, your teen girl's prefrontal cerebral cortex is developing and is not fully formed or fully capable of making sound decisions or using good judgment. This lack of maturity is most obvious online if your daughter has ever posted a mean comment or a provocative pic and later had remorse. The brain is also making neural connections at a rapid rate. If she is constantly connecting to multiple social media sites at one time, the brain learns to divide attention. Over time, and with much repetition, this becomes her new normal. And with each "like" or "comment" that your daughter earns on social media, the "feel good" chemicals—namely dopamine (a neurotransmitter contributing to reward-motivated behaviour)—is released. This surge feels so good it's inevitable she will seek out more. She will almost always get what she is searching for, but at what cost?

EVERY PARENT I meet tells me the same thing: they are less worried about how tight their teen daughter's jeans are than about how to get her to look up from her screen and break the spell of virtual reality. Most come with a host of questions related to this online activity: "Who is she talking to?" "How is social media influencing her character?" "Is she being safe?" "How do I protect her or educate her?" "Is there such a thing as responsible social media use?" They feel misinformed, frustrated, and afraid. They worry about what their daughters are doing online, what they are viewing and posting, and how their current digital footprint could affect their future endeavours. As well, sexting (sending sexual images) is a major issue for parents to grapple with and bears its own discussion. I'll talk more about it in chapter 7.

Many parents understand that their teen daughters are overly attached to their devices; they also understand that their teens are taking the first steps toward independence. As a result, parents are often conflicted about whether they should be stricter with monitoring usage. Should they impose time limits, remove her phone periodically, or allow her the freedom to navigate on her own? Should they simply allow her to make her fair share of mistakes and suffer the natural consequences (like being exhausted after staying up way past bedtime to text chat), and trust she will find her way through? It probably doesn't help parents making these kinds of decisions to know that some girls have what's called a Rinsta (a real account) for themselves and a Finsta (a fake account) just for parents; others even have a backup device. Clearly, and not surprisingly, a teen girl's phone is her life—an integral, even necessary, part of her day. She would be lost without it. Only you can decide if your daughter needs a phone, but you can expect her to constantly try to convince you it is as vital as the air she breathes or the water she drinks.

Consider for a moment what it is like for your daughter not to have a phone, especially in her social context. My usually timid and reserved student Eshana told me that she needed to get a phone because "it's really embarrassing when you are at soccer practice and meet new girls you want to hang out with. Everyone gets out their phones to enter your number in their contacts and you get out your sticky pad and pen." Funny but not funny. Eshana may have a point. Sameness matters when it comes to fitting in and avoiding potentially socially awkward moments like this one. Other girls tell me they need their phones to find friends at lunch or else "you spend the entire time walking around the school alone when you could have found your friends instantly via texting or apps that show location." Her phone really can seem like her lifeline. She can live without it but it's difficult, if not impossible, in our technologically dependent society.

Her First Phone

Parents usually get phones for their kids for one practical purpose: to be able to contact them when they need to. But this isn't necessarily how your teen daughter sees her phone. Before you even acquire a phone for your daughter to use, think about the guidelines you want to hand over with it. If your daughter shows she's mature enough to handle the responsibility that comes with having a phone—and as her parent you know your teen best—then give it a try with these provisions:

- Have a serious and ongoing conversation about her level of usage and finding balance between a screen and the real world (more ideas at the end of this chapter).

- Consider refraining from buying a data package when you first get her a phone. Although she can still talk and text, her on-the-go internet usage is restricted to Wi-Fi outside the home.

- Explore apps such as iKeyMonitor, mSpy, or Spyzie that can control how much she is using her phone and how her phone time is allocated. Most home modems can be programmed to turn off access to Wi-Fi at certain times.

- Create a monitoring system that works for your family.

After you've established some ground rules for phone use, the next issue to sort out is how much involvement you should have when it comes to her social media. I was once certain that parents should definitely not be scrolling through their daughter's social media feeds, but I've been enlightened by parents who have helped me change my stance. Your teen's social media accounts—unlike a private, old-school paperback journal—are very public. I no longer see parental monitoring of a teen's social media activity as "snooping" or an interruption of her ability to connect with others in her own way. Instead, I now find myself aligned with parents who profess a need to know what their daughter is putting out into the wider world—because she will not always be aware of the messages she may be sending.

Your daughter, especially if she is new to social media and in the thirteen-to-fifteen age range, will need support. The best way to provide this is to consider a balanced step-by-step process that offers her the scaffolding for gradual online independence. You can negotiate how much support is needed based on her comfort level and experience. It is reasonable to periodically check her feeds and to ask her questions to clarify what you don't understand. It is also important to have serious conversations with her when you feel she has either posted or commented inappropriately or when someone has been inappropriate with her. In cases of cyber bullying, for example, she may need to block, unfollow, mute, or even report that individual. As with many things, teens do need practice to understand what healthy phone use looks like. Work on modelling this yourself and make patience and trust a necessary part of your toolkit.

All Social, All the Time

If you are like most parents around the globe today, you are baffled, bewildered, and bothered by social media. You may feel that you are on an incredibly steep learning curve as you observe her doing homework while simultaneously using social media, texting her friends, and streaming music. To compound your confusion, there is a growing concern that smartphone use is undermining self-regulation and emotional control, promoting tech addiction, and exponentially increasing exposure to pornography, online predators, narcissism, and disturbingly violent videos—all of which affect her health and happiness. You may feel you simply can't keep up with new concepts she tells you about (Google Hangouts, IGTV), the filters she is excited about trying on her VSCO app, or her references to catfishing or trolling.

Parents wrestle with opposing views of social media. Is it an amazing place where girls can connect with others, share ideas and life experiences with new people, and keep in touch with far-off friends? Or is it simply another arena in which she feels pressured to be perfect and constantly keep up with and compare herself to peers, and where she experiences the sting of inevitable rejection or cruelty? You may not know how to start talking about device use with your daughter. You may be torn between letting her figure it out on her own or helping her to figure it out by removing her device and limiting access to the internet at home. This conflict is not surprising considering that social media use has been linked to an increase in unhappiness, risk factors for suicide, sleep issues, and teens feeling left out or isolated from peers.[3] Since girls are spending an average of eight hours each day using social media, let's take a closer look at the statistics:[4]

- 92 percent of teens report going online daily, including 24 percent who say they go online "almost constantly."

- 43 percent of parents think the negative aspects of their child's social media account outweigh the benefits.

- 58 percent of parents believe their child is too attached to their phone or tablet.

- 78 percent of parents have logged in to their child's account to check their posts, or simply follow them on accounts of their own.

- 32 percent of parents have deleted a post about their child, fearing it was oversharing.

These are eye-opening stats, and they may help to illuminate your understanding of a girl's online world. But although parents often focus on how much teen girls depend on their phones, and legitimately so, it is also important to consider that healthy device behaviour begins with role modelling. Our phones are important parts of our connected lives, but it is real, live connection with family and friends that takes the hit.

Have you ever complained that your daughter is on her screen too much only to have her respond, "What about you?" She's not wrong. One girl told me that she begs her mom to look up when she is trying to tell her the details of her day. Her mom always apologizes, puts her phone down, and gives her undivided attention for about five minutes, when she grabs her phone again. This teen girl feels frustrated by her mom's distracted attention span and misses talking to her. She added that she doesn't want to talk about logistics like her bedroom that needs to be cleaned or her homework that needs to be completed. She wants to talk about how she is feeling overwhelmed by life lately, how she is falling behind her friends in terms of academic success, or how she spends her days dreaming of travelling the globe rather than paying attention to her mundane social studies class. Giving some thought to how connected you are to your own phone may be the catalyst for a discussion with your teen that has positive benefits for both of you.

Most parents today are mystified by their daughter's obsession with and passion for her social media sites and status. There's a simple reason for this, says Rachel Simmons, author of *Enough as She Is*: "Social media rewards behavior that girls have been long primed to express: pleasing others, seeking feedback, performing and looking good."[5] And yet, this is exactly the kind of behaviour that can negatively shape identity and body image in a teen girl. If you feel you have lost your daughter to the perils of social media and text messaging, you are not alone. One mom emailed me with this suggestion for my session with her daughter: "She recently got an Instagram account ... Although we have some rules about how to use it, I am sure you have lots of clever tips for young girls about how to use social media responsibly and respectfully and how to keep away from the drama, gossip, bullying that can go on in this virtual world I feel so far away from! Something tells me that has to be one of your hot topics!"

I do have some ideas for parents later in this chapter. First, though, I want to check in with girls on this hot topic. The teen girls I spoke with held a strongly divided love-hate relationship with social media. Although they love their phones, they felt equally pressured to keep up with peers and constantly polish their online profiles. My view is that girls engaging with social media is not necessarily the problem. The crux of the matter is how girls use their online time, how much time they invest, and the value they give it.

Girls Heart Social Media

Whether your daughter is thirteen (or younger) and just entering the world of social media, fifteen and full of robust social media acumen, or seventeen and slowly becoming more aware of her digital footprint, the story is the same: her life's narrative is being told through pictures and posts. Girls thoroughly enjoy this social media world—the connection to friends and, yes, to strangers, the entertainment value and fun, the videos that make them laugh, following stories and other people's lives, and the inspiration they get from quotations and images.

Girls love social media for various reasons. It is fun and entertaining; it can be inspiring to look at other people's pictures and lives and to edit and then post their own photos; and it is a great way to connect with people and meet new friends. It allows girls to create personas that are living the lives they want, not necessarily the lives they have—a modern version of show and tell where girls can highlight the best parts of their life experiences. Lola told me, "I love that you can connect with people all over the world, you can see what other people are doing, and you can learn a lot from social media." Girls also go to social media to connect, to feel included, and to feel normal, as well as to relieve stress. After a long day of school or a fight with a friend, they often want to dive into social media to find someone who understands them, and to relieve their mounting stress. Jill says, "Sometimes, social media seems like my only option for community. You know, somewhere I will be accepted and not judged." A teen girl may find community, as Jill says, but mindless scrolling to alleviate boredom merely magnifies her insatiable need for any kind of connection. Whether she's logging her hours snapping, messaging, or "talking" with friends using a secret lexicon of text-talk or emoticons, or taking part in more daring pursuits such as sexting (see chapter 7), she does feel she is connecting and that her connections are real.

I have learned to take the best that social media has to offer, but I do not agree that virtual chats are as good as in-person conversations, or that social media is harmless and a great stress reliever. Social media is neither of these things. In fact, social media is a stressor, as it will never replace true friendship or live connection. It is also distracting and addictive. But for an entire generation of girls, social media is all they know. Later in this chapter I will talk about how to counter the effects of social media in your teen's life. For now, I want to share a positive social media story about Chloe.

Chloe, who came to see me for help with academic enrichment and fine-tuning her social skills, is by far my best example of a teen who was using social media to enrich her life (and the lives of others) and not as her lifeline. She decided to curtail the traps of social media (seeing posts that made her unhappy, following accounts that made her feel she needed to be someone she wasn't, and comparing her body and success with others) by posting only positive quotations to uplift her followers. She chose to respond only with positive comments to her friends' posts, affirming their successes with "great job" and a thumbs-up emoji or complimenting them with "I love this" coupled with a heart emoji. I asked her how she felt and whether this was easy or hard for her. "I know I'm different from other girls, but honestly, I feel so happy to help," she told me. "My friends get so stressed and worried about mean comments and not getting enough likes; that's just not me." There was one problem, though: Chloe's time commitment.

Chloe spent a lot of time posting positively, upwards of five hours a day. We talked about why she was so committed. She said that she felt obliged, but did want to decrease her time investment. What did she come up with? Limits. She told me about an app that her parents could use to set a limit on her access to social media: she suggested two hours a day, and that it be password protected. I learned a valuable lesson from Chloe about how teen girls are aware of the time investment they make in social media. Over time and as they mature, many girls will realize that they are perhaps spending too much time in the virtual world. But you can help this process by understanding why social media holds such great appeal and gently encouraging her to consider creating balance between her real and virtual lives.

Girls H8 Social Media

When asked why she hated social media, Natalia told me, "It's a lot of pressure." Although girls love social media, they also find it stressful. This stress can come from not knowing whom to trust online, trolling (a deliberately offensive or provocative post intended to offend or upset), and clickbait (an enticing ad or link that can lead the viewer to explicit, offensive, and inappropriate content). And let's not forget the difficulty discerning what's real and what isn't. Teen girls feel judged and subjected to harsh criticism. If their social media account doesn't look good enough, they fear they will be cast aside.

Not only do teen girls have to keep up with their own online profiles, but they also have to constantly create "better." Ruby puts it well: "People's social media accounts are only representations of what they choose to highlight—it will never be their real life, but the life they want us to see. So, it's an illusion. It's fake. Yet we all believe the hype." Think of social media as your teen daughter's stage and her followers as her audience. She needs to keep her performance strong so her audience will be pleased, and so she can capture the approval for which she is longing. Simultaneously, she can spiral into a cycle of comparing and competing when someone else's post makes her feel not good enough, and she can experience the very real FOMO (fear of missing out).

Girls tend to use social media most when they are bored, lonely, or stressed—sometimes when they want to share, sometimes when they want to boast, and occasionally to inspire and encourage other girls. They soon discover that the online world is yet another place full of people who are prettier, fitter, sexier, smarter, richer, and more popular or successful than they feel. Most bothersome is how the likes and followers that are an integral part of social media have become the most prominent measure for a girl's self-worth, attractiveness, desirability, and popularity. These days, girls can even purchase followers to make themselves appear more popular to fellow viewers. And they learn quickly: if they don't get enough likes on a photo quickly enough, they can either delete it or be more edgy, creative, or provocative. Many girls are on a mission to amplify their numbers: likes, followers, tags, and subscriptions.

Despite that need to improve their social media presence, girls also recognize the damage and toxicity social media participation can cause. "I hate that people corrode social media feeds with negativity, inappropriate images and language, and insults," says Iris, "and it's the worst when you are 'ghosted' [the sudden and often abrupt ending of all communication with someone]." The conflict Iris and other girls are contending with is abundantly clear: I want social media because it's so interesting, but I don't want social media because it creates too much pressure.

If the pressure gets too intense, some girls may eventually ban themselves from social media so they can spend some time in the real world. Older teen girls, usually those over the age of sixteen, often come to realize that social media is a time waster; they want to focus on more serious goals like playing competitive sports, taking on leadership roles, and getting the marks that will help them in their post-secondary school plans. This change can be indicative of her changing brain. As your teen girl's prefrontal cortex develops, she gains a much wider perspective. She is consequently better able to weigh social media's pros and cons, and make reasonable decisions about what she wants to view and how much time she wants to allocate to her device. Girls who have reached this stage want to step out of the perpetual game of seek and find. They know they need a good night's sleep and that this is easily thwarted by the blue backlight of a smartphone, which sabotages the release of melatonin (the sleep hormone) and tricks the brain into thinking it's time to be awake. They come to see the value in unplugging. With parental guidance and a growing awareness of the more sinister effects of smartphone use, I hope this approach will become the new normal as teens develop. Until then, it will take concerted effort, diligence, love, and understanding on your part to correct the course, as well as an awareness of your own social media use.

MIA

I like social media because I learn about my friends' interests and their personalities. It helps me to know what kind of people they are. I also like posting my own stories and interests. Social media is just fun. I like the option, too, of blocking people who seem unhealthy. I don't like when people choose to do bad things on social media. I worry that I may get into trouble through association (because I follow them). Posting rude pictures of people without their permission, texting rude messages and using mean words, and some people make fake accounts and try to befriend you—these are the hard parts for me.

Selfies and Self-Obsession

The other day I saw this post on Instagram: "Find yourself behind the selfie." Selfies are an interesting phenomenon when it comes to teenage girls. At first glance, you might simply conclude that girls love how they look so much that they want to share their beautiful faces on their social platforms. And some girls do report that selfies boost their self-confidence. In some ways, a selfie is a "look at me" message declaring she knows, loves, and accepts herself. However, when girls become obsessed with posting images of themselves—in front of the mirror, or with friends at the beach or a party; eating, smiling, happy, and loving her life—I wonder if they are in fact becoming self-obsessed (borderline narcissistic). I wonder if we are looking at a generation of girls who are actually self-loathing. In this scenario, the "look at me" post is code for "Please know, love, and accept me," and the selfie is, in essence, an attempt to have the outside match the inside: "I know how to look happy, I want to feel happy, but I don't (yet)."

Photos can be land mines when it comes to self-doubt. And the fact that everyone accessing social media platforms post selfies— peers and celebrities alike—only adds to the pressure. The more girls look at other people's posts and pictures, the more likely they are to compare themselves to what they see and feel unhappy about their own appearances and lives (read: not good enough). Counsellor Julia Kristina Mah told me that girls can be negatively affected by their own selfies for one of two reasons:

> If a girl thinks she is not bad in the looks department but then sees a photo of herself (with a bad angle or lighting), without a strong sense of self, she may be stunned that she is not as attractive as she once thought. She will spiral. She will wonder what that means and how she could have thought she was beautiful in the first place. Or, more extremely, a girl who does not think she's good-looking

from the start could use an unforgiving photo she sees as a reason to feel even worse about herself, affirming her own feelings of ugliness or low self-worth. In fact, the latter girl could avoid getting her photo taken altogether.

So, what may begin as seemingly harmless "selfie fun" can become extremely damaging to a teen girl's self-image and self-esteem.

You don't have to scroll too far through apps like Instagram or vsco to see girls posting starlit pics of themselves. Many of these selfies are masterfully taken, digitally edited with filters, and altered with apps such as GoCam. Girls are fast becoming experts at lighting, makeup, and working their best angles, and they don't hesitate to use selfie sticks and tripods. Selfies are fun, interesting, and can entertain a girl for hours. They are conducive to creativity and can be a safe haven from her hectic real life. In some ways, selfies may even help with body image concerns (p. 60). I spoke at length about this with my photographer, Lexa. When Lexa is engaged in the work she is most passionate about (the SHE Project), she talks to her clients about proper lighting and body posture. This helps them learn that what they see in content imagery on the internet is planned. She encourages her subjects to show up authentically and project their confidence for the best results in all photographs and in the images they create together. That said, we need to look deeper into the "why" of teen girls' posting activities and the "who" she really wants to be when she is projecting.

False and Fabricated: Celebrities and Micro-celebrity

According to a survey about media use among tweens and teens, youth who use social media place a much higher value on fame than those who do not use social media sites.[6] The obsession with fame is so high, and the democratizing influence of the internet so powerful, that we now have individuals who deliberately craft a public identity and brand to create a fan base and, eventually, become "famous." The term "micro-celebrity" was coined by Theresa Senft in *Camgirls*; it describes a new form of identity linked inextricably with the internet and the use of still images, videos, and blogging to create a sense of celebrity. It's not that teen girls want to be famous; it's more like they want to *appear* famous and glean the attention that follows. Micro-celebrity gives girls a taste of fame by allowing them to gain an audience outside of their circle of family and friends—the now-attainable "Instagirl" experience they see in action when they follow popular product endorsers like Kendall Jenner, Gigi Hadid, and Joan Smalls.

Teen girls are also fascinated by movie, TV, and music personalities—Selena Gomez, Emma Watson, Jennifer Lawrence, Demi Lovato, Zendaya, Rihanna, Lorde, Taylor Swift, Lady Gaga, Hailee Steinfeld, and Lilly Singh, to name just a few. Teen girls follow celebrities in part for the same reasons adults do: interest and entertainment. But when we probe deeper, we discover that many teen girls are not just obsessing over what famous people are eating, wearing, and doing with their lives—they secretly wish to be one. Girls are keen to emulate celebrities. They find themselves caught in the vortex of posting, promoting, and pleasing, being as "celebrity-esque" as possible, all while sinking into deeper dissatisfaction with their plain-by-comparison lives.

How is this particular strain of online activity—spending countless hours creating a brand of their own—going to affect our girls? From where I stand, girls are focusing too narrowly on the allure of celebrity status and are unknowingly intoxicated with all that comes with it (what I and others call the Kardashian Effect): attention, money, free stuff, parties, fame, a laid-back and enviable lifestyle, and, ultimately, a happy and perfect life. They don't know about the dark underside of celebrity and micro-celebrity status: the pressure to keep up with the demands of being famous, the difficulty in figuring out the difference between a real friend and a fan, the temptations of drugs and alcohol, the addiction to constant approval, and the demands of management and their entourage.

Like you, I understand the appeal of celebrity; I get why many teen girls are chasing the illusion. And like you, I also understand that an adolescent girl is often only able to see half of the equation; what she sees are all of the benefits and none of the drawbacks. We can take that understanding and step into action.

Distracted, Disengaged, Disconnected

Whether your teen daughter is online seeking wealth and fame or just popularity, the obsession with social media is ultimately damaging.

First, girls are distracted. The constant need to check her phone—to click, tap, scroll, snap, post, tag, like, comment, delete, and then repeat—is taking up a great deal of her day. Time looking down at her screen is time that could be spent paying attention to the life around her: sunshine, crisp leaves, people, current events. Whatever she could be looking at or learning from, she is missing it. At school, there is a direct link between being distracted (by her phone or her own thoughts) and the inability to focus, pay attention, concentrate, and learn. I know how much girls pride themselves on their "talent" of multi-tasking. "I can scroll and listen at the same time," they tell us. This is just not true. Her brain may be learning that this is the new normal, but that doesn't mean it is healthy or helpful. In fact, the brain is actually rewiring as it becomes accustomed to attending to multiple streams of stimulation. The downside of this rewiring is divided attention, unfocused energy, and hyperarousal.

Second, since girls are used to engaging on social media by clicking and sending, they are increasingly more disengaged from real conversations, not to mention the much-needed opportunities to practise their social skills. They are "talking" to peers via text message (often sitting side by side) and yet missing the chance to experience someone in real time. They are depriving themselves of the benefits that come with eye contact, body language, voice, tone, and of the energy exchange that naturally occurs when in close proximity with others. I worry that girls' social skills are diminishing, and they do not know how to converse and be present with one another. They are out of practice when it comes to offering undivided attention, care and genuine concern, empathy and understanding, and they do not know how to work through conflict as it arises. It is easier and quicker to chat online. But easy and quick are not the ingredients for any solid relationship. One dad told me that he isn't overly concerned that his daughter is online; he worries more about the fact that all of her "friends" were made through chat rooms, and she almost never spends time with them in person. He didn't even know if these people were real. In a recent interview, comedian and podcast host Joe Rogan and American volleyball player Gabrielle Reece talked about how a tricky thing for the iGeneration will be connection—being able to have real conversations and to concentrate long enough to be with somebody.[7]

Finally, when girls don't take time to be device-free, it means they are disconnected from themselves. I am forever talking to girls about the benefits of downtime and quiet, a chance to simply be—without doing anything—so they can process their busy day, re-evaluate priorities, and give themselves an opportunity to ask deeper, reflective questions: "What am I most proud of?" "What am I thankful for?" "How did I learn and feel today?" She cannot get to these questions about her feelings, thoughts, and potential if she is always "connected" online. Any time a girl is focused more on being someone else or selling her own hype, she is negating her own identity; she is actually drifting further from, not closer to, knowing and loving herself. She needs time to do nothing, recharge, be with herself, and just be.

Whenever girls are distracted, disengaged, and disconnected from real life and themselves, the potential exists for a darker side effect to emerge: addiction. I'm sure you've had many conversations with your teen girl where the challenge is not the conversation itself (no matter how awkward or uncomfortable) but getting her to look up. Not only is her device tethered to her hand, but her eyes are fixed on a screen that seemingly holds all the magic she is looking for. Round and round she goes, bouncing from texts to emails, from Instagram to Twitter, from Google to Snapchat to see what has happened or who has noticed her. And if she's not looking at her screen, she is quite possibly experiencing the anxiety that can come when she is away from it.

Not sure if your daughter is addicted or merely interested? One of my astute Grade 11 clients recalled a time when a girl in her class had her phone taken away. With the phone in sight, but carefully placed just out of reach on the teacher's desk, this friend's anxiety spiked. "It's like she went into withdrawal: she was shaky and sweaty and just couldn't concentrate on anything else." This is a visceral reaction. This is addiction. To test addiction, see what happens when she misplaces her phone or "loses" it somewhere between home and school, or you need to take it away while she is studying for her exam tomorrow. In one hour, the answer will likely be obvious.

Frequently, I tell girls that I feel addicted to my phone—as in, I really can't be without it. This confession permits me to ask them if they feel the same way. Some girls answer in the negative and couple that response with disapproval and wrath. But I also get confirmations from girls who either believe or fear that they are addicted. If you suspect that there is a deeper issue that may be fuelling her reliance on her phone for connection, I urge you to seek professional help. For those girls who want to evade addiction and feel good in healthier ways, here are a few ideas:

- Find a way to replace the dopamine (p. 106) that spikes in the body with each like or comment. She can naturally increase the levels of dopamine in the brain by exercising and by eating foods such as dairy products, fish, turkey, nuts, and dark chocolate.

- Teach her how to generate joy through creating. She may find joy doing arts and crafts, baking and cooking, building, or doing graphic design.

- Help her find moments of flow—when she is so immersed in what's she's doing that she doesn't notice time—and to discover what she is most passionate about doing. This can take some exploration and experimentation.

- Guide her to help someone else by volunteering or organizing a community event.

- Talk to her about self-care practices such as stretching before bed, getting a massage, taking an evening bath, using a face mask, or reading a good book.

- Encourage her to get outside and move her body (p. 64).

- Make time for a heart-to-heart conversation (with you or someone else) where time is irrelevant; check in with her on some deeper topics, such as her future plans and dreams (p. 226).

MISHA

Finding balance with our screens is a struggle I know a lot of people have. I feel what's most important in order to feel balanced is to get enough sleep and not to fall asleep stressed. I have some ideas when it comes to responsible and balanced social media usage: first, use it as a tool to find cool coffee shops or new local stores; second, learn to create a business with it; third, use it as another communication platform (like text or iMessage); fourth, create things for yourself—if you have an idea, just go for it and enjoy but don't create something for someone else; finally, if you reach a point where you feel like there's no joy in using social media, it's okay to stop and do something else you like.

Searching for More Ways to Connect

Clearly girls are using social media to search for something. Is it simply attention and approval? Popularity and friends? Acceptance and belonging? A sense of normalcy? Or is it something deeper, such as love? I'd argue that it's all of the above. The less secure and solid she is feeling in herself, and the more stress she is encountering, the greater her desire will be to search outside of herself for something, anything, and anyone—and social media and her phone are there to answer her need. But what she is really searching for is inner contentment and, most importantly, connection. To find that connection, she needs you to help her navigate and manage her time on social media. It's possible to do that by sharing the world that she loves and keeping her rooted in her own circle. Here are four ways to make it happen:

Learning

If you want to better understand your daughter's infatuation with social media, take the time to get familiar with its ever-evolving language. Give Instagram and Snapchat a try so you can see what she sees. You don't need to be an active participant or even have a public account, but you will benefit from exploring these sites.

Learning the language is one way to get to know and understand her. You may already be familiar with jargon such as "snapstreak," "Snap Maps," and "Insta story," and abbreviations like LOL (laughing out loud), JK (just kidding), BTW (by the way), BRB (be right back), PM (private message), DM (direct message), and IRL (in real life). But what about HTH (happy to help), NVM (never mind), OMW (on my way), TBH (to be honest), TTYS/L (talk to you soon/later), or CD9 (code 9/parents around), PIR (parent in room), and POS (parent over shoulder)?

Ask her to teach you a trick or two. She'll likely jump at the chance, because she will feel that you care about what she is interested in. Warning: she will be fast with her fingers, so ask her to slow down. Teaching you is a refreshing change for her, a chance to shine in an area where she excels. As you learn more about social media, you will gain insight into its allure and appeal as well as its pitfalls and perils. And that knowledge can inform your guidance in positive ways.

Educating

Your daughter may know a great deal about social media, but she still needs to be smart online and social media literate.

Girls are often oblivious to the insidious ways in which feelings of insecurity and self-doubt can be triggered. Every day she is consuming perfected images and "perfect lives," which may be how she comes to measure her own self-worth. There are so many opportunities for her to question and feel bad about herself. Speak with her about filtering her feed and editing her media. She should decide who and what she views with some key criteria as a foundation. Here are some questions to get her thinking about this:

- Who and what do you want to see?
- Does who you follow help you to feel better about yourself or worse?
- Who and what brings you hope and optimism?
- Who can you follow to bolster you instead of bringing you down?

Prepare her to respond appropriately when she is affected by what other people put out there—edited and shiny versions of themselves that are simply not real. Remind her she has options: she can unfollow, block, delete, report abusive or inappropriate content, or take a social media time out.

Reassure her that you are her safety net, that she can come to you at any time to let you know what's bothering her without judgment or criticism. She will appreciate knowing she has you as her lifesaver (just in case), and that you are there to help her navigate these turbulent waters. At the same time, she needs to be responsible for her own content and practise intentionality. What she posts online matters, so suggest she ask herself these three questions:

- Are my pictures appropriate and a true representation of me?
- Are my intentions good?
- What effect might my words have on others?

Posting to share, celebrate, or inspire is different from boast-posting with the intent to garner attention or insult other girls. If she is cutting down others or criticizing online, this behaviour reflects her character. A smart rule of thumb is to be kind and respectful. Advise her to wait three seconds before posting and to take this time to consider how she'd feel to be on the receiving end of her own post.

Developmentally speaking, teen girls do have a difficult time looking too far into the future. It is therefore a parent's job to make sure she is aware that what she posts today can drastically affect her future options, including getting into post-secondary education and getting a job. People will judge her by her online accounts. What she posts may be forever because any social media post can be screen-shot and shared by a follower without the owner's permission. It is imperative she thinks before she posts, and that she chooses who she is online wisely. With your guidance and understanding, I hope she will choose to be her best self.

Collaborating

Your teen daughter may be making more and more decisions about what she wants for her life: what she eats, who she hangs out with, how she spends her Friday nights. But she is still a part of the family and thus needs to follow family rules. There is a great need for social media guidelines, and the earlier this conversation takes place, the better. Most teen girls prefer guidelines, despite the complaints, and they need rules to keep them safe on the internet. When your daughter feels included in the creation of rules, she feels respected and valued, and she is more likely to commit to following them. The investment will be worth the return. At the end of the day, you make the final decisions, but when you enter into this conversation ready to listen and consider her ideas, you are much more likely to get her essential buy-in. Here are my suggested guidelines for internet and social media use:

- Negotiate the time of day she uses her device. I suggest avoiding first thing in the morning and just before bed. You can program your modem to cut off internet access at certain times, or to allow access at a specific start time in the morning.

- Strategically place multiple charging stations around the house. Ask her to place her phone in a charging station an hour before bed each night so she can wind down.

- Use downtime settings and app limits to remind her of the guidelines.

- Practise the 1:1 ratio: balance every hour of virtual time with an hour in the real world.

- Establish where she can use her phone, laptop, or computer; in shared spaces like the living room or office, for example, but not in her bedroom.

- Create timelines for when she can use her device, such as when homework and chores are done. Since most girls use their devices for homework, remind her that homework gets done quicker when she is not on her phone at the same time.

- Ensure she is staying safe by using privacy and location settings and not sharing too many personal details.

- Set and maintain boundaries around who she allows to follow her, and help her find safe sites and secure chat rooms by looking at her phone with her and monitoring her activity on an ongoing basis.

- Talk with her about being authentic and not contributing to the false reality of social media.

As much as parents have a responsibility for setting and maintaining boundaries for social media and internet use, I believe that girls have a responsibility to do so as well. It's admirable how much time they invest in crafting images and creating witty comments, but these can perpetuate the cycle of toxic perfectionism.

I am not saying that she shouldn't care or that she should share everything with her friends and followers. However, she should be aware that the more "perfect" she tries to make her life (and her feed), the more pressure she will feel to attain her own standards—and this perfectionism is infectious. Challenge her to acknowledge her "uglier" sides that make up the rest of her life. A teen girl can be real, even vulnerable, by sharing her good days and her bad, her edited and unedited photos, her #justwokeupthisway or #nofilter. She is so much more than a "brand," and she needs to know how to keep it real, in life and online.

As you talk to your teen daughter about these various guidelines, explain the "whys" as you listen to her rationale. The result will most likely be some compromise, but guidelines will be set. If nothing else, this can promote self-awareness and small changes.

Empowering

Empowering your teen girl can begin with the creation of a simple check-in: "How am I feeling about myself?" If she's not feeling great, social media is not the remedy; real connection is what she needs. Talk about how there is a big difference between using social media *because* she feels good (it's fun, interesting, and entertaining) and using social media *in order to* feel good (searching for validation, approval, love, and belonging).

Girls so easily give up personal power by searching outside of themselves, especially online. They follow what everyone else is doing. We can give their power back to them through two fundamental ideas: adopting new metrics of self-worth, and seeking life balance (real versus virtual).

Today as never before, girls are measuring their worth by their numbers. Recognizing the connection between low self-esteem and mental health concerns amid teens, it is imperative we help a girl find new metrics for self-worth. That metric might be who she is— her kindness, her sense of humour, her ability to take risks and show bravery, her care and compassion for a friend who is struggling. Or it might be her skill set, which could include singing or playing an instrument, writing a story or a song, building a robot, leading a group activity, babysitting, driving, or refereeing a lacrosse game. These are real measures of self-worth.

A second way she can empower herself is to seek life balance— using social media sometimes but not all the time, and deciding how (and for how long) she wants to use it. She may hop online for an hour of Google searching but then step away to spend an hour on another activity, whether that is baking a cake, exploring a park, walking the dog, having a conversation with you or a friend, cleaning and organizing her bedroom, reading a book, or perhaps even doing nothing.

PHONES AND SOCIAL media are not going to disappear any time soon. This means that parents need to know how these devices can affect teen girls and how to teach them to be intentional about their time online. I have high hopes that we can influence and change the relationship our girls have with their phones and social media—but it's going to require some changes and compromise on all sides.

Although you don't want to take this lifeline of connectivity away from her (you still need to reach her, too!), you also don't want the phone to rule her life and become a source of obsession, addiction, and low self-worth. You may not be able to keep up with your daughter's online life, but you will always have more life experience. Your teen girl sees her virtual world as one of endless possibilities and potential. Understand that for every possibility, there are potential drawbacks and downsides. You can support her because you have something she does not—perspective.

How Parents HELP Growth	How Parents HINDER Growth
• Staying aware of your phone use and distractibility	• Looking at your device while she is trying to talk to you
• Modelling how to turn away from your phone and be present	• Resisting learning about her social media accounts and online life
• Seeking to understand her screen habits and social media usage	• Removing her phone as a consequence, despite knowing that it's her social lifeline
• Sharing stats and facts about screens and social media as a catalyst for change	
• Participating in ongoing conversations about screen use, social media, her intentions, and internet safety	
• Practising the 1:1 ratio: one hour of real time for every hour of virtual time	

5

THE KALEIDOSCOPE
OF TEEN RELATIONSHIPS

"FRIENDS ARE THE most important thing you can have," said Peyton, when I asked what friendship means to her. "I feel so lucky to have a close-knit group of girlfriends who are there for me and always will be. I love the moments where you can be entirely yourself and completely accepted."

In contrast, Alicia answered the same question in this way: "Your friends won't always be there for you; they'll throw you under the bus and can be 'hot and cold.' If you are lucky, you'll find the odd true friend, but it's not easy."

An adolescent girl's kaleidoscopic social realm, with its various shades and hues, is never the same. It's constantly changing in often unanticipated and unpredictable ways, and it can prove to be painstakingly challenging at times. The juxtaposition of the comments from Peyton and Alicia highlights that unpredictability. Although I'm gladdened that Peyton feels a sense of genuine belonging, Alicia's cynicism broke my heart and left me flooded with a wave of compassion and disbelief. How could these two girls have such diametrically opposed views of relationships? Borrowing a popularized cliché, the only conclusion I can make is that "it's complicated."

Teenage girls' relationships are as complex as they are contradictory. Complex because every girl is on an individual journey of growing, maturing, and becoming; they are figuring out whom they want to spend time with, who truly supports them, whom they can trust, and who earns membership in their "tribe," "squad," "gang," or "posse." Girls are simultaneously balancing themselves within interconnecting circles of friendship. They covet authentic friendship, and yet they are sometimes exposed to girls who are bullies, girls who don't have boundaries, or girls with impenetrable borders. Often relationships are devoid of parity.

Girls can be closely and intimately interconnected, but these close connections can also be a web of damage and destruction. At their best, relationships help girls feel included and supported. Positive friendships can empower girls to take constructive risks and embolden them to show all their colours. At their worst, relationships can make girls judge themselves and each other harshly. Amid the betrayal, backstabbing, ghosting, and psychological manipulation, the negative aspects of relationships can leave them feeling stressed out and overwhelmed, uncertain and insecure—a nobody in a class of somebodies.

Relationships, like girls' moods, seem to come and go. They can change daily, and oftentimes drastically. At the end of the day, there seems to be no rhyme or reason to the social circles and categories girls create, or the ones they destroy. The people closest to her may be cheering her on; it's also possible that, propelled by jealousy, they may be the greatest threat to her well-being, with the potential to deeply hurt her. Other girls can make her feel strong and supported, pushing her to grow into who she is becoming. Or they can make her feel vulnerable and uncertain, pulling her to become who others want her to be.

Parents can at times struggle with the revolving door of friend-ships: How can she spend every day with a friend—and be constantly messaging when they are not together—and then suddenly declare, "She's not my friend anymore; she changed"? Possible translations: "She got popular and left me behind," "We had a fight and talked it out but I don't know what to do now—it's just awkward," or "I am uncomfortable with how she's grown and it's easier to break the friendship than to face my own insecurities head-on." Girls often internalize and blame themselves when this happens. Their self-talk is self-directed, as in "I must not be enough."

I field these feelings of inadequacy daily from puzzled girls, and I know how concerned and stressed out they can be as they navigate the oh-so-unpredictable waters of relationships—frenemies (friends one day, enemies the next), yo-yo friends, mean girls, good girls, queen bees, and all the ensuing girl drama. Although some girls make friends through domineering tactics, abusing their power to force loyalty, others can be kind, caring, and generous. Still others can be passive followers, often giving up their voice and values to fit in. When a girl does that, she is choosing the comfort of conformity over the discomfort of standing alone. Whatever her way of making and keeping friends, it remains clear that what matters most to girls is meaningful connection.

Why Girls Need Connection

Prehistorically, social connections increased survival rates for humans. We are literally stronger and better together as we work to avoid conflict and fight danger. As a result, the human brain is extremely evolved for emotional connection and relationship. From a scientific perspective, connection contributes to emotional, physi-cal, mental, psychological, and spiritual growth and health. Physical and emotional closeness connects us. Feeling connected causes the brain to release "feel good" hormones such as endorphins, serotonin, dopamine, and oxytocin. Connection feels good. At the same time, it lowers the brain's stress response system while soothing the parasympathetic nervous system. This is conducive to self-regulation and feeling calm and confident. Secure relationships, therefore, offer feelings of warmth, belonging, safety, and love.[1]

With close friends, girls feel they can be themselves—unguarded and unpretentious. These friendships provide a place where girls can say anything, where they can express their deepest feelings, secrets, and insecurities and still feel seen, heard, valued, validated, and encouraged. In this safe circle, where the air is rare, there are shared interests and hobbies, values and beliefs, and experiences. There is security, familiarity, and closeness. Girls long for inclusion, and they need it to relieve their stress and lower cortisol levels.

At the same time, this quest for closeness can also cause them the most distress, especially when connection goes awry. Sometimes teen girls have a toxicity tolerance that makes it impossible for them to see or feel true, authentic, reciprocal relationships. This means that girls will endure unhealthy relationships for far longer than they need to because they either don't know better or don't yet know they are worth more. Often, these kinds of relationships are based on the adage "someone is better than no one." Toxicity in friendships is not always immediately obvious; it can happen incrementally over time and often so subtly that a teen girl will not recognize it.

JORJA

Friendship is a relationship with you and another person who cares for, loves, and adores you. In a friendship you should feel you can tell them everything; it is a person you can rely on and can count on, that will be there for you no matter what. I think that a healthy relationship is where you and the other person are honest. Where you can trust them and they can trust you. I think an unhealthy relationship is where you are not honest and when you lie to the other person. When you can't trust them and when they bail on you a lot. I think that the best aspects of a friendship are that you have someone you can always talk to and have someone that is always there for you. You have a person to hang out with and get to do fun things with. The biggest thing that I worry about in a friendship is if the other person will judge me and see me as different. I worry that they will laugh at me and think less of me because I learn differently than other teens.

What Girls Think about Friendship

What's interesting to me is that girls are not always aware that they aren't meant to connect with everyone. Connection takes time and needs to be nurtured (which requires effort beyond clicking on her device). You cannot force or fake connection, and disconnection is normal—sometimes she'll have to disconnect, and at other times someone will disconnect from her. She needs to see relationships as fluid and flexible so that she is less blindsided by the drama and also prepared for it. One mother told me she advised her two teenage daughters "not to get caught up in the drama of what might be going on around them, and that if it does not affect their lives directly, to stay out of it."

What They Like Best

The special bonds formed during the teen years can last a lifetime. Girls know this. Girls love this. They want this—the BFF no matter what, the experience of comfort and closeness with the tacit understanding of reciprocal care, concern, support, and loyalty. When girls are close friends, they are sharing, connecting, understood, and accepted; they are having the "me too" experience—the realization that "I'm not the only one feeling this way," and the relief that comes along with that. They are building trust with one another through laughter, fun, exploration, and experimentation, and also, sometimes, through tears, hurt feelings, and conflict. Through it all are moments—immeasurable moments—of unspeakable joy as they navigate the ups and downs of the teen years together. Girls tell me how much they appreciate having a group of friends who "have my back just in case I am picked on or left out." A social media post I recently viewed sums this up by turning FRIENDS into an acronym for Fight for you, Respect you, Include you, Encourage you, Need you, Deserve you, Stand by you.

What They Like Least

Girls have a plethora of reasons for why they love relationships, but they can counter each one with something they loathe. For starters, girls (and most of us) hate working through conflict. They will tell everyone else about a problem, but they'll avoid talking directly with the person who upset them. They feel frustrated by the frenemies— so kind and fun and interesting until they turn against them on a dime, becoming mean, distant, and, most harmfully, passive-aggressive.

Beyond this confusing yo-yo type of friendship dynamic, teen girls are petrified of the bully. Bullies can be overtly mean—calling her names to her face or behind her back, gossiping, spilling secrets. They can also be covertly mean—telling girls to ignore someone or whispering cruelties as the intended target walks by. A classic "bully move" is gathering in groups and fervently telling secrets, but going silent as the picked-on girl approaches. Little wonder that girl concludes she is the topic of conversation. If confronted by a teacher or parent, the bully will hide behind the colloquial expression "just kidding," or she will go on the offence, labelling other girls "too sensitive," "too weak," and "unable to take a joke."

Making life harder for teen girls these days is that bullying is so easy to do online. Bullies search for power and dominance to feel secure but also to hide their own deep-seated fears of being left out or bullied themselves. If you think little girls can be mean, know that teen girls can be vicious. In *Little Girls Can Be Mean*, Michelle Anthony and Reyna Lindert discuss how social struggles like bullying take their toll and affect every aspect of the victim's life. They also challenge us to consider this: "Sadly, friendship struggles, relational aggression, and girl bullying are glossed over because girls have had no language or framework to understand what is happening to them. They have not realized that such events warrant discussion, support, and, at times, intervention in order to be resolved."[2] Though our teen girls need to learn the life skill of working through problems without the language or necessary practise, their default is silence.

Girls also hate separation. But walk into any school cafeteria and the divisions are obvious. The "us" vs. "them" dynamic of the teen girl population is built on race, class, appearance, maturity, intelligence, gender preferences, interests, and sexual experiences (or lack thereof). Separation is alive and well. Many teen girls also have a hard time when they experience a new social situation. Teens recognize the need to show their game face and look as if they know exactly how to handle themselves. Truth be told, so many of them are navigating unfamiliar social territory without the appropriate tools. Whether she experiences an embarrassing call-out among peers or a rejection when she asks someone out, a girl can feel mortified but still keep her cool girl mask firmly in place.

Finally, girls hate the social hierarchy and its built-in quest for popularity—though sometimes I sense that they secretly want this popularity as well. The idea of popularity, or relevancy, has allure. Popular girls appear to get all the attention, notoriety, and happiness an adolescent girl could ever want. Yet with popularity comes a surprising amount of pressure to keep up on social media, with peers, and with trends—to be "on" all of the time. One false move, one social blunder, and down the social hierarchy she will plummet. When I asked girls if they were popular or relevant, or if they even wanted these social labels, they were united in their responses. They told me they liked the upside of popularity—being known, respected, and "liked"—but they didn't want the downside, which they identified as "too much pressure to be someone you are not." One of my clients, Grace, offered this advice to girls chasing the idea of popularity: "Don't be friends with someone who is trying to be 'popular,' or even 'cool' for that matter, because they will step on you to gain access into the more popular crowd. Instead, choose to be friends with people who are happy with who they are and their social status."

What Girls Learn from Friendship

Mostly, girls learn how good they can feel when they are in relationships that boost and buoy them, opening them up to a whole new world. The girls surrounding your daughter can help her see parts of herself to which she's blind. They can bring out the best in her—her subtle but witty humour, her insightful observations, her adeptness at gathering people together. Other girls can be a tremendous sense of support, strength, encouragement, and comfort. Some will be the social mirrors she needs to further grasp her burgeoning identity. They will teach her how to behave, to communicate by talking and listening, to share her feelings instead of opting for silence or pouting, to be empathetic by imagining what it's like to go through a breakup or a breakdown. As she is learning the art of friendship, your teen girl is also looking for loyalty. Nothing will test trust and loyalty like a challenge or tough time. "Who is really there for me when I need them to be?" is an important question she should learn to ask herself.

Relationships also teach girls some tough and painful lessons, especially when it comes to social graces. For example, girls learn early on which social behaviours are considered positive and friendly (not interrupting or talking over someone, for instance, or not stealing someone's thunder when listening to a story). They learn that it's not appropriate to insert yourself into a group of girls talking in low voices, or make plans in front of girls who aren't invited, or put someone on the spot among peers. In contrast, some girls will learn that cruelty and gossip provide a boost in confidence and power, albeit temporarily. Additionally, girls learn that they will need to walk the delicate line between wanting to celebrate victories and feel proud of themselves and coming across as arrogant or rude. Too often, a fear of being unfairly judged results in a girl downplaying her success or dismissing compliments.

For some, friendship is challenging and takes more time (and trial-and-error learning). Others, like my outgoing client Elle, find it less difficult. "I love my friends and feel I can be myself," she told me. "I don't find it hard to make friends; it has always been easy for me." But what if your teen girl is not social? Some girls I work with are just not interested, while others don't have the social skills or confidence to know how to make friends. Truthfully, some of them are inappropriately loud or odd because they don't yet have a robust social skill set. Others might be on the autism spectrum. Still others prefer their own companionship or the company of older people.

Although you may worry about a lack of sociability in your teen girl, let her choose how social she wants to be. One mom I know often pushed her daughter into social situations, such as a pool party with the popular girls. The mom was deeply disappointed when she picked her daughter up and found her reading at the edge of the pool, a safe distance away from her peers. Later, the daughter told me she'd had a great time, and was confused by her mother's reaction. For this teen girl, being at the party around the other teens was more than enough socializing. The mom, caught up in her own expectations, missed that her daughter was socializing in her own way—as a quiet observer and a casual participant.

Friendship will teach your teen girl both positive and negative behaviours. But as she grows and experiences more, and with your calm guidance and support, she will learn what she wants and doesn't want out of her friendships—and who will always have her back.

Truth and Lies

Nothing pulls a girl further from the centre of her own circle than the dramatics, distinction, disillusionment, and disappointment that can emerge from relationships. She can easily become disconnected from the person she is trying to become. How do parents help their teen daughter return to resilience when she grows distant? How do we teach her to stand up to peer pressure, not fall prey to it? How do we guide her to be resilient and true to herself when she is constantly pushed to be a version of everyone else? Let's focus on one imperative strategy: truth.

Take some time to remind your teen of her truth: who she used to be and how far she has come. Perhaps she was light-spirited and giggly as a little girl, or the one with small hands and big ideas. Maybe she was bookish and reserved, or excitable and silly. Whoever she was is still within her, masked by the oh-so-serious, unfazed teen image she feels she needs to show. Remind her of the interests, hobbies, and passions that used to make her happy. Affirm her growth by pointing out that while she's certainly gotten taller, she's also more confident, or smarter, braver and bolder, or kinder and more generous, or more musical or artistic.

Truth is the ability to use discernment in relationships. It's paying attention to what others show her and their true characters (behaviour is consistent and then predictable), and knowing the difference between the lies girls are taught to believe and the truths they need to know. There is no better person to bring her clarity on this one than you, and you alone can prepare her to see the lies and to believe the truths instead.

Here are five of the most common lies I deconstruct with teenage girls. You can use them as conversation starters in talking with your daughter.

Lie: *I need friends; I cannot be alone. Some friends are better than no friends.*

Truth: She is enough. Being alone and true to herself will always be hard, yet it will feel better than having unhealthy, unsupportive friendships that can create insecurity rather than strength. Being alone can feel lonely, but so can being in a group that doesn't see, hear, or value her for who she is as a person. Girls who get comfortable with being alone—strong and rooted in their own incredibleness—do not stay alone forever. In fact, they tend to attract girls just like them. I often suggest girls work on developing their skills as a way to build up their competence and thus confidence; this often creates organic opportunities for girls to meet others who share the same interests.

Lie: *My friends define me.*

Truth: She exclusively defines herself, exactly as she chooses to be.

Yes, her friends can influence and shape her, but at the end of the day, she decides the kind of person she wants to be and the values and beliefs she wants to live out. Her character is designed by reflecting on who she is and who she wants to be. She is growing in both self-awareness and inner confidence. Her character becomes her reputation. At any moment, she can re-evaluate, reprioritize, and redefine who she wants to be. She is never stuck and always has the ability to decide who she wants to become.

Lie: *Popularity is everything.*

Truth: Popularity can create more anxiety and stress than the chase to achieve it.

Being popular or relevant sometimes means pretending to be someone she is not; it can mean changing in ways she doesn't want to, taking on a persona that no longer feels like her, and doing and saying things that are not what she wants. Popularity is a facade—and a lot of work to keep up. Girls who once wished to be popular and have had this wish come true often tell me it wasn't what they thought it would be. If you suspect your teen girl is focused on being popular, remind her to focus instead on being a good friend and on being relevant to herself and close friends.

Lie: *What people think of me matters more than what I think of me.*

Truth: Her opinion is the only opinion that matters, and she needs to stop caring what others think about her. People will always judge, criticize, and tell her what they think. Although this is much easier said than done, she can learn—over time and with practice—to say "who cares," and to not be bothered or waiver when those around her are telling her what they think. What *she* thinks is the most important thing. What *she* thinks is all she needs to focus on. Her unique opinion, perspective, and voice are things she should be proud of—without apology, without compromise.

Lie: *Girls are stronger and better together.*

Truth: Sometimes girls are stronger and better together, but sometimes girls are also cliquey and exclusive. Oftentimes, a group of girls can create a culture of superiority and toxicity. The appeal of having a group of girlfriends to chat with, confide in, and be with is magnified by what a teen sees in the media and popular culture. Without knowing it, she may have internalized the idea that this group will be there for her, no matter what. She may not have considered that relationships can come with a great deal of disappointment. If your daughter doesn't have a "girl group" of the type so often idealized on television, she needs to know that is okay. She may find one or two good friends, and that may be a better fit for her. Girl groups can look like fun, but they are not always healthy. It's much healthier for her to focus on her expectations of herself, which will help attract the right people who share those values.

Teach Her to Be a Friend

Parents can have a major impact on their daughter's ability to be a friend as she becomes more aware and intentional about the kinds of friends she wants in her life. You can teach her to collaborate and co-operate, to encourage and support other girls, to compliment and remind each other that they are all important and valuable, in different ways. You can also remind her that competing for power or attention, criticizing or condemning, or being jealous and insecure can be a serious threat to her equilibrium. This wisdom may be met with a serious eye roll, but it will nevertheless let her know that she doesn't need to be this way.

If a teen girl's friendship drama becomes damaging and destructive, many parents are uncertain as to when to listen and when to advise. You can discern this by paying attention. One parent told me, "I really keep my ears open when she and her friends are discussing issues and step in if I feel the need. If it's nothing major I will just listen and let them sort it out." Another mother makes sure she plans regular activities for her and her daughters to do together. "I love our weekend outings because that time in the car or at the restaurant table is often the time she decides to tell me things. I am also always happy to be the group driver—the picker-upper—or I suggest they have their party at my place as this gives me a better idea of what her friends are like, what the relationships are like, and what they have going on."

When deciding whether to talk with your teen daughter about her friendships, here are three points to consider:

- You don't need to weigh in on every issue or solve all her friendship problems, but you do need to be available to connect when she needs to.

- Remember that these are her choices for friends, not yours.

- Avoid allowing your experience to influence her experience.

What Makes Healthy Relationships?

Beyond the basics of respect, care, kindness, loyalty, support, empathy and understanding, and reliability, girls also need to know that healthy relationships are founded first and foremost on trust. She needs to know how to measure the ways in which that trust shows up.

Respect for Boundaries

She can trust a girl who keeps her secrets, who respects her boundaries (such as when she says she doesn't want to drink or hang out with certain people), and who speaks the truth even though this can be difficult at times. Clear communication requires honesty and the ability for girls to share what's really on their minds, what they want, and what they need. So often, girls hold back for fear of being misunderstood and rejected. When they speak up, though, it can make relating to others so much easier. There is simplicity in clarity. At the same time, we can make clear to girls that when someone doesn't respect their boundaries (by not listening or pushing them beyond their limits, for example), they can set firmer boundaries, or even borders, as necessary.

My student Rachel is sweet and kind and occasionally too nice altogether. One day she came to me distraught because a friend had been repeatedly asking her for help with her school work. Rachel knew she was smart enough and capable enough to help, but she had so much work on her own pile! She was tired and torn. As a nice person, she wanted to help, but at what cost? Her energy and her time. Rachel needed help with boundaries. We practised saying no without adding too much of an explanation or too many qualifiers—devoid of a story, and with absolutely no apologizing. This was incredibly difficult for Rachel. To start, we wrote out five different ways to say no tactfully, including "No, I just don't have time today," and "No, that won't work for me." Next, we practised. I asked her for a sip of her water. She squirmed and wiggled before murmuring, "No, that won't work for me." We kept practising to cut out her unneeded apologies. We worked at it until she felt confident that she had every right to guard her time and protect her energy, and that she did not have to feel obliged to help.

Balanced Communication

Healthy relationships need to be balanced in terms of talking and listening, but also with respect to giving and taking, compromising and collaborating. No one girl should always be giving or always be getting. No one girl should always be the initiator or always the follower. Equilibrium comes when both girls show up in the relationship and do their part. There is shared power and the sharing of ideas and insights. Yes, sometimes one girl will have more of a need to talk, usually when there is something pressing on her mind. But girls need to ensure that there's no "always" or "all the time." To promote equity in relationships, I teach girls the simple strategy of mirroring. Girls feel empowered by the idea that they can match what they are given. If her friend is offering her ideas and support, by all means, she can offer her ideas and support back. And if she's not receiving much input from her friend, or feels she is doing all the heavy lifting in the relationship, she can just as easily pull back.

Active Participation

Relationships require time and effort; there is no such thing as "Insta friends." Help her shift her perspective on friendship from "What can I get?" to "What can I give?" Girls need to see themselves as active participants in relationships and, by extension, in their own happiness. So often girls tell me, "Nobody talks to me." My response is always "Can you try talking to them?" When girls see themselves in charge of cultivating connection, they feel empowered.

Here are some of the simple ideas I suggest to girls for positive connection with others. I offer them along with gentle reminders to be active participants in relationships (not passively waiting to be talked to) and to find the balance between talking and listening. These all work beautifully and can be another way for her to feel competent and confident.

- Start by saying "hello" and "how are you?".

- Listen to the answer and respond appropriately rather than making the conversation all about you.

- Practise empathy. This shows up in phrases like "I understand why you'd feel so frustrated," or "That must be so uncomfortable for you."

- Notice something about another girl, like a new haircut or funky nail polish—"I love your hair," or "Great nails!"

- Look for strengths in others and compliment them; for instance, "You are really good at ignoring the boys when they tease you," or "You are fierce on the volleyball court," or "Your Insta posts of nature are amazing."

- Initiate conversation by asking questions like "How has your day been so far?" or "What are you doing this weekend?"

- Share a detail of your day: "Today was up and down. I felt off first thing because I slept in, but then I learned my bio test was bumped to Monday."

- Suggest plans; for instance, "Do you want to eat lunch together today?" or "Should we study at the library?"

- Speak in a clear, concise, and confident way, and don't use filler words such as "um," "like," and "you know."

Fun and Authenticity

Healthy relationships—and here I am talking about in-person inter-actions as opposed to internet interactions—are infused with fun, authenticity, and common interests and activities. They should feel good, without exception. This is non-negotiable. The litmus test I suggest to girls is this: After spending time with someone, do you feel better about yourself or worse? Do you feel uplifted or drained? With these thought-provoking questions, girls can make a choice based on the effect another person is having on her.

JORDANA

I think as girls we are all insecure, deep down, and it is easy to take our own insecurities and project them onto others. I also think there is a level of com-petition that comes with this and leads girls to not working as one and being dishonest. It is easy to say what you think the other person wants to hear. When you are in a position where the consequences of a situation could be detrimental or dangerous, you need to speak up instead of saying what you feel you "should" say. Looking back on the old times and how things used to be can keep us attached to a false reality of what the friendship is now. Letting go of something is scary, and the social structure you once knew may need to become different. I'd rather wait for a good friend than settle. I like to keep in mind the expression "When one door closes, another one opens." You need to put effort into friendship. It is not enough to know you have a friend-ship with someone; you need to continue to make it a priority to grow with friends through life. You need to be honest with yourself and others.

Avoiding Unhealthy Relationships

Connections that are not life-giving are life-draining. Yet unless teen girls know how to define what an unhealthy relationship looks like, they can easily become trapped in toxic friendships. Unhealthy relationships are out of balance and out of sync with what a girl is looking for; oftentimes they are out of control. There is no worse feeling for a teen girl than being stuck or "this is as good as it gets."

Unhealthy relationships often include all or several of these behaviours:

- confusing communication
- passive-aggressive behaviours
- boundaries that are ignored and disrespected
- constant competition, comparisons, and judgment
- meanness, jealousy, and a culture of gossip and degradation

You can help your teen daughter to avoid toxic friendships by encouraging her to do the following:

Look for the Like-Minded

You want her to surround herself with like-minded, like-spirited friends. That doesn't mean she and her friends will always agree. However, because these relationships are founded on shared interests, similar life approaches, and common values, friendship challenges among like-minded girls are not always deal breakers. Respect and trust are high, which in turn promotes forgiveness and understanding. Guide her to be on guard for a "leader" who dominates the attitudes and values of her peer group, often using threats to ensure loyalty.

Create Variety

In *No More Mean Girls*, Katie Hurley echoes my sentiment when she says, "When girls have the freedom to try out a wide variety of friendship and showcase their interests and talents, they learn to blaze their own trails and take pride in their individual differences."[3] Encourage your daughter to gather a variety of friends: girls who are older than her and who can serve as mentors; girls who are younger than her and whom she can mentor; girls from school; girls from her after-school activities; girls who are just like her, and girls who are nothing like her; and boys. Sometimes she needs a logical, pragmatic, and solutions-focused friend; other times she needs an empathetic, compassionate listener. The wider her circle of friends, the more protected she is from losing a BFF (the unhealthy, unrealistic best friend forever).

Have the Courage to Let Go

Friendships are fluid: they come and go, and the earlier your teen girl understands this, the better. But one of life's toughest friendship lessons is learned when your teen realizes that she is in an unhealthy, unfulfilling relationship and needs to let go. Letting go is loss, and with loss comes uncertainty. It's so hard for a teen girl to see beyond her current circumstance. There is inevitable discomfort, but as you can gently remind her (at the right time), this feeling does not last, and it opens the door for something better. Letting go of unhealthy friends is not easy, but it will allow her to gain a wider perspective on people and life. You will need to tread carefully to avoid giving off a lecturing or "I told you so" vibe, or possibly appearing happy that a toxic friend is no longer in her life (even if you do feel this way!). Remember to do more listening than speaking, offer more understanding than questioning, and allow her to draw her own conclusions in her own time.

Trust Herself

We can teach girls to work through difficult situations by encouraging them to trust themselves when something feels wrong. She can then decide how best to express herself or if the situation is worth her words. Here are steps for doing that:

1. Get her to take charge of her own feelings. Whether she is angry, frustrated, or confused, she needs to own her feelings and express them. You can help her extend this prompt into "I feel" phrases such as "I feel [fill in the blank] because..." Here are some examples:

   - "I feel anxious and excited at the same time about starting a new school this year."

   - "I am so worried about my test today because I feel I bombed but I don't know for sure."

   - "I am angry when you tell people my stories before I get the chance to. This frustrates me because I would like to share my stories."

   - "I am hopeful I got the job at the kids' camp because I rocked the interview today."

   - "I am afraid to go kayaking with my class because I've never kayaked before and I don't want to be bad at it."

2. Encourage her to be empathetic by asking her to consider the situation from another perspective. For example, when she is disappointed that a friend cancels plans with her because she has too much on her plate, ask her to imagine one of her busy days, when she would appreciate the grace of a friend if she had to cancel. My client Tyra often complained that her friend Alex was "always cancelling on her." When I asked her why

Alex cancelled, Tyra had no idea. Upon further probing, Tyra discovered that Alex was going through a lot: her parents were divorcing, so she was bouncing between two households; she was preparing for her spring dance competitions; and she was dealing with school demands and a part-time job at the local bakery. Considering what her friend was going through allowed Tyra to have more than a little empathy.

3. Let her know that working through conflict ends with stating—not asking—what she wants using "I need" statements. Here are some examples:

    - "I need you to hear my opinion, though it's different from yours."

    - "I would appreciate your full attention when I am telling you some exciting news because I feel unappreciated when you are only half-listening."

    - "I need you to stop assuming that I will agree to all the plans you make. Please ask me first."

    - "Please don't make my experience about your experience. Please listen."

4. Encourage her to claim the power of choice: Does she want to find compromise within the relationship? Is it worth her while, or does she want to end the relationship and focus on what matters more to her?

Boyfriends and Girlfriends

Having a boyfriend or a girlfriend is on a lot of girls' minds, and the energy of anticipation is palpable as she awaits her "firsts": first time holding hands, first kiss, first date, and first romantic relationship. Unfortunately, many teen girls feel pressured into dating, mostly because everyone else is talking about it and some are starting to experience it. That's the social reason they show interest in dating, but there is a biological element to this interest as well.

Once a girl gets her period, she experiences an increase in estrogen production. At the same time, she also experiences an increase in the production of dopamine (a neurochemical) and oxytocin (a neurohormone), which can provide her with an urge for intimacy. With these hormonal surges comes a rise in sensitivity, self-consciousness, and self-criticism as well as a new attraction to the opposite or same sex.[4] Girls may or may not want to date, but they do want to feel close and connected. Sometimes, dating—and that new attraction to the same or opposite sex—gives her the intimacy she feels she needs, along with the sense that she is "walking on air" or "over the moon." Girls can become overly exuberant and affectionate, hugging everyone!

For some girls, the interest in dating spikes early on; for others, it is later. It all depends on where they are on the maturation spectrum. What I know for certain is that teen girls are considering and entertaining the idea of having a relationship, and exploring the direction of their sexual preferences.

Dating

Teen girls' experiences with the opposite or the same sex (more on same-sex relationships in chapter 7) may begin with secret infatuations with actors, pop singers, or sports heroes—crushes that are as innocuous as they are fleeting and fun to gossip about over cafeteria lunches. Bonding over unrequited love is another way to connect and feel included (even if she's not ready for something real). Her "love" of a famous entity is far removed from her reality, a safe way for her to practise liking someone without the awkward face-to-face encounter. Crushes become more serious when they are on actual humans, even if said boy or girl has no idea who she is. Her radar is on full alert for teasing, flirtation, and attention: a look, a smile, a "hi" between classes, the light graze of a hand on her shoulder. She'll spend hours texting or messaging friends about what this all means.

Things start to change for teen girls when hanging out becomes more serious—when it becomes "dating." I know many parents have mixed feeling about this, and some are averse to their daughters dating, especially if she's interested in someone who isn't a parent's "cup of tea." What do you do when your daughter brings home the rebel boyfriend or girlfriend who is two years older than she is, the one you warned her about, or the sleazy guy from her math class who you know is only looking for one thing? What do you do when you have no idea if or who she's dating because she's not telling you a thing? Many girls have secret boyfriends or girlfriends, relationships that their parents will never know about.

When parents ask me about their teen girls and dating, especially in the early stages, I tell them that their best strategy is to remember they are on the periphery—they don't have the veto power they may have had when she was little. Your parenting "power" is the ability to observe what kinds of people she chooses to date and to be curious about why. Gentle, non-judgmental questions about her love interest may help you better understand her choice. She may opt for someone who is completely unlike her and brings her out of her shell, or she may choose a person who dotes on her and makes her feel special. Your job is to focus on the relationship you share so that you can be there for her through the ups and downs of her dating experiences. Remember, you are her safety net.

I'm open to girls dating; some are ready to feel close to a special someone—an important developmental juncture. Maturity has led them to want more from relationships. However, I worry about girls who want to date because they are lonely, looking for attention and approval, or feel pressured to date or "hook up." Often there is a subversive and unspoken undercurrent of competition with other girls for the same dating partner. Although one girl may "win," she may "lose" her once close-knit group of girlfriends, who will let her know that she betrayed them. Girls will turn against the girl they feel is turning her back on them or advancing beyond them. Lost loyalty and insecurity are pervasive. The competition is fierce, and girls in relationships don't help themselves to feel any more secure by peppering their dates with compare-and-contrast questions: "Do you think she's pretty?" or "How am I different from your last girlfriend?"

It is vital that girls know they will be okay without a boyfriend or girlfriend, despite societal ideas that being in a relationship is a significant marker of maturity and being a "someone." Standing tall and independent means knowing who she is, having her own opinions, and making her own decisions based on her values. From this strong stance she can step into interdependence. What you want to discourage is dependence and an over-reliance on a relationship (of any kind) for her value and fulfillment.

During the high school years, dating can be a great way to get to know peers without feeling trapped or obliged to any one particular person, and without missing out on different relationships. But dating can also take away from this opportune time for teen girls to learn who they are and to enjoy the full breadth of high school. Limiting their choices too soon can cause feelings of regret. Why not work on friendship instead?

Just Friends

Hands down, boys—and specifically the male demeanour—may offer something girls cannot always offer each other. Girls who jump into boys' worlds through conversation or activities soon learn that boys do have feelings. Boys can be sensitive, and they, too, have a complex inner world—though it's different from a girl's in its lack of theatrics. "They may not get caught up in the drama of the day, but they do care," one fifteen-year-old girl told me. "When I talk to boys, they are good listeners and make me feel better."

Friendships with boys are an appealing change of pace for some girls. If a guy has a problem with her, he'll tell her straight and then move on. Guys often focus on activity and doing things over talking in circles. This is refreshing to girls, especially to those who haven't yet bought into the "perks" of gossip. Guy friendships are sometimes necessary and welcome alternatives for girls caught up in circles of rumour and gossip. Many moms and dads have told me that they encourage their daughters to hang around with boys as friends. "I even signed her up for co-ed sports," one says, "and I let her know that it's great to be friends with guys, as they are different than girlfriends. She has several male friends, and she's learned a lot about guys and what they like and want."

RELATIONSHIPS ARE NEVER easy, even for adults. But they are especially fraught for adolescent girls, who are learning to navigate their social world. Regardless, your teen girl's relationships are essential to her growth and understanding of herself. Her relationships sustain her in trying times, comfort her through trials, and offer her celebration in her triumph. Ultimately, a teen girl's relationships are woven into the essence of her identity and her ability to transform her strength and power into purpose and passion. In the end, how nourishing her friendships will be is a result of how well she navigates the changes and challenges, and if she makes healthy relational choices. As a parent, you are uniquely positioned to nurture that growth by paying attention and keeping the door open to conversation without judgment and criticism.

How Parents HELP Growth

- Understanding that her relationships are complicated
- Being there for her and listening without judgment through the complexities and tough lessons
- Assuring her there is nothing wrong with her if she has few friends, and discussing how to let go of unhealthy relationships
- Keeping the door open to talk about bullying, both in person and online
- Talking to her about being ready to date

How Parents HINDER Growth

- Judging her for who she is spending time with
- Trying to hang out with her and her friends
- Influencing her relationship choices
- Weighing in on her friendship concerns and trying to solve her problems
- Getting caught up in the drama of the day

6

PRESSURE FROM PEERS

IMAGINE YOU COME home from a busy day at the office to see your daughter's backpack, shoes, and jacket dumped in the entryway. Exhausted, you start to clean up before turning your attention to dinner. As you pull out the backpack's contents one by one, you see the expected collection of half-used lip balms, smelly workout gear, and crumpled permission slips, including one for the school's year-end camping trip. Then you find something unexpected: a turquoise piece of paper, carefully folded up. Curious, you open it up to see a bolded title—OUR SUMMER GOALS—followed by a list of five items:

1. Stay up all night.
2. Send a partial nude text.
3. Steal makeup from the drug store.
4. Get cross faded [getting drunk and high at the same time].
5. Have sex.

Stunned and speechless, you stand frozen. Is this really your daughter's list for the summer? You were thinking she'd be going to camp, having her first kiss, and, hopefully, maturing as she prepared to start Grade 10 in the fall. Clearly, she has different ideas about how she's going to spend her break from school.

You may not find a list like this in her backpack, but chances are, your daughter has some sort of list of her own, a list that is likely the result of feeling pressured by peers—her fellow list makers. Your teenage daughter is under pressure to keep up in many areas: school, work, appearance, activities, volunteering, and social media. Most heavy is the pressure she feels from peers to look, speak, and act in accordance with social norms, which is exacerbated by social comparisons. As she advocates for more time to spend with friends, and not family, you may have a list, too, filled with questions: What decisions will she make without me? Will she do the right thing? Will she be safe? Will she be able to withstand the pressure from peers, or will she cave in when pushed? Have I taught her enough and prepared her for what she will face? Only time and experience will tell, but there are specific things you can do to help your teen girl deal with peer pressure.

Girls strive for acceptance and approval as their social circles expand beyond the classroom to after-school hangouts at the mall, parties, and many other daily adventures of teenagehood. With this bigger world come more opportunities to grow and a greater risk of not belonging. For the most part, a girl takes great pains to look like everyone else, dress like everyone else, talk like everyone else, and be like everyone else—sometimes at the cost of her own identity and integrity. You see evidence of this in what she chooses to wear, how she talks to peers, and how she acts—being "cool" but still following social mores. There are some exceptions, of course, but most girls feel desperate to blend in, and they understand that sometimes they need to change to belong.

Peer pressure is at work when teen girls feel pushed by members of a group to a point where they feel discomfort, worry, and angst;

it's also at play when she feels inner conflict between wanting to be true to herself and fearing ridicule and rejection. Peer pressure can be about breaking rules (skipping school or sneaking out past her curfew, for example), experimenting with fashion trends or musical tastes, or dating. Typically, teen girls will encounter a variety of pressures to varying degrees.

MALIA

To me, peer pressure means that my peers (classmates, allies) are pressuring me into something I didn't want to do. I have felt pressure from peers, but I always stay true to myself and stand up for myself and others who are going through the same thing. Consent is key.
I have never given in, I'm proud to say, but I have definitely seen others being peer pressured and influenced or giving in to peer pressure. I see peer pressure happening all the time. But if I know the person being pressured and know that they would listen to me, I would encourage them to stick to their own gut.

Sometimes these pressures can lead a teen girl straight to behaviours such as smoking and vaping, drinking, sexual activity, and rebellion. Teen rebellion is not new; what is new(er) is that the teen experience is now magnified on social media, which constantly tells her how she should be acting and models the life she should be living. When I asked parents about their strategies for peer pressure, one mom told me something that was echoed by many others:

"They need to self-discover this part of life to understand it better. If I told them to never do this or that—then they would never learn. This has served me well because my girls have never abused the power I have given them." It's a smart strategy, as teens are contrary creatures, and one I'm convinced is worth adding to your teen toolkit.

Before I explore some of these pressures—and offer strategies for helping your teen girl manage them—it's important to be aware of two considerations when it comes to teen girls and peer pressure: the first is her longing for connection and inherent need for inclusion (see p. 135); and the second is how the teen years often culminate in a "perfect storm" as her emotional brain overwhelms her logical brain. During the teen years, your daughter's brain tends to rely more on the limbic system (the emotional accelerator) than the prefrontal cortex (the logic "brakes"). This means the decisions she makes may be impulsive and lacking in sound judgment, and she needs higher doses of risk to feel the same rush as adults.[1] At the same time, the upsurge in her brain's production of oxytocin (the bonding hormone) receptors peaks at the age of fifteen and increases her need to be close to others.

It is almost inevitable, then, that teen girls will yield to pressure and take risks in order to belong. Connection is everything to them. Girls simultaneously long for and fear connection, and this can often lead them to follow their peers even when their instincts (and you) tell them otherwise. Given a growing girl's brain development and self-consciousness, not to mention her sensitivity to and fear of rejection, the stakes are high when it comes to disconnection. Feeling unseen, unheard, and neither valued nor validated is a teen girl's worst nightmare, and can lead to very real physical responses. When a girl is feeling disconnected, her stress response systems (both the amygdala—the part of the brain involved with experiencing emotion—and the hippocampus—the part of the brain that is associated with memory and that regulates emotion) are activated and on high alert. She is keenly paying attention to every nuance in communication: a sigh, a sideways glance, a look of disapproval, words spoken and unspoken—this all must mean something. She scrambles to make the most of these signs. Concurrently, due to an amygdala that is more easily activated than in her male counterpart, she is much more attentive to potential dangers, including someone mocking her, shunning her, or deserting her.

Thanks to social media, girls have a multitude of platforms where they can see what their friends are showcasing and boasting about. They can see what their peers are posting, commenting, and even saying about them, and they are aware of what events they are left out of and who has unfollowed or unfriended them. This is a firestorm of intensity, and it explains why girls can feel pressure to do "anything" for connection. In turn, this means that when you cut off connection with her friends, she may choose to do things that are risky. Taking some time to think carefully about how you manage the results of peer pressure may prepare you for the inevitable collisions.

How Peer Influence Challenges Her Growth

Peer influence isn't all bad. It can lead, for instance, to social mirroring—when a teen copies what she sees and emulates others to fit in. It can encourage her to do something she normally wouldn't do because she is influenced, even inspired, by others. Friends can help your daughter in all the right ways. They can push her out of her comfort zone to learn a new activity or meet new people. They can inspire her to feel safe enough to show more of her personality and be more outspoken, to be adventurous and get more involved. Her peers can lead her to notice what they are doing—volunteering, perhaps, or seeking a part-time job—and ask, "Why can't I?"

With peers, she is exploring and experimenting in a whole new world, but within the safety of a group (as in "We are all in this together"). There is much bonding over trying new things—different foods or sports or music—and, yes, even in taking some risks, in trying what may seem scary in order to widen her circle. But there is a distinction between peer influence and peer pressure. The trick is getting the balance right between being herself and finding her place with others.

How Peer Pressure May Sabotage Her Growth

Peer influence becomes peer pressure when it is negative or dangerous, and when the risks are too high. You may notice the negative effects of risks taken with peers when your daughter's mood and demeanour drastically change (she's surly and self-deprecating), when she withdraws from her usual activities (quitting teams and clubs or skipping school), and if her health declines (too much or too little sleep, too much or too little food). At the same time, we have to remember that an adolescent's cognitive capacity is developing and that her prefrontal cortex is lagging behind in its development growth. This means that she doesn't always have the ability or experience to think before deciding, to consider the consequences of her choices, or to fully understand how her actions will affect or even harm herself and others.

Moreover, anything that affects her developing and oh-so-fragile brain—whether it's drugs, alcohol, or the toxins of cigarettes or e-cigs—is directly damaging her brain cells and thus its very structure, not to mention the potential of her brain's overall health. Without grasping the dangers these substances pose to her growing brain, she's likely to take uncalculated risks. Why would a girl even want to get drunk or high, inhale fumes, or harm her body in any way?

Working with teen girls has helped me to answer that question. Often, they are trying to extinguish the stress that accompanies dealing with a new social scene, the intensity of school work, the pressure to be involved in extracurricular activities, maintaining high or at least decent grades, and her own internal drive to succeed—to look right, feel right, and be right. Sometimes, teenagers embrace the social imperative of "now or never" when it comes to having fun and experimenting. This YOLO maxim—"you only live once"—can drive rebellious actions. Other times, teens are born into families with addiction, and they learn to emulate what they observe. They see how stress is managed with escape.

When I talk openly and honestly with teen girls about their experiences, they invariably ask how I behaved in my teen years and about the pressures I felt. I tell them my parents set out guidelines for my sibling and me to follow: to be home at a reasonable time, to never drive with someone under the influence, and to call them for a ride home if we drank. Because I was guided and not forbidden, and given a safety net, I was able to make smart choices for myself. I do tell girls that although I concluded that drinking wasn't for me, I was thankful for the freedom to try. I give them the gist of my experiences, and explain how I learned invaluable life skills about holding my own and handling myself, thinking quickly on my feet, and trusting my gut when a situation felt wrong. You may choose to share stories about your own teen choices and rebellious acts, as much as you are comfortable doing. Don't worry that this will somehow give her "permission" to make her own risky choices (she's already thinking about it anyway); sharing stories is simply about relating to her and showing her your vulnerability. It makes you "normal" in her eyes, and shows her that even you faced peer pressure "back in the day."

Let's start our exploration of peer pressure by looking first at the behaviours parents most worry about: smoking and vaping, alcohol consumption, and drug use. For each of these behaviours, I have created a list of things your teen girl should be aware of. Find the right time to suss out her knowledge about the topic; ask her low-key questions about what she does know, without judgment, and use her responses to figure out what she doesn't know. If she mentions something that happened at school, make it an opportunity to discuss the consequences of the behaviour in question. This will be an ongoing conversation, so take care to listen carefully. She may even teach you a thing or two.

Smoking and Vaping

Cigarette smoking and the now-trendier vaping almost always happen as a result of peer pressure. Girls often begin smoking because they think it looks "cool," and what teen girl doesn't want to look chic and stylish among friends? Cigarette smoking, then, can be a way to fit in—although it can also be a way to deal with stress over body image. Many girls believe that smoking is an effective way to maintain their weight, so it can seem like a good idea. The appeal of vaping with e-cigs is even greater, and this smoking alternative is fast becoming the new normal. Many teens believe that there is "just flavouring" in this product and that it is harmless (which is not true).[2] Teens are more likely to smoke e-cigs than cigarettes, but those who do are also more likely to eventually smoke cigarettes. Since teens often emulate the actions of the adults surrounding them, they are likely to follow your example if you smoke or vape. Please be mindful of the fact that your daughter is going to do what you show her more often than she will do what you tell her.

What she needs to know about smoking:

- Smoking can negatively affect athletic performance.
- Smoking leads to bad-smelling breath, clothes, and hair.
- Smoking leads to greater risks of body injury and slower recovery times.
- Chemicals in cigarettes, like nicotine and cyanide, can harm health in the short and long term.
- Smoking is addictive.[3]

What she needs to know about vaping:

- E-cigarettes are often not regulated.
- Vaping is no safer than smoking cigarettes.
- Chemicals in e-cigarettes, like nicotine and antifreeze, can harm health in the short and long term.
- Vaping is addictive.[4]

As concerned and proactive parents, you want your daughter to make healthy choices. Despite the social stigma that now exists, smoking and vaping are still seen as viable and enviable options for adolescent girls. What you can offer her are the facts about both, the encouragement to make healthful decisions to take care of her body, and perhaps even the motivation to be "cool" in alternative ways.

Alcohol Consumption

A few years ago, I worked with some parents who were called late one night to pick up their very drunk daughter from a friend's house. The friend's parents were away for the weekend, and in an attempt to impress some boys, Ava had started to drink without knowing how much her body could handle. To make the situation worse, she was drinking several kinds of hard liquor: a shot of vodka, then tequila, and then some brandy. Ava felt fine until she stood up, fell over, and started vomiting. Because she hadn't eaten much that day (on the recommendation of friends who'd told her she'd get drunk faster this way), she was essentially throwing up stomach acid. Ava's parents were grateful their daughter was safe and that she had called them. They immediately picked her up and put her to bed. Then they deliberated suitable consequences.

Every family must choose what's best for them, but I do believe it's important to prepare girls where alcohol use is concerned. Here's why: Girls tell me constantly that they only drink because everyone else is doing it, and also because alcohol alleviates any social anxiety they might be feeling. In new and sometimes overwhelming social scenes, alcohol provides a way to feel more comfortable and equipped. Drinking helps the outgoing girl become wilder, the shy girl become more outgoing, the reserved girl become more boisterous, and the nervous girl become braver. What they don't anticipate is the poor decision making that can result from drinking too much: making out with the wrong person, saying or doing something she later regrets, and feeling sick the next morning. Drinking on a Friday or Saturday night can become a habit; worse yet, it can turn into the more dangerous problem of binge drinking. Sometimes, girls drink to feel better socially, to become their "best social selves." Other times, they drink to forget their problems, to escape into a drunken stupor, and, ultimately, to hurt themselves because they don't have any alternative coping tools. This can, potentially, set them up for alcohol addiction.

Addiction to alcohol can happen. Underage drinking is glamorized and glorified on your daughter's social media feeds (more reason to help her choose healthy feeds), and she is vulnerable and impressionable to drinking and becoming addicted. Addiction to alcohol could set her up for much greater problems—a compromised quality of life, poor coping skills, body and brain damage, behavioural problems, mental health concerns, and even death.

So what were the consequences of Ava's drunken episode? Ava's parents were not prepared for this moment; their eldest daughter, Hadley, was far less social and hadn't had this experience (at least that they knew of). But liberal by nature and open to thinking outside of the parenting box, this is what they decided to do: a few weeks later, they sat down with both girls to drink. That's right, they drank together, as a family. They felt that in the safety of their home—where they could carefully monitor their daughters' alcohol consumption and, specifically, tolerance—this could be an essential teaching moment. They could empower their daughters with the knowledge of how much they could drink and how they felt as they drank. Armed with this information, Ava and Hadley would be at an advantage the next time they were at a party or out with friends. They would know their own limits and be ready to use phrases like "I'm cutting myself off now," or practise fake drinking (taking tiny sips to give the appearance of drinking while remaining in full control). It may sound unorthodox but it worked. Both girls felt ready and confident for the next social situation.

Other families might find this idea ludicrous. Instead of drinking with their daughters, they would opt to talk instead, maybe offering up a story from their own teen years (but only if asked), or referring to a movie where the main character drank and made compromised decisions (kissing her friend's boyfriend or girlfriend, or drinking alone to lessen loneliness). Some parents I spoke with had decided not to talk about the subject at all; they wanted to assume their child did not and would not drink. In the end, you choose the approach that works for your family, but my opinion is that you need to guide her with information.

What she needs to know about drinking:

- Alcohol is a depressant, which slows the central nervous system and blocks messages trying to get to the brain.

- Alcohol may alter vision, hearing, perception, emotions, movement and reaction time, and judgment.

- In small amounts, alcohol may lead to feelings of excitement, or lessen anxiety.

- Overdrinking may lead to overtalking or yelling, staggering, poor coordination, and slurred speech. More seriously, it may also lead to low blood sugar levels, seizures, alcohol poisoning, or death.

- Alcohol is addictive.[5]

Drug Use

I distinctly remember a conversation with Kaia, one of my most outgoing and daring clients. She told me about a recent experience in which she and a friend had done "shrooms"—and then freaked out because they thought they'd overdosed. I was not surprised that Kaia had tried mushrooms or that she was pushing the drug-taking envelope. What startled me was the calm and casualness with which she told the story and that the experience hadn't freaked her out enough to make her stop trying any kind of drug ever again.

Even though I was not impressed with Kaia's lifestyle choice— actually, I was deeply disappointed—I knew it was essential to maintain relational connection and calm. But I also didn't want to come across as endorsing her harmful behaviour. I found myself asking questions to get her to think: "How do you think experimenting is affecting you?" and "Are you concerned you may seriously harm yourself or worried something really bad could happen to you?" I also reminded her how much I (and so many others) cared for her. I talked to her parents afterward (our sessions are confidential except when it comes to possible self-harm). Together, we discussed what was happening with Kaia, the reasons for her choices, and a plan to set her up with some counselling sessions and additional support systems.

I will never forget the day a colleague told me his kids' favourite babysitter had died at a party over the weekend after she tried opioids for the first time. This tragedy was devastating and inconceivable for both her family and his, and it left me wondering—not for the first time—why girls are pushing their own boundaries when it comes to drug experimentation? Are they simply curious or bored? Are they oblivious to the dangers and perils of taking drugs? Do they feel invincible, believing that "nothing will happen to me"? The truth is that girls are trying drugs of all sorts—from marijuana and prescription painkillers to opioids and fentanyl. Some are using cocaine or ecstasy to enhance their lives in some way, whether that's providing focus and energy to meet their demanding schedules or decreasing their inhibitions during sexual experiences.

Although some girls absorb the warnings and advice about drugs and decide they never want to try them, others may find themselves drawn into drug use for different reasons. Escapism is the big one. With mounting pressure from family, school, and peers combined, your teen girl may feel compelled to practise escapism. Most will find healthier options for dealing with stress, such as physical activity, listening to music, or just hanging with good friends. For some, though, drugs like marijuana may prove to be the stress reliever she craves in the face of her "too much to handle" reality. And for others, drugs may become a way to avoid "doing" life. It may be easier to get high than to face her problems—a fight with a friend, parents who don't understand her, the constant nagging of teachers, or counsellors who tell her she could "do better" and set a "higher standard for herself." Consequently, many girls today are abusing drugs like Adderall (an ADHD medication), or even caffeine beverages mixed with cough syrup, in an effort to stay alert and focused and to continue juggling their activities and competing demands.

What she needs to know about drugs:

- Drugs are chemicals that change the way the brain and body work.

- Drugs may intensify or dull the senses, leading to hyper-alertness or excessive sleepiness and decreased physical pain.

- Drugs can affect the ability to make healthy choices.

- Drug users are more likely to get involved in dangerous situations, drive under the influence, or have unprotected sex.

- Drugs are highly addictive.[6]

Addiction

Addiction comes in many forms—from less stigmatized addictions to exercise, shopping, or playing video games to highly stigmatized addictions to pornography, drinking, and drugs. As a parent, what should you do when any or all of these addictions—but specifically drinking, drug use, or smoking—dominate your daughter's circle? You act. Now. This is where you must put the notion "power to parent" in motion, because you know better and you are the help and support she needs. This will not be easy. In fact, your teen girl may be deep in denial, fraught with pain, and oblivious to how she is hurting herself, to the fact that she could die. You will both need the support of a professional, and I encourage you to seek this kind of help if you believe your teen girl is exhibiting addictive behaviour.

Early risk factors for addiction include:

- a family history of addiction
- abuse, neglect, or other traumatic experiences
- mental disorders such as depression and anxiety
- early use of drugs
- intensifying methods of administration—smoking or injecting a drug may increase its addictive potential[7]

Signs of addiction could include:

- neglecting responsibilities such as chores, school work, after-school activities, and work

- skipping classes or shifts at work and frequently getting in trouble

- secretive or suspicious behaviours

- sudden changes in mood and demeanour, friends, favourite hangouts, hobbies, and interests

- relational difficulties: constant fighting and conflict with family, friends, teachers, and employers

- experiencing trouble at school, such as poor attendance, failing grades, not following school rules

- consistent use and overuse of drugs and alcohol

- physical symptoms: bloodshot eyes; dilated pupils; changes in sleep or eating patterns; deterioration in self-care habits; unusual breath or body or clothing smells; slurred speech; or impaired coordination

- withdrawal symptoms: restlessness, agitation, insomnia, anxiety, and depression

Experimenting with Sex

Teen girls have an automatic "dare to compare" mechanism, and this applies just as deeply to the pressures they may be feeling around sex. We will explore peer pressure in relation to sexual experiences more in the next chapter, but for now, let me just say that teen girls, surrounded by their friends, hear all about sex—who is doing it, and what with whom. Although this gossip is likely to be exaggerated and even fabricated, girls do feel pressured to keep up or catch up with girls already claiming to be having sex. Your teen daughter will need you to guide her, or at the very least to talk with her about sex as much as is possible. Please see chapter 7 for more discussion on conversation starters around sex.

Rebellion

As I have said, teens are meant to push boundaries, and it is likely they do this more when surrounded by friends who are also pushing limits. Rebellion is a natural extension of this pushback and can range from an annoying stretching of boundaries (challenging house rules, staying out past curfew, refusing to join your family for mealtimes, or boycotting family movie night to continue playing on her device) to more serious behaviours such as stealing small items from the grocery store, skipping school to hang out at a friend's house, or cheating on an exam with the justification that "my teacher doesn't teach science very well." Rebellion is part and parcel of the teen years, and it can be a positive step toward independence and figuring out what feels comfortable and uncomfortable. Yet rebellion—like the list of summer goals early in this chapter—is often amplified when peers are standing close by.

Rebellion comes with a natural curiosity and wonder, not to mention inescapable lies and mistruths—"We just drank a little";

"We didn't know she was going to steal the makeup; we thought she'd pay on our way out"; "This isn't my vape; it's my friend's." As one small lie becomes a larger, more convoluted lie, and as she is forced into more surreptitious activity to cover it up, a girl is further uprooted from her truth. Sometimes girls get so caught in their own web of lies that they keep at it simply because they don't know how to get out. You may need to help them deconstruct their fabrications—but do so calmly and with compassion. When I know a girl is lying, I don't challenge the lie; instead, I focus on the truth. Let's say that I know she's lying when she tells me her teacher didn't give her the information for the assignment we are meant to be working on. I may say, "Teachers always give us the information we need. Why don't we try to find it?" She may tell you she couldn't find her new shirt, so she's wearing the favourite one you happen to hate. Your response might be "Actually, I saw it under your bed. Please run and grab it." In this way, you help her shift away from the lie and toward the facts.

The Confusion of Competition and Connection

Peer pressure often manifests in the arena of school, where your teen faces a multitude of pressures: to perform and achieve, to fit in and belong, and to look like she knows exactly what she's doing. Girls feel pressure from peers to earn positions on sports teams or clubs, be popular, and earn good grades. Some of this pressure can serve as healthy competition, pushing her to develop new skills and reach new milestones. But some of the pressures that come with comparisons can lower her self-esteem and debilitate her own development. Girls can push each other to grow, and they can also cause stagnation.

But here is the paradox: although girls want and need connection with their peers, they are also keenly aware that there is an inherent and simultaneous process of competition and comparison. Girls are taught to be close with other girls and "play nice." At the same time, they are absorbing cultural messages to "go for" what they want and do what it takes to be better than other girls their age. In conversations about women, this dynamic has been referred to as "bitch culture," or survival of the fittest; it is no different among teenage girls. The problem is that this paradox is a less obvious form of peer pressure. Parents should keep an eye open for situations in which the "stronger together" message is combined with intense competition within girl groups, and results specifically in the additional pressures of jealousy and judgment.

The Power of Jealousy and Judgment

The effects of jealousy can be intense, and I have yet to work with a girl who sees other girls achieving and automatically utilizes this feeling as a motivator for her own achievements. Instead, she'll conclude that she's coming up short. What's at work here is essentially the fear of her own inadequacy. She feels powerless, and sometimes the quickest, easiest way to gain power is to put someone else down. This may mean undermining other girls' accomplishments ("Everyone can do that") or planting seeds of doubt ("Do you really think that your outfit's appropriate?" or "Why would you want to get a job there?").

She sees other girls having fun at parties, laughing with friends. She notices the girls who have "hot" boyfriends, and she will experience the fear of missing out. She notices advancement in every way and will compare herself and compete for the success she believes is real. She will automatically categorize girls as either better than her, so that she feels inadequate, or worse than her, so she feels a false sense of superiority. Unfortunately, neither category will help her to feel her own value or to feel good. If your daughter is experiencing this type of peer pressure, you will hear it coming out in her language: "She's so much better at dance than I am," or "I'll never be as outgoing as she is—she's not afraid to talk to anyone." Jealousy can be seen as proportionate to a girl's exposure to and inability to deal with peer pressure. Many teen girls grab the tool of judgment to deal with their feelings.

Time and time again, I have had conversations with girls about other girls. Mostly, I hear from the girls who are being judged for being too tall, too smart, too rich, too friendly, too popular, or too likeable. Or maybe it's too sexy, too pretty, and too slutty. What they have yet to learn is that other girls' judgment is a shield. Girls judge before being judged. They hide behind their judgment to protect themselves from the pain of being hurt and from the vulnerability that could come with being known. Nothing leads a girl to feeling more disconnected from others—and likely herself—than judgment, criticism, and the ever-so-lethal "silent treatment."

The psychological effects that girls can suffer from being judged are potentially damaging. Whether she is being shamed ("You are so skinny—don't you eat?"), shunned, left out of every group and conversation, or talked about behind her back, she often feels blindsided; she doesn't know what happened or what to do. When working with a girl in this type of situation, I help her to see that other girls' problems with her are not her problem. Let me say that again: *other girls' problems with her are not her problem.* I empathize ("I know this is tough"), but I also emphasize that most girls exhibit some level of jealousy at one time or another. They are jealous when other girls garner attention or grow faster, whether academically, socially, athletically, musically, artistically, financially, or romantically. A girl seeing another girl succeed may trigger insecurity and push her to judge—it's simply a way to gain power when she feels devoid of it.

In the act of changing and improving, she will likely trigger other girls' doubts and fears as well. I constantly remind girls that their number one job is to be aware of this—and then not to change, hold back, or compromise their own goals or growth for fear of triggering another girl. Second, they need to keep on stepping up toward a better, greater, and more-than-they-first-thought-imaginable version of themselves. Third, girls need to stop judging. Yes, a teen girl should practise discernment and evaluate whether she wants to be in certain relationships. But she needs to refrain from judgment—as in condemnation—and seek to understand, empathize, and connect with other girls. Girls have the power to lift each other up. Melinda Gates says it best in *The Moment of Lift*: "Because when you lift up women, you lift up humanity."[8] When girls lift up other girls, they live out the very definition of "girl power."

Unfortunately, when girls don't follow the practice of judging other girls, they can be ostracized. It will be a challenge for you to convince your teen daughter that it is better for her to stand alone—strong and rooted in her own circle and in her value and worth—than to surround herself with other girls who will not build her up but tear her down and make her feel disconnected. "Stronger together" only works when all the girls are, in fact, strong together. This means that girls have to keep their insecurities in check and feel good about themselves first.

MAXINE

Peer pressure is when you are influenced by other members of a group who push you into doing things you might not want to do and that you don't feel comfortable doing. The result could be negative and harmful—like pressure to talk to someone you don't feel comfortable talking to, breaking rules or skipping school, or maybe even going out with someone you don't know or like—or it can be positive, as in learning a new skill, listening to certain types of music, working hard at school or in sports, being more positive, or trying something that seemed scary and having fun. I have realized I feel the most pressure around guys: I will act differently. I am more hesitant and careful with what I say, I wonder what I should say, and I am worried if I say something wrong, they will tease me. This feels like peer pressure.

Girls Under Pressure

Peer pressure is going to be part of your daughter's journey, but what kind and to what degree can depend on how resilient you can teach her to be. A girl under pressure from peers can easily unravel, losing herself and what matters most to her. As a strategy for minimizing the effects of peer pressure, let's look at what you can do to build up her resilience and show her that she has choice and ample opportunity to grow in the face of that pressure. Here are three steps to explore with your teen girl: prevention, practise, and recognizing her potential.

Prevention

The expression "an ounce of prevention is worth a pound of cure" is apropos when it comes to peer pressure and what you can do to help your daughter. When you talk to your teen girl about the potential peer pressures she may be exposed to—pressure to do what she's not comfortable doing or to take risks she's not yet ready to take—you are getting her to start thinking. This matters. Not only will she be able to predict the pressure she's likely to experience, but she'll also be able to prepare herself for it. For example, she can start planning what she will say when asked to skip class, have a drink, send a sext message, or when a friend tries to convince her to shoplift because it's "just candy" and "no big deal." Girls have helped me come up with so many phrases that work—casual enough to remain "cool," serious enough to be heard, and without any hint of moral superiority. Lines like "No thanks, I'm good," "Not today," and "That's not for me, but you go ahead" get her to feel ready so she will be ready.

Practise

Standing up to teen pressure is a challenge. You can recognize this by telling her, "Look, it's not easy, and I trust you to make the best decision you can in pressure situations." Or you could say, "Sometimes you will have the luxury of time to think about what you want and how to respond. Other times you will be at a disadvantage, and it may be hard to think straight, but you can always do the best you can."

Thinking on her feet is tricky. Here, I'll offer you strategies for two common situations where girls get stuck: the pressure to drink (or do drugs, smoke, or vape), and the pressure to make out or go "further." You can use these to help her practise her response.

When it comes to avoiding illicit substances they have no interest in trying, girls have told me that pretending is key. Have a cup of beer in hand and "sip" it occasionally, or vape without inhaling. It's not ideal, of course, but temporary participation may appease peers until they become distracted, and this will allow her to stay true to her decision to abstain.

When it comes to not wanting to be more physically connected, saying "I don't want to" should be enough. But if she gets caught in a moment, a white lie allows her the out she needs. She can say she has her period, she didn't take her pill, or she has something to do. A practised girl is a comfortable girl.

Potential

Finally, you can talk to your daughter about her potential. Explain that as much as you make mistakes as a parent, she will make mistakes as a teenager. The screw-ups needn't be the focus for either of you. More important are the comeback rate and the potential to learn and improve. Say your daughter gets caught in a fabrication—that she was staying over at her friend Jasmine's house when she was really at her boyfriend's place. You could choose to lecture her about lying, and demand that she respect family rules. Or you could work with her through this mistake. Girls know when they've screwed up, and they need to be held accountable for both their actions and any consequences. Sometimes they will lose friendships; other times they will lose trust. Girls need to learn how to say "I'm sorry" and take full responsibility for their roles in the circumstances. At the same time, you can give her a chance to explain herself, respond, and redo a moment. Chances are, you will only be having this type of conversation because she got caught, since it's unlikely she'll tell about the times when she gave in to pressure or stepped too far out of her comfort zone. That means she is already likely in shame mode—sometimes this is enough of an uncomfortable consequence.

Try steering the conversation to a question—"If we could rewind the moment, how would you do it differently?"—and give her the chance to be reflective. She may better learn how her choices went awry and where she could have chosen better. In my experience, girls don't mess up on purpose. Rather, they get caught in the messiness of peer pressures. Another option is to ask your daughter growth-mindset questions. No matter what she did or did not do, queries like this teach her to think: "How could you have handled this situation better?" "What choice did you make that felt right for you?" "What did you take away from this?" "What could have helped you in this situation?" In talking to her in this way, you become part of the change process, and not the police, standing against her.

Recently, I had a consultation with a family who felt their daughter's recent truculence was the direct result of her new best friend, Megan, who was already categorized by the other parents as "nothing but trouble." Their daughter, usually on the obedient side of the rebellion spectrum, was now talking back, proclaiming they were "dinosaurs," and not keeping up with her chores. In short, she had changed, and they were worried. This is going to happen, and it's no doubt difficult. Yes, it seemed to these parents as if their daughter's friendship with Megan was influencing her, but that's not to say they couldn't influence her as well. I advised them to highlight her character over her behaviour (even though, admittedly, she was not presently showing her "best"). If and when they noticed her demonstrating positive behaviours, they needed to point these out. Every kind word and right action was therefore a chance to highlight her values, not her misbehaviours. Then they practised leaning into conversations about making smart choices, choices that would let her feel good about herself—including choices about who was worth the investment of her time. These conversations would never have happened if the parents got caught in the vortex of highlighting her faults and flaws. Most likely, that would have elicited her instinctive shut-down response. By contrast, these conversations happened because these smart parents chose to focus first on their daughter's strengths.

This doesn't mean, however, that rude behaviour is acceptable. Every teen girl needs to understand that there is a definite expectation for her to be respectful. But instead of drawing a connection between a peer and her change in behaviour, remind your teen girl that she becomes just like those she spends time with and that positive influences will always serve her well. Ask her which of her friends she feels is positive and how she feels after spending time with certain people. She will discover, on her own, who positively shapes her. When you tell her who to hang out with, she will spite you by spending even more time with the person you veto. It's what teenagers do! Encourage her to check in with herself about who feels best for her and she will discover these truths on her own. Remind her about integrity. At the end of the day, only she is accountable for her character.

TEEN GIRLS WILL face pressures of all kinds: pressure to take risks and rebel, as well as pressure to make social comparisons and to compete, which often triggers jealousy and promotes judgment. No teen girl wants to be outshone, outranked, or one-upped. Many girls do and say everything right but still get stuck under the pressure exerted by peers. Girls need a second (and sometimes third and fourth) chance to figure out how to handle that pressure, and they need to know they have choice for a do-over. Prevention, practise, and potential are the three Ps that may support her as she tries to find a balance between herself and identity, and forming healthy relationships with peers—relationships where there is connection and inclusion, and, yes, even a list of summer goals!

How Parents HELP Growth

- Normalizing pressure so she knows everyone feels pressure from peers
- Talking about possible pressures so she knows what she can expect
- Sharing your own stories of peer pressure, if appropriate
- Distinguishing between positive peer influences and negative peer pressure
- Giving her the facts about substance use, abuse, and addiction
- Holding her accountable for her actions and any resultant consequences
- Preparing her for the pressure situations she may encounter by equipping her with language to use and practising getting out of sticky situations
- Using missteps as growth opportunities

How Parents HINDER Growth

- Avoiding discussions about pressure
- Assuming she'll find her way without support
- Telling her your stories with too much detail
- Placing added pressure on her in the form of academic or extracurricular expectations
- Comparing her to peers or siblings
- Making assumptions about her rebellious behaviours without context or questioning
- Threatening, forbidding, or scaring her when it comes to drinking, smoking, vaping, and sex

7

LET'S TALK ABOUT SEX

ECENTLY, ONE OF my clients, Charlotte, told me a story about how she and her friends played a game called "Most likely to..." Obvious prompts such as "most likely to become a lawyer" or "most likely to be famous" were quick to come up, and the girls would pick someone in their group who they thought matched the description. One prompt, though, took me by surprise: "Most likely to have sex this year." The girls did not hesitate to point at Cameron, known to be popular among the boys and also the most physically developed in this group. Charlotte went on to tell me that some girls looked completely embarrassed and immediately looked down and giggled, but others yelled with excitement, "I can't wait" or "I want to have sex now!" What is interesting about Charlotte's story is that she and her friends are fourteen years old, and most of them didn't even need to wear bras. Yet here they were, already predicting which of them was going to have sex first. For me, the game underscored an important fact: young girls are talking about sex—and parents, and other adults, need to accept this. We can either get ahead of these conversations (and resultant life choices) or risk the consequences.

Language is the starting point for thinking about and then stepping into the sexual arena. On the playground, or in the safety of their unicorn-decorated bedrooms, young girls are talking about sex even though they may not truly understand a concept so abstract. Still, they are learning the vernacular; they are being taught what to want and what to put on their list. Though many young girls are curious and naive about the details of sex, you can see the influence of it in how they choose to be "sexy." In their valuable book *So Sexy So Soon*, Diane E. Levin and Jean Kilbourne talk about how girls are still being groomed to be "pretty, be coy, and often even be saved in the end by a handsome prince. In today's popular culture, these gender stereotypes and sexualized messages are everywhere."[1] Despite the #metoo movement and girl power campaigns that attempt to instill in girls the inner fortitude to know that they are in control of both their bodies and their lifestyle choices, girls are still socialized to be desirable for others. In younger and preteen girls this usually plays out in the mimicking of a beloved pop star who struts the stage in provocative clothing while shaking her booty. They quickly learn that this brings them attention and that attention feels good.

Teen girls want this attention as well, and as they grow, they begin to wonder about sex in less abstract, more tangible ways: "Will I ever have sex? With whom? When?" They worry that it will hurt or that they'll be "bad at it." They are simultaneously excited and impatient, and want to know how sex will play out for them. The flip side of this is that they are afraid and often hold erroneous (yet understandable) misconceptions that sex will give them what they want: love, belonging, and acceptance. Not having sex is a blatant reminder, much like her social media feed, that she is not good enough or not measuring up to her peers or to society's measuring stick. Adolescent girls often feel they are missing out, assuming "everyone is doing it" except them. They grapple constantly with conflicting messages: they are not mature enough to have sex, but they are physically ready for it. Our sex-soaked culture does not help them with these feelings of inadequacy. Sixteen-year-old Isabella told me, "Sex is what all my friends are talking about and feel they are missing out on. I want to wait, but they see this as weird."

Wouldn't it be great if girls felt informed enough and ready to make decisions that felt right for them? Decisions based on their individual timing and grounded in facts rather than socio-cultural pressures? That's exactly why this chapter will be so honest and clear, real, and raw. My intention is to convey what I know about sex so you can be ready, willing, and able to talk to your daughter about it without feeling awkward.

The Culture of Sex

We live in a sex-saturated world. Ubiquitous marketing, advertising, pornography, objectification, and explicit and implicit expectations cajole our girls into believing that being sexy is a requisite, that they should be sexy in a certain kind of way, and that they should have amazing sex. These powerful and enticing messages can leave young, impressionable teenage girls feeling confused—and asking themselves why "hooking up" and indulging in the moment can leave them feeling so empty and alone. All they want is to connect and be loved.

From a parent perspective, talking about sex clearly and without illusion when your daughter is immersed in constant sexual messaging is a challenge. In *Redefining Girly*, Melissa Atkins Wardy poignantly reveals her concerns about raising a daughter in today's hypersexualized era: "I know moms and dads all over are talking about the sexualization of childhood but feel isolated and powerless to do anything about it. Parents are not finding enough ways to aggregate our voices, and we are unsure of how to combat this media and marketing juggernaut we know to be unhealthy for our kids. We have to figure all this sexualization garbage out on our own, and then we feel like we're standing on an island once our eyes have been opened."[2] I want to help you and your teenage daughter and commit to ongoing, open-ended conversations about sex so you can get off that island.

As we've seen, girls learn early to focus on being beautiful and appealing to others. Girls are overexposed to commercialized and hypersexualized versions of girlhood, and then womanhood, that focus on appearance over character. "Sweet and pretty" pink and purple tutus, jewellery, and hair ribbons eventually become "sassy and sexy" midriff-revealing crop tops and booty shorts. This focus on early sexualization can exacerbate health problems, including but not exclusive to eating disorders, anxiety and depression, self-harm, and drug and alcohol abuse.[3]

Ultimately, early sexualization undermines a girl's self-worth and value and objectifies her as the target of others' desires. Many women tell stories of being whistled at or hearing catcalls, even as young girls.[4] As girls are objectified, they can quickly learn to self-objectify—internalizing others' perspective of her physical self and the idea that girls are objects to be looked at, admired, evaluated, and valued. Girls self-objectify without the awareness of the downside: making themselves look desirable as a means to feeling desirable rather than reflecting on how they truly feel about themselves.

Lucy told me about her group of friends, who intentionally "show a lot of skin and let their bra straps hang off their shoulders to garner attention from anyone."

These girls—and others like them—have bought in to society's idea of sexualization. Every time they make a purchase to help themselves look better (instead of feel better), every time they try to change their bodies to be thinner, sexier, and more beautiful, they are embracing this unhealthy dynamic. Self-worth diminishes every time they search for external sources of attention and approval, rather than looking within.

Unequivocally, the sexualization of our girls affects their sexual identities. The omnipresent media emphasis on beauty and sexiness distracts girls from focusing on how they truly feel about themselves as human beings rather than sexual beings. Girls are forced, often prematurely, to believe their sexual self is decided by what others want for them. This can lead them to give up what they want and give in to being pleasing, to performing. More disturbing is the exposure to pornography and an ideal of female sexuality that explicitly includes degradation, subservience, and violence. Teen girls are "taught" sexual expectations, and teen boys expect girls to comply.

In the midst of all this "noise," our daughters need the opportunity to form healthy attitudes and beliefs around their sexual identities. Unfortunately, pre-existing cultural standards envelop them long before they even consider themselves to be sexual. Parents should bear in mind that girls often have sex because they are asked, and not because they truly want to. "I wish I had waited" and "I was too young" are the regrets I too often hear from teen girls.

MAGGIE

I think girls want to get it over with and be like everybody else. It's what everyone is talking about, and they feel they are missing out. Girls I know get really stressed about not having sex and they want to just "get it done." It needs to be natural and happen when it's supposed to happen. Girls believe the upsides of sex are bragging rights and making them feel good, happy. The downsides are not being ready and so many unknowns, such as what it will feel like, the after part, not feeling good enough about their bodies, whether they are good at it, if a guy will judge her and then talk to his friends about her performance and her body.

Ideal vs. Real

In my ideal world, teen girls would hold off on having sex until they know themselves well, feel comfortable in their bodies, and feel ready both physically and emotionally. They would abstain until they were in a committed relationship with another person, a relationship founded on mutual trust, respect, and love. I wish every girl would wait to have sex until she really knew what she wanted and needed. Delaney shared with me that some of her friends have definitely thought about waiting to have sex for one or all of these reasons: respecting their socio-cultural beliefs, wanting to find the right person, and feeling ready enough so that "you don't have any regrets."

However, given the current landscape around girls and sex, my hopes are idealistic, wishful thinking—especially as research tells us the chances of girls partaking in sex, becoming victims of sexual assault, or being exposed to sexualization is staggering.

- Girls as early as fifteen are having oral sex.[5]

- Girls as early as seventeen are having vaginal sex.[6]

- Over eleven thousand sexual assaults of girls under the age of eighteen were reported to police in Canada. Since only about 10 percent of assaults are reported, the actual number is much higher.[7]

Given these statistics, I will trade in my "wishing and hoping" for education and empowerment. As the author of *Girls & Sex*, Peggy Orenstein shares how, like most parents, she struggles with raising a teen in the current culture: "I, too, was just trying my best to raise a healthy daughter at a time when celebrities presented self-objectification as a source of strength, power, and independence;

when looking desirable seemed a substitute for feeling desire."[8] Parents are up against strong societal messages, and somewhat mystified as to how to help their daughters in the sexual atmosphere. I am convinced that with knowledge and choice, you can help her feel prepared and equipped to enter the sexual realm of the teenage years.

Your teen daughter lives in a world where she is at least interested in and curious about sex, though she may not be having sex as early as her peers claim that they are. She may even have asked you questions about it. Most girls I spoke with—though certainly not all—talked about sex casually, which may explain the current "hook-up" climate. As Zahara explained, "It's something to be done, and you want to get your first time over with so you have the experience and know what to do the next time." Amanda told me, "This generation of girls sees sex as no big deal, because that is what we are taught to believe in this patriarchal society. Although losing your virginity is supposed to be a big deal, sex is seen as something that is normal and mandatory."

Many girls today do not view sex as something you wait to have or an experience to be treasured. Although sex is a natural part of life, I believe that treating it like the latest video game or a casual sport is damaging. Many girls have confided that they weren't ready for sex when they had it, and nor did they feel it lived up to the hype. Translation: "I was so disappointed that it happened so fast and didn't seem to have any 'fireworks' or magical moments." Unfortunately, many early sexual encounters for teen girls take place under the influence of drugs or alcohol. Sex may feel less awkward this way, and a disappointing experience can be easier to dismiss with a trite "Oh well, I was really drunk."

Girls should not have to navigate this minefield alone, but more often than not, this is precisely what happens. Talking to your teen daughter about sex can be empowering for her. When we provide girls with information, we build up their resilience to social pressures and help them make the best decisions for themselves. Sure, she may be able to obtain the basic facts about sex through her school's sex-ed curriculum, and yes, there is a wealth of knowledge on the internet, where she can ask any questions she dares. But there is a lot of misinformation out there, too. In the end, there are two key points that you must communicate to your teen daughter: (1) only she will know when sex is right for her, and (2) sex is meant to feel good in a relationship of equanimity. The responsibility that comes with sex should not fall on her shoulders alone. It really does take two to tango.

Same Sex

Your daughter may share with you (or blurt out) that she is "bi" (or bisexual), lesbian, gay, or perhaps that she is transgender, questioning, or non-binary. If this happens, how you respond is critical. Parental acceptance, and the maintaining of relational connection, is paramount in these kinds of conversations. Teen girls who are questioning or exploring their sexualities may be feeling peer pressure in the form of teasing, not to mention cultural pressures arising from the dominant heterosexual paradigm. Wherever your daughter sits on the sexual spectrum, she will need to talk and she will need the freedom to explore. The critical conversations you have with her, just like any other conversation about relationships, can focus on what feels right and best for her.

You may not know a lot about same-sex coupling or gender transitions. You may be from a more traditional relational framework, or you may not want to know about her sexual preferences. Thus, these conversations may be the most difficult of all. Remember, the focus can be on love and her definition of being in a loving relationship. Girls who are figuring out their sexual identities—both in terms of what sex means to them and with whom they want to be intimate—crave support. You can help her by providing it, either on your own or through another trusted person. Not being able to talk about her journey of self-discovery can lead to shame, self-deception, or self-deprecation, and often forced furtiveness. Freedom to talk about connection and different types of relationships helps her explore her feelings and experiment with who she is becoming in this realm.

"Let's Talk About Sex"

Conversations with your teen about sex can be awkward, but they can also be awe-inspiring. Sometimes, these conversations will happen naturally and spontaneously (I call these "moments of unplanned magic"). Other times, your gentle questioning may be met with nothing but a mile-thick brick wall. Trust me, I've experienced this with clients on more than one occasion! But since we know girls want to talk—need to talk—let's not hesitate to talk about sex. Avoid making the conversation about you. Steer clear of stating your opinions or describing your experiences unless she asks you to. Then tell her the truth. She needs to hear the truth. This is not the time to instill fear or coerce her to abstain. Now is the perfect time to talk about getting ready or being ready and about her individual journey into the realm of her sexuality.

"I was only fourteen," Sarah-May told me during a conversation about girls and sex. "I was only fourteen when I had sex and I was not ready." When I asked her why she'd gone ahead if she wasn't ready, Sarah-May continued to explain. "I felt I had to or I'd get dumped, and honestly I had no self-esteem. It was too early, and I wish I had waited." Sarah-May was not the first girl to trust me with deeply private, delicate information. And although I was initially surprised by her confession, I was also ready. I felt honoured. I listened. I asked more questions. I let her tell her story. Then I asked some questions to get her thinking: "What did you learn about yourself and how do you approach sex now?" "Are you better able to use your voice when it comes to asking for what you need and saying when you are ready?"

Like Sarah-May did with me, your daughter may surprise you from time to time by sharing some unexpected details of her life. You can prepare for this by giving some thought to how you might answer questions (more on this later in the chapter). You can also pause to breathe before you respond—a technique that will allow you to gather your wits so you can speak to her calmly and with confidence. Keep in mind that the purpose of dialogue with your teen daughter is not to debate or to lure her into a moral argument. Instead, you want to nurture a conversation in which she is thinking about her decisions, processing aloud, and perhaps considering the consequences, too. I learn far more when I ask girls questions and show genuine curiosity than when I lecture them or make decisions for them. What I have discovered is that in many cases, girls have already thought about a topic, and when they start to talk, they are merely weighing their options. Often, girls are wondering if sex is right for them (or if sex was right for them). You are gently guiding them to think things through.

This doesn't need to be a conversation left only to mothers. When I asked fathers to weigh in on conversations about sex with their daughters, some became uncomfortable and quickly responded with phrases like "Oh, I leave that to her mother," or "This is not my territory. My job is to teach her to drive!" Other dads were willing to work through the discomfort and head into unchartered territory. One dad told me what he tells his daughter about guys: "Sex. Sex. Sex. This is what guys think about and talk about. I tell my daughter this straight, so she knows that guys don't think like girls and so she is ready to be approached and pursued. Oh, and then I tell her she can start to date when she is twenty-five!"

The majority of dads I spoke to wanted to be involved in the "sex talk," but they often didn't know where to begin. It does take some finessing and awareness to get this conversation flowing. You may find it happens in bits and pieces over time or that a specific situation opens a door. Tune in to what is happening with your daughter when you broach the subject. Be aware of when she might be shutting down, and be ready to talk when she is.

Although the questions below appear to endorse teenage sexual activity, that is not the intent. They have been crafted based on the reality—discussed earlier in this chapter—that teen girls today are most certainly talking about and considering sex. Your opinions around the right time and right way to have sex are not paramount here. It is more important for you to help your teen girl embrace how she is feeling about her sexuality and to consider what matters to her in this arena. So, here are some ways to start the conversation about sex—whether you are a mother or a father or any other person supporting a teen girl.

Start with what she knows: She may surprise and impress you. Try asking a question such as "You may know more than me but I'm curious, what do you know about sex already?" In doing so, you are giving her the chance to share and creating a space for her to be heard. From this starting point, add what you know and correct any inaccurate information she may have.

Reassure her that she has a choice: You can also say something like "I am sure your friends are talking about sex, but it's so important that you know the sex facts and that you keep your sexual journey about you—meaning you should not feel rushed or pressured by all the talk." Reassure her that no matter what conversation is encircling her in her peer group, or what she is seeing on social media, she is in control of having the right information and in control of her own choice about what she feels ready to try.

Remind her of her individuality: Her body is unique, wonderful, and beautiful, so her sexual experience should also be unique, wonderful, and beautiful—provided she honours her own body and her readiness to participate. Suggest that she does this by listening to her body, trusting herself, and paying attention to her comfort level.

Other questions to consider asking:

- Do you feel ready?

- How are you feeling about having sex?

- What seems comfortable to you right now, and what feels uncomfortable? (How far are you willing to go?)

Ask her about waiting to have sex and her potential participation:

- What are some of the pros and cons of waiting to have sex?

- It seems you are ready for sex. Can you name a few pros and cons of engaging in sexual activity right now?

Ask questions about other girls, her friends, or even girls as they are portrayed in movies:

- These girls seem so young to want to lose their virginity. What are your thoughts on this?

- Is anyone at your school slut-shamed or prude-shamed? How do you think that person feels?

- Does anyone talk about going too far and regretting it later?

- How do you think girls can avoid feelings of regret?

- Are there lessons to be learned, even when mistakes are made with sexual experimentation?

- What would happen if you or one of your friends became pregnant? Who could you talk to, and what would you do?

Many parents are concerned about the negative consequences of sex—namely pregnancy and disease—and for good reason. But that can mean that the joy and fun of sex, as well as its relationship component, are negated entirely. Your conversations should include the positive parts of sex as well. You could say, "Relationships matter in sex. It's so important that you show and are shown care, kindness, and sensitivity, and that you and your partner focus on mutual respect, communication, and pleasure." This kind of general conversation may make you both blush, but it will make things less awkward for her later as the questions become more focused and intense. As well, your conversation likely will get her thinking about the deeper meaning of being intimate; it may even influence her to wait until she's ready to talk about sex before she actually has sex.

Girls want to have this kind of conversation with their parents, and they want to know much more than the basic mechanics. What they most want to talk about is the relationship, the connection, and the emotional aspect of sex. They want to discuss how to use their voice and speak up for what they want and don't want—and how to make their wishes known—without a partner being mad or disappointed.

When these conversations happen naturally and frequently (driving home from karate, book club, or rugby practice, for example, or in the kitchen while preparing dinner), they tend to be less awkward than formal sit-down talks. Over time, you want to add the topic of sex to the regular roster of things you discuss with your teen, including school, her friends, and how she's doing. You may be intentional about wanting to talk to her about sex at a particular time, but she doesn't need to feel your urgency. If you find your teen is evasive or shows discomfort when talking with you about sex, it could be that this topic is best handled by someone else. Ask her about it in this way: "You may not want to talk to me about sex. Do you want me to find someone who you can talk to instead, or can you think of someone?" That person could be a doctor, a relative, or even a family friend.

Think of these conversations like an exchange of ideas, and come to them with an open mind. Stick to the facts about sex, not opinions. Ultimately, you want her to form her own opinions and make the best decision for her—with a little guidance from you when it comes to being safe and smart. And, yes, she may be awkward; you may be awkward too. Who cares? Just talk about sex.

How to Answer Questions about Sex

Many girls tell me, "I'd never talk to my parents about sex! No way!" So I ask, "Who do you talk to then?" With great sighs of relief, they tell me how thankful they felt to have a family friend, an older sibling, or a "cool" aunt who opened the door to this conversation. Whoever your teen chooses to talk to about sex, it should be someone she trusts, is comfortable with, and feels she can ask anything. And I mean anything—from "How do you put on a condom?" to "What is an orgasm, exactly?" What you want to avoid is your daughter searching for answers on the internet, where false information is a click away. Here are some of the questions teen daughters most frequently ask their parents (or others) about sex, along with some answers to guide you.

Q: *Does sex hurt?*

A: For some girls, sex does hurt; for others, it doesn't hurt at all. The truth is that sex can hurt your first time, but it doesn't have to. It really depends on lubrication and comfort level. If you use lubrication and if sex is right for both partners in the moment, most likely it will not hurt. Also, you can speak up. If anything hurts, say so, and then figure out what you need to feel good.

Q: *Why should I worry about sex? Everybody's doing it.*

A: Not everybody is having sex. Some teenagers are having sex, but not that often, and the average age for a first sexual encounter of any kind is seventeen years.[9] I know girls I grew up with who waited until they were older and more ready, perhaps after high school. You may find this hard to believe, but others held off until they were married! You have to know this: some girls just boast that they are having sex. In my experience, those who are most insecure tend to talk the loudest. You don't need to compare yourself to other girls because the choice is individual—you are the one having sex. And the right time for you is never too late.

Q: *Is giving oral sex considered sex?*

A: The short answer is yes, but what's more important is your consideration of what sex means to you. Some people have broad definitions that include all kinds of sex; other people have specific definitions, including that sex is vaginal only. I need you to spend time thinking about how you want to define sex. This is also a chance to consider your boundaries. Your definition may change as you grow, so I'd encourage you to be ready and to be flexible in your thinking.

Q: *What does it mean to lose your virginity? Does it include intercourse?*

A: Virginity is defined differently by different people according to their values. For some girls, "losing their virginity" happens only when they have vaginal sex for the first time; they believe they are still virgins if they have only oral or anal sex. Others feel that participation in oral or anal sex counts. What does virginity mean to you? I want you to value yourself and always respect your body and your timing.

Q: *My friends told me that only guys orgasm. Is this true? Is there a right way to orgasm?*

A: Everybody, girls and guys, can orgasm (if physically able). If your partner is attentive to what you need to orgasm—whether that's oral sex, mutual masturbation, or intercourse—then orgasm can happen during sex. However, sometimes it doesn't happen at all, and that's okay. There is no right way to orgasm. Bottom line: sex should feel good, and feeling good takes time and exploration between partners.

Q: *Can you get pregnant even if the guy wears a condom?*

A: Yes, because condoms are not 100 percent foolproof protection.[10] The best protection is not having sex. There are ways you can protect yourself other than condoms, and we should explore your options. There are pros and cons for each; so again, it is going to come down to what feels best for your body. There is the birth control pill, the birth control patch, an IUD, a diaphragm, or a vaginal ring. Early withdrawal or the pull-out method (when the guy pulls out of the vagina just before he ejaculates) is another option, but it's riskier because sperm can still be deposited in the body even if there has been no ejaculation. Please remember: you can refuse to have sex with a partner who refuses to protect both of you when he does not wear a condom or says he doesn't have one. That is why I want you to make sure you have your own supply of condoms.

Q: *Can you get pregnant from oral sex?*

A: Nope, you cannot become pregnant from oral sex.

Q: *What if I get pregnant?*

A: Good question. It is possible, even when you are careful and cautious. Again, the only way to guarantee you will not get pregnant is to not have sex. Pregnancy does happen, though, and I am glad we can talk about it. If you were to get pregnant, I'd want you to tell me or another reliable adult so we could discuss your options. Likely, we'd go to the doctor to get more information. Then we would have to look at what is best for you and your body. Of course, you will be guided, but ultimately, you will have to consider what you want for yourself and for your future. I will be here for you and you will be supported in the way you need.

Q: *Can you get an STD or an STI if you have oral sex?*

A: Yes. Sexually transmitted diseases (STDs) or sexually transmitted infections (STIs) can be passed from one person to another during vaginal, anal, or oral sex. That is another reason to be careful. Always use protection and always ask guys to wear a condom before giving oral sex. If you don't feel comfortable making this request, I feel you are not yet ready to be responsible for sex.

I know these questions and the ensuing conversations are bound to feel awkward and be uncomfortable for both of you. Still, I'd rather have you work through the discomfort of talking about sexual preparedness than have to work through the discomfort of any negative effects of her having sex without knowledge and confidence. These conversations are not meant to happen all at once; it is best if they are woven into opportune moments when they present themselves. And sometimes you will find these talks are not awkward at all; your daughter may really enjoy and appreciate talking to you about the intricacies of sex. It is equally essential that we speak to our girls about consent.

Consent

A recent social media post showed a teen holding up a pair of lacy black thong underwear. The caption read: "This is not consent." This is absolutely true—clothing choice should never be considered consent—but it is still important to discuss with your teen daughter what consent is as well as what it is not. Girls need to know they can say no and that their decision should be respected no matter what is happening in any given sexual situation. Sex should feel good and be comfortable for both people involved. But many girls I spoke with have had sex numerous times when they didn't want to. They went ahead because they felt pressured to be cool or get it over with or they worried about how their partner would react.

So what is consent? Consent is based on open, honest, and constant communication between two people. Consent is when both partners agree to the level of comfort and the speed and type of intimacy, whether it's touching, kissing, hugging, oral sex, anal sex, or vaginal sex. Consent is freely given and specific. Consent is not only agreement but willing enthusiasm and desire by both partners—a

"100 percent yes!" It is also reversible: either partner can change their mind or stop what they are doing *at any time*. Sometimes girls will initiate and offer consent, and sometimes their partners will ask for consent: "Is this okay?" "Are you sure you are ready?" "How does that feel for you?" Consent is a mandatory precursor to sex, and clear consent is a requisite for sex the entire time, every time, no exceptions ever. This is what consent can sound like:

- "Yes, that feels good."
- "Yes, I want to do that."
- "Yes, I am ready."
- "Yes, I feel comfortable doing this."

However, consent is not indicated by the kind of clothes a girl chooses to wear, or if she is high, drunk, or passed out. Even if a girl doesn't say no explicitly, or if she says nothing, her partner should never automatically assume she means yes. I'll talk more about how to set sexual boundaries later in this chapter, but here I want to address how even the most assertive girls are sometimes lost for words when asked to have sex. Where does the confident, self-assured, "I've got this" girl go? What happens to her voice? She is engulfed by fear—fear of disappointing or being rejected, fear of getting a reputation for being the girl who wouldn't oblige. This fear has a strong hold on many girls. They believe it is easier to give in and give up than be labelled as "that girl"—the one who said no. This is why parents need to talk to their teen girls about consent. Here are the guidelines I share with my clients:

- Believe that you have the right to decide for yourself whether you want to participate in a sexual activity.

- Communicate clearly what you want along the way—whether that is yes, no, not yet, or that you've changed your mind.

- Make sure that your boundaries are heard and respected, whatever your decision.

- Think about the outcome or consequences of your words and choices.

- Get comfortable with being uncomfortable; practise does make progress when it comes to speaking your mind and making yourself heard.

- If possible, stay clear and uninfluenced by drugs or alcohol.

- Ask for accurate information about a potential partner's health and to see the results of an STI test (also called "making sure he's clean").

- Bring protection and know what protection is best for your body.

- Avoid situations (when possible) where you may experience the pressure of unwanted sexual activity.

- Practise phrases for the "out" option, such as "I am not ready," "I changed my mind," or "I just remembered I have plans at 8 p.m. and have to leave now."

Setting Sexual Boundaries

Consent matters. So do sexual boundaries. Setting sexual boundaries can help your teen daughter proactively prevent unwanted sexual advances and activity. The greatest gift you can give her in this area is to role-play. Work through various situations where she first gets the chance to feel uncomfortable and then practises using her voice to stand up for herself. Whether she is saying, "No, I don't feel like doing homework together," or yelling, "Get away from me!" she needs to be clear (loud enough), concise (short and direct enough), and confident (strong enough). Why? To keep her safe. To help girls use their voices in the sexual realm, they need to set boundaries, and I insist they practise. Practise with her or show her how and let her practise on her own: in her bedroom, in her head, with her friends—wherever, whenever, and however.

Here are some suggested practice situations you can role-play with her or that she can think through herself:

- Someone gets too close to her at a party.

- A stranger offers her a drink.

- Her boyfriend lifts her skirt and she doesn't feel ready for more.

- Kissing becomes petting, and she wants to go back to kissing.

- A guy in the line for the movie is standing too close behind her.

- At a school dance, a guy starts kissing her neck and she's not into it.

- She says yes to sex and then doesn't want to go through with it (regardless of the reason).

Here is what setting sexual boundaries can sound like and look like in situations like these:

- "No."
- "Don't."
- "Stop!"
- "I don't want to."
- "That is not comfortable for me."
- "I'm not ready."
- "Get your hands off me."
- "Leave me alone."

Encourage girls to use the power of repetition. This requires no thinking on her feet for diplomatic ways to rebuff an advance, which can be difficult under duress. A simple "No," followed by "I said no" can be the most effective.

Or you can start with three phrases, such as "No, I am not comfortable with this," "Get out of my way!," and "Stop. I said stop." Go through the phrases with her, one by one. With each repetition, give her positive feedback: "That was good. Let's try again." "Okay, now louder. Now stronger. Now use your body. Now say it like you mean it." Working through the role-play and these phrases may save her from discomfort or even harm. She needs to tap into her anger and use it as her power. Anger means something is wrong, and she has to fight by setting a clear, firm, not-to-be-stepped-over boundary. We owe it to our girls to prepare them for these worst-case scenarios.

All the phrases mentioned above are more effective when coupled with her pulling her body away, removing a hand from her thigh, or holding her hand out to create space and distance. Girls may giggle during these role-plays, and you may temporarily lose their eye contact or their willingness to try. But I guarantee you this: if you can show her exactly how to set these kinds of boundaries in the safety of your presence, she will be ready if and when she needs to set them in a less safe situation.

Sexting

"What exactly is sexting?" one mom asked me the other day, with a hint of embarrassment. I assured her she had nothing to feel embarrassed about, as the digital lexicon changes as fast as her preteen's moods and energy levels. I explained that sexting is any sexually explicit content sent via text message, Snapchat, FaceTime, or video; it can range from provocative poses in revealing clothing to seminude or even nude poses.

For many teen girls, sexualization begins with sexting, and it is on the rise among teens (both boys and girls).[11] At best, this form of sexualization limits a teen girl to strive to be sexy and hot. At worst, it morphs into dangerous territory such as pornography, sexual abuse and assault, prostitution, and sex trafficking. At first, teens can be merely obsessed with selfies (see chapter 4). Sexting can be an easy next step toward sexual exploration, and it happens fast. If she is posting, she is more likely to eventually sext. Sometimes this begins as a quick way to get attention, or it's a joke that turns into something more serious. Many girls feel as though they are expected to sext and that this is the new normal.

Girls feel pressured to sext as a way of pleasing and complying with requests from others (both in real life and online). Girls tell me that sexting is a means of feeling sexy and hot, a primary way to get attention. Often, they use sexting and experimenting with sexy video chatting as a way to explore their sexuality safely. For some, sexting can be seen as "just fun," as harmless flirting. But beyond the fun lurks a dark and dangerous reality. Not complying with a sexting request can result in rejection and social isolation, which can be a catastrophe for a teen girl. In *Girls & Sex*, Peggy Orenstein reports that "coercion into sexting appears to cause more long-term anxiety, depression, and trauma than coercion into real-life sex."[12] Moreover, sexting can be a gateway to sexual objectification, and, even worse, sexual abuse or exploitation.

Take my client Deidre, who was texting with a boy from her chem class whom she found delightfully charming. They had witty banter and a snapstreak that was up to 251 days. But one day, he texted something outside of their usual banter: "Hey, send me a pic of your boobs." Deidre told me that "WTF?!" is what came to mind first. Then, she started thinking: If she didn't send him a pic, he could ghost her, and she might never hear from him again. Or he might participate in locker talk with the other guys about how frigid she was. If she did send him a pic, she had no idea what he'd do with it, who he'd show, or if he'd even respond. She was torn, stuck in a "Should I or shouldn't I?" situation that is all too common for teen girls, and that simply feels like a lose-lose situation. She sent the pic and waited. Nothing. Silence. She freaked out, questioning her own sanity, and sitting in worry and anxiety. Not two days later, he was dating her friend. Deidre was mortified and ashamed, and she decided in that moment that she'd never sext again, no matter what. Tough lesson. Tough reality.

When I ask girls why they sext—and when they are willing to have these kinds of meaningful conversations—I receive responses such as "It's fun," "I want to fit in," "Because everyone else does it," and "If I don't, I'll be left out." Not a single girl admitted this, but what I sensed from all of them was a mounting pressure to text (and sext) to feel good about their bodies, and to curtail any hint of disappointing others or feeling rejected. Assuming you are not privy to her phone and her sexting behaviours, and knowing sexting isn't always harmless fun, it is imperative she understands how to be sext savvy. You can support her by providing the information she needs. She may feel sending sexts is harmless and fun. She is wrong. Over half (57 percent) of teens from a 2012 survey reported they had been sent sexts. Eleven percent of girls ages thirteen to sixteen have been involved with sending or receiving sexually explicit messages.[13] Initially these statistics will be irrelevant to her, so here are a few ways to make them make sense for her.

Ask her to think independently from the girls around her: Sexting is dangerous. Sexually explicit content often ends up on the screens of people other than the intended recipient, as screenshots can easily be taken and redistributed. Girls can feel pressured to send sexts and to keep up with peers, but this drive to keep up can blind her from considering what is best or right for her. Ultimately, pressure to sext could result in harmful outcomes.

Explain the consequences of sexting (intended and unintended): Tell her that what she puts out there and shows people is how people will see her. If she is sexting, it is quite likely others will see her as someone who is willing to take risks; they may even think she's up for possibly riskier behaviours. Let her know that sexting can be emotionally harmful and can often lower self-esteem and self-worth. The reason for sexting may seem reasonable, but the result can feel awful. Afterward, she may feel sad, lonely, embarrassed, and vulnerable—all because she pressed Send.

Help her make healthy choices: She has choices, and she can feel empowered as the designer of her own story. Instead of focusing on forbidding her to sext or restricting her device use, give her alternatives. Suggest that she focus on feeling good about herself, and specifically her appearance, by increasing her self-care practice. This could mean more downtime and rest or being more physically active and eating nutritionally balanced meals. Instead of obsessing over her appearance, foster her focus on her personal growth and development: her skills, her talents, and her life experiences.

Deepen your conversations: Ask her how she is feeling about her growth and her achievements, what she is proud of, and what is next for her. Affirm her effort and work ethic over her appearance. Ask her if she's interested in being her own publicity person—how amazing it is that she can create an authentic image that truly represents her personality, values, and beliefs. Together, create responses to suggested sexting so she feels armoured. For example, she could say, "I will not be sending private pics," or "My body is for real time only," or simply, "Not interested."

Please know this truth: your teen daughter will more than likely be sexted or will send a sext message. Let's prepare her for this experience so that she'll know what she needs to do.

EMILY

Sexting has become so popular mostly because this is the age of the internet. People are able to connect so quickly and easily have conversations with each other through their phones. Now more people than ever are in long-distance relationships and are using sexting as a way to be intimate despite distance. The biggest pro about sexting is that it is so easy, and is also easy to hide behind. A person can send whatever they want and modify it however they want with little consequence. However, one of the cons is when these private conversations become public. People can face lots of criticism and backlash and can have their reputations ruined over this. It is ironic that when a girl refuses to sext someone, she is shamed for being too prudish or too modest. It is mostly girls, though, who face the consequences of sexting, if they occur.

When Sex Goes Wrong

The topics I'm about to cover are heavy and may feel far removed from your daughter's reality. But over the years, conversations with parents have helped me to see that talking about when sex goes wrong is something we don't do enough. Although an in-depth discussion of sex abuse, assault, and the sex trade is beyond the scope of this book, I do believe that girls can get caught up in these dire situations unknowingly and unwittingly. And I believe that teaching teen girls to understand both the severity of these hard issues and how to protect themselves is the best approach. So please do have conversations around online safety and street smarts. Your teen girl needs to be aware of how what she posts online may be received, and she needs to know how to be street smart in the real world, too: observant of people and potentially dangerous situations around her, quick to react should something feel amiss, and equipped to act immediately by running away, screaming for help, and using her body to fight back, if necessary.

Sexual Assault

For most of her high school years, shy and sweet Addison had the hugest (albeit unknown to him) crush on Devon, a tall, good-looking, oh-so-charming athlete who was one year her senior. Everybody loved Devon; he was Mr. Congeniality. Occasionally, Devon would say hi to Addy in the halls as they went to their classes, or he'd give her a quick wink or nod before basketball practice. Either would make her heart flutter, and she'd spend days texting her friends, analyzing and scrutinizing what this all could mean. A few years later, Addison found herself at a party with Devon. As the party dwindled, it ended up being a foursome for some drinks and swimming. Addison was full of anticipation: this could be the night she'd get to kiss him, and maybe even reveal that he was her secret crush back in high school. As the night wound down, Addy found a bathroom where she could take a quick shower. As she finished drying off, Devon entered and instantly pressed himself against her. She was shocked, but she went with it. They began kissing, and she now recalls the conflict this caused: "I remember thinking, 'Oh yeah, we're kissing,' and 'Finally,' but I also remember feeling that I wanted to talk first; it was too much too soon." Devon's aggression and speed felt wrong for Addy, and so she politely asked him to stop by playfully pushing him away and asking, "Can we go slower?" He didn't listen. "That's when I pushed him, hard, and remember screaming, 'Get off me now.' I ran out of the bathroom and straight to my car. I knew I shouldn't have driven home, but I felt I had no choice. It was run away or be harmed."

Here is my question: Is Addy's story a story of sexual assault? The definition of sexual assault is not always clear in a teen girl's world. Here's what they need to know: Sexual assault is *any* violation; *any* undesired sexual behaviour of one person upon another, often by force; *any* type of sexual activity that is not agreed upon. Sexual assault can be verbal or visual; it can be inappropriate touching, or actual penetration and intercourse.

Sexual assault can occur with strangers, within families (a close male or female figure), with people you know well or whom you are dating (a boyfriend or girlfriend), and with acquaintances. Sexual assault can occur in public or private, and in any situation. *All* sexual assault is a violation of basic human rights and dignities. *All* sexual assault is unacceptable and deplorable dehumanization.

Is Addy's story sexual assault? Yes. And she's not alone. In 2008, more than eleven thousand sexual assaults of girls under the age of eighteen were reported to police in Canada. Since only about 10 percent of assaults are reported, the actual number of assaults is much higher. Girls experience sexual assault at a much higher rate than boys: 82 percent of all victims under the age of eighteen are female. When girls are assaulted, over 80 percent of the time the perpetrator is someone they know.[14]

What Devon did to Addison was assault. Period. Girls need to know the gradations of assault—it can be someone feeling them up on the bus, or it can be violent rape. They also need to know that sexual situations may start one way but quickly develop into something else, which is why this issue can be confusing. To help protect your daughter against sexual assault of any kind, please refer to the section on consent (p. 204).

Rape

Rape is a form of sexual assault. It is nonconsensual sexual intercourse, often committed through force, threats, and fear. Statutory rape is unlawful sexual activity with an individual who is below the legal age of consent (typically between adolescence to age twenty-one, depending on the laws in various locales).

When I spoke with Ciara, a beautiful second-year university student who was taking a gap year, I was brought to tears. In Grade 12, Ciara had decided to move away from home for post-secondary schooling. She was excited and ready for the fresh start. School began, and Ciara was impressed with her ability to stay focused amid so many opportunities to socialize. One night, Ciara was at a dorm party when she realized she'd forgotten her phone. She ran back to her dorm room to get it, and while she was there, she was surprised by Jeff—an acquaintance from high school. After chitchatting, Ciara told me, "He grabbed me hard, threw me on the bed, and pulled up my skirt. I didn't say no because I didn't have time to think. And just when I found my words, it was too late. He was inside me. Just for a minute, but it happened." Jeff freaked out and ran away. Ciara was left silent and afraid. She didn't tell anyone. In fact, she wanted to get back to "normal" as fast as possible. She showered and crawled into bed. She went to class on Monday. She saw Jeff. She even said hi to him.

What if this was your daughter? What would you do? It's frightening to even fathom. Here's what I tell girls: "You know how at school there is an earthquake plan, just in case there's a natural disaster? Well, you need a rape plan in case *this* kind of disaster happens. We need to plan and be prepared." Then I take them through these steps:

- First, it is *never* your fault. Don't let anyone tell you it is.

- Second, tell someone—anyone—and be supported.

- Third, do not shower or change your clothes, and do seek medical attention for a rape kit. You do not need to share the details of the rape. Many girls are most afraid of having to talk about the incident.

- Fourth, report the rape to the police. Take someone trusted with you for support.

- Finally, but most importantly, seek the comfort and support of a mental health professional and surround yourself with close friends and family.[15]

Ciara started seeing a therapist, and they specifically worked on boundary setting to understand that what happened was a violation of her boundaries. She also worked on rebuilding herself. "It has taken so much time," Ciara said just a few months ago. "But I feel so much better, so much stronger now. I'd love to confront Jeff and tell him what he did was wrong, but I don't think he'd get it. He didn't seem to feel any regret or any remorse." For now, Ciara is in the process of communicating with the university to report Jeff and to have her transcript wiped clean so she can start fresh at another school.

The Sex Trade

Prostitution. Pornography. Human trafficking. These are society's shames and a parent's worst nightmares. You may feel far removed from the very thought of the sex trade and believe it is not happening in your neighbourhood. Truthfully, the sex trade happens locally and globally. A recent report by the United Nations informs us that human trafficking of girls is on the rise and at a thirteen-year high.[16]

Many of the girls who end up in the sex trade are vulnerable. They may be from minorities or from lower socio-economic backgrounds. They may be on the run from broken, abusive, and violent homes. With no money or resources at their disposal, these girls can turn to the sex trade to survive. Many are targeted by pimps or madams who "shop" online.[17] These men and women use social media or chat rooms to lure girls into the market. Girls can be seduced by a warm bed and clothes, or simply by someone who shows an interest; before they know it, they are expected to "pay back" whatever has been given to them with forced labour in the sex trade.

Should we be talking to our daughters about the sex trade? I believe that with knowledge comes empowerment. Depending on your teen girl's maturity (not necessarily her age), these conversations can happen, and they can be eye-opening. That said, there's no need to expose a girl to life's darker side if she is not ready. This conversation should be about informing her, not scaring her, and once again, you are the gauge of when and how much to talk. Most parents I've spoken with want to give their teen girls the tools they could need to navigate the world of sex; they want their daughters to be resilient in the face of this world's dark side. That's why I want to talk here about some new "selfies."

The New "Selfies"

Teen girls today know a lot about selfies—and as you've no doubt seen, they love to take them! Let's connect the selfies they know and understand with a few "self-ies" they may not yet have considered: self-worth, self-knowledge, and self-advocacy, and trading her focus on self-portraits for a new focus on self-growth. To get the conversation started, you might want to say to your teen, "You've put a lot of time into mastering the selfie. Can I introduce you to some other types of 'self-ies'?" These new "self-ies" give your teen girl power. They steer her away from the cultural pressure to please and perform and toward the driver's seat of her self-worth.

Once there, she can carefully consider, and then choose, what she wants.

Self-Worth

Every girl has worth. Every girl has value regardless of age, cultural background, socio-economic status, religious affiliation, race, creed, or sexual orientation. But how do we convince girls to truly believe in their own worth and value when they live in a society that imposes objectification and sexualization, that teaches them to self-objectify? How do we teach her to avoid basing her worth on her appearance, achievements, and accolades as opposed to her true inner value as a human being?

Girls who know their self-worth believe in themselves as they are, and they believe in who they can become. When girls believe in themselves and their worth, they can honour and respect themselves in all areas of their lives, from setting boundaries with friends to setting sexual boundaries. Low self-worth can lead girls to give up what they do not want to give up and are not ready to give up. Seeds of self-worth can be planted in the form of positive power statements such as "I will always listen to my body," "I will trust myself," "I will speak up until I am heard and understood," and "I will not do what I am not ready to try."

Self-Knowledge

Girls need to know their bodies intimately. For example, they need to be aware of the hormonal changes within them that may be affecting how they feel. Most importantly, teenage girls need to learn to track their periods, especially if they are sexually active, so they know when they are most likely to get pregnant. Understanding her unique cycle serves to help her understand herself, and may explain a lot when it comes to shifting moods, energy levels, and needs.

At the same time, girls need to know to check in with their bodies. This can take place through an inventory of sorts, where she gauges her stress levels and feelings as well as bodily needs such as hunger, thirst, and fatigue. When girls know what is happening in their bodies, they also know what they need. Meeting those needs can involve making a request of another ("I need a hug," or "I'd love to chat with you about how I am feeling"), or it can mean taking some time for self-care (nurturing and nourishing herself with a bubble bath, some quiet reading time, a face mask, a manicure or pedicure, or some extra sleep). She can give herself permission to relax and to rejuvenate. When girls trust in and rely on their bodies, they become more self-assured; they know they are taking care of their needs. Reassure her that in the context of sex, only she gets to decide how her body is feeling—what feels good and what doesn't—and that this can change in any given moment and with any given partner.

To promote your teen's self-knowledge, encourage her to check in with her body as often as she can. She can do this by asking herself the following questions: "How am I feeling about my body?" "What do I want and need?" "If I am not feeling good in a particular moment, what do I need more or less of?" Examples of "more" could be more sleep, more water, more healthy foods, more rest or downtimes, more alone time, or more healthy distractions like music or playing with her dog. Examples of "less" could be less processed foods, less time spent staying up late on her device, less stress or fewer items on her to-do list, or less noise and distraction.

Self-Advocacy

When girls know their self-worth and have self-knowledge, they can feel ready to self-advocate, to speak up for themselves and others, to know they have power over injustice and that their voices will be heard. She needs you to tell her that she has the right: the right to speak up when she feels uncomfortable; the right to change her mind when she doesn't want to have any kind of sex; the right to her own opinion about her body and her sexual comfort level; the right to ask for what she wants and needs before, during, and after sex; the right to feel safe and secure when she is sexually intimate; the right to be respected and valued in a sexual context; and the right to stand up for herself if she feels violated. There is no time like now to grow her self-advocacy by asking her to use her voice with you to prepare her for speaking up with others. Ask her to practise on you by using phrases like "I need you to _____," "No, I don't want to, and here's why: _____," or "Yes, I can, but with these changes: _____."

WE LIVE IN the real world: a postmodernist, post-feminist, post-sexual revolution—a world full of challenges for young girls as they begin to navigate sex. It would be nice if we could comfort ourselves with visions of the ideal, where she would wait until she knew and loved herself intimately before becoming intimate with another person. But we live in the real world—as do our teen girls. This means we have a responsibility to them: to educate and empower them to be safe and smart when it comes to sex. All girls have the potential to be caught in dangerous circumstances. Many girls have regrets about having sex. All girls will make bad decisions. How do you support your teen girl?

Give her the facts and blow up the falsehoods. Prepare her to be uncomfortable when she has to confront a difficult situation, and perhaps take the time to work out a pregnancy and rape plan with her. Talk to her openly and honestly. Remind her not to compare herself to other girls her age but to focus on *her* body and *her* timing. If images have power, let's power up her potential to see herself as a strong, competent, capable, confident, and valuable young woman when it comes to sex, and when it comes to life. When we believe in her, she will believe in herself.

How Parents HELP Growth

- Making time for consistent, honest conversations about sex—starting out with general topics and becoming more specific when she's ready
- Asking her what she already knows about sex, and adding or correcting what she tells you
- Encouraging her to check in with herself about sex readiness and comfort
- Ensuring she has someone trustworthy to talk to about sexting, sex, STIs and STDs, pregnancy, and intimacy
- Helping her to practise what consent means and sounds like: being clear, concise, and confident with her words

How Parents HINDER Growth

- Allowing her to navigate sex on her own
- Being unavailable for her to ask any questions she has about sex
- Showing judgment and criticism
- Making the conversations around sex about you (unless she asks)
- Being closed-minded to the idea of her becoming sexually active
- Shying away from tough conversations about sexual assault, sexual abuse, trafficking, pornography, and rape

PART THREE

READY

When your teen girl is rooted in her identity, focused on her journey, and able to see her strengths, passions, uniqueness, and goodness—will she be ready for the future?

Will she be ready when she is resilient in the face of challenges? When she can resist the pressure to fit into a stereotype or a certain dress size? When she can stave off social pressures to follow peers, take risks, or silence her voice? When she pushes back when pushed beyond her sexual comforts?

You need your teen daughter to be ready for the twenty-first century: ready to be brave and bold, with imagination and passion; ready to be her best (not perfect); ready to believe she deserves an extraordinary life that only she can create.

You can prepare her for her own potential. You can inspire and motivate her, letting her know that no dreams are too big and no aspirations too high. When you help her eliminate her own barriers, and to know that anything is possible, she no longer needs to get ready—she will *be* ready. Ready to flourish and ready to fly.

8

TWENTY-FIRST CENTURY GIRL

WHEN YOUR CHILDREN are young, you get used to making all of the key decisions in their lives. You probably chose your daughter's school, and perhaps even her extracurricular activities. You likely bought many of her clothes and no doubt cooked most of her meals. But around the time she celebrates her thirteenth birthday, things start to change. All of a sudden, she wants to make more decisions for herself—and this means you will need to make fewer decisions for her. Remember that parenting a teen is all about working from the periphery, helping and guiding as you follow her lead. Talking and thinking about the future can be challenging—whether you are discussing getting her driver's licence, her first part-time job, or her post-secondary plans. For some girls, the conversation you start about her future will be the first time she's even considered it. She may find this scary or intimidating. For others, these conversations are a continuation of the talks she's been having with you since she was little. She may feel more comfortable. What's important here is that you can start preparing her for the future today, regardless of conversations that have or have not yet happened.

Girls and parents alike often ask me, "How much future talk should we have?" I say talk about the future a little every day, as often as possible—enough to get her thinking in a fun, playful, and curious way, but not so much that her head starts spinning because she's overwhelmed. With younger teens, you can ask open-ended questions like "What are you dreaming about?" With older teens, try posing more intentional questions, such as "When you imagine your future self, where does she live, who is she surrounded by, and is she happy and doing what she loves?" Remember, her future includes both the short term (getting her driver's licence; her first kiss and relationship; her first part-time job; accumulating more likes and followers on her social media accounts) and the long term (earning her way to post-secondary school; exploring and obtaining a career; possibly getting married and having kids of her own).

The more you talk about the future with your teen daughter, the more comfortable—and less fearful—she will become with her future self. Pumping her up to feel confident and excited will help catapult her into her future, rooted and ready. Now is the time to be an active listener and supporter of her future planning, no matter how silly or outlandish her ideas may be. Let her talk it out, and work on responding rather than reacting: "It's interesting that you want to be a barista/ballerina/business owner. Tell me more about this choice."

Be the Dream Booster, Not the Dream Buster

Harper told me one day that she wanted to be a doctor. "That's fantastic!" I said. "When did you decide this?" I knew Harper had recently been obsessing over *Grey's Anatomy*, watching the entire fifteen seasons three times over. Now, I know Harper pretty well. One: Harper doesn't enjoy science. Two: Harper is apathetic toward school in general. Three: Harper is a bare-minimum kind of girl. Is it realistic that she will suddenly develop the ambition—not to mention the passion for science—that is necessary to become a doctor? It may not be. Still, when girls confide in us like this, they create opportunities for us to listen and respond to their dreams, no matter how unrealistic and even ridiculous those dreams can sound. So how did I respond to Harper's declaration? I asked about the reasons behind her decision. They seemed well-thought-out. She told me the work seemed interesting, she enjoyed helping people, and, in some ways, it looked like fun (TV shows have a knack for making demanding jobs look fun!). Next time I saw her, in the spirit of being a dream booster, I showed her a simple graphic of the human skeleton, thinking I could help her start to learn the bones in the body. At the sight of this first step toward her new career choice, Harper said, "Being a doctor seems too hard for me," and swiftly started telling me about her new crush in math class. I will never be the one to squash a dream.

The dreams of our teen girls need to be heard, validated, and oftentimes, further explored. This needs to happen without minimizing or modifying, and also without diminishing, comparing, or competing with the dreams of others, especially her friends or family. Girls need to believe in their dreams, whether they want to be a marine biologist on the West Coast or a wife and mother of two with a dog and a big house—or both. You support them best by believing in them too. Focus on listening, be curious, and foster her interests. Release yourself from being the voice of reason, even when you worry about her unrealistic or idealistic dreams. Over time, girls see for themselves what is realistic and what is not.

Focus on Being over Doing

Wherever your teen daughter is in her planning for the future, one thing is certain: the world will tell her what to be, whether that's a doctor, a lawyer, a dentist, a teacher, an engineer, a champion, an advocate, or a change maker. The world will also tell her *who* she should be: pretty, polite, and placating; high-achieving, happy, and exemplary all of the time. The definition of girl power has become so big and broad. This is hugely progressive, but it is also far too much to ask of any one girl. This is exactly the pressure girls are feeling—not only to be something but to be everything.

What if she (and you) focused on her being over her doing? Take a moment to ask your teen this: "Who do you want to be? What kind of person?" The message inherent in these questions is that who she is becoming matters far more than any achievement; and it matters more than the pressing messages she will receive from the world to be a title, a position, a salary, and a status. Reflect positivity back to her by saying, "I like who you are becoming," and by asking questions from time to time to stimulate her thoughts. These could include:

- What is influencing and inspiring you?
- What are you learning about?
- How are you growing?
- Where are you thriving? Where are you failing?
- How can you push yourself just a little bit more?
- How are you daring to be brave?
- What brings you joy?
- What do you dream about?
- Who are you becoming?

When you focus on who she is becoming, you instill the inner confidence that who she is has greater value and longevity than any of her accomplishments ever will.

ELLA

I really want to go to university. That's what I've been working toward all of my school years—getting good grades in elementary school so that I can get into a good high school that will help me get into a good university. University will shape the rest of my future, and my education now is what will determine whether or not I get into university. I really need consistent school habits to have what I really want. I can't get another chance if I mess up. I'm worried about my future and my education. Right now is the future, and it determines everything. If I mess it up, I won't get another chance. In the future (after university), I see myself in a huge house, maybe really close to where I live now, with a good husband, and two kids, and lots of pets. I will hopefully be a successful, highly paid lawyer, and I will still be really good friends with my best friend. Advice that I would give not to my younger self but my past self would be not to change myself for anyone, no matter who they are. A new piece of advice that I would give myself would be to tell someone about how I was feeling, because they could've helped me sort out how I was feeling faster than I did.

Girls Tell Me...

When I asked girls questions about their future, I was impressed. Answering my questions meant they had an idea of what that future might look like (and sometimes many), though some of them told me they hadn't really thought about their future self. These teens, ranging in ages from twelve to eighteen, told me they really, really,

really wanted to be happy and successful. They wanted a good job and enough money to live a similar lifestyle to what they had now. They wanted to try new things and have long-lasting friendships. They didn't want to be judged or criticized, left out and left alone, and nor did they want to experience self-doubt, unhappiness, or financial stress. They dreamed about buying their first car, graduating, moving out, travelling, finding meaningful work, being more independent (even though this means taking on more responsibilities), and living lives of joy and happiness.

However, they also worried about not knowing what their future might look like. They worried about not being happy, not having a good life or enough money, never finding a job that fulfilled them, being a disappointment to themselves and their parents, not meeting their own expectations, and failing to achieve. Most notable was the girl who told me, "I am scared that people might enter and leave my life, and this gives me an air of uneasiness that I will screw up relationships."

I asked how they felt their parents helped them to prepare for the future. Their answers were wide-ranging: allowing them to be more independent, letting them figure more out but helping when needed, inspiring them with ideas and stories, hiring professional support such as tutors and counsellors, and teaching them key values such as kindness, generosity, and work ethic. They also felt their parents hindered their preparation for the future in different ways: by "helicopter parenting" and being too involved, asking too many questions, being too negative and critical, planting seeds of doubt instead of nurturing pursuits, not leaving them alone, stressing them out with adult worries and problems, or showing little interest in the things they like to do.

Of all my clients, Niveah seemed the most worried about her future. Perhaps this was because she was already twenty, or maybe she was anxious by nature. She astutely told me, "Honestly, the world I was born into doesn't exist anymore. We are changing, and figuring out how to fit in with our evolving society is scary. It's not an easy topic to think through without becoming slightly overwhelmed." To help Niveah feel less inundated with worry, and more calm and in control, we decided to spend time thinking about what she could control. Here is what we came up with: Niveah could spend one hour each week taking steps toward developing her future. She could do this by talking to people about their careers and, more fundamentally, their paths to these careers. She could work toward creating a diverse support circle of women and men who could help her in different ways, such as creating a resumé, doing research, or going with her to the schools she was interested in. She could continue to develop a skill set after work each day, learning new programs online, furthering her art portfolio, and tightening up her computer acumen. And she could stay current by staying abreast of world news. Niveah felt that her anxiety was creeping up because her mom tended to dig for information. What she was able to articulate to me was this: she needed a parent who could be supportive without prying.

Parents Tell Me . . .

Parents tell me they do try to talk to their teen girls about the future, but that their daughters often respond with unrealistic goals such as being "rich and famous." Or they are apathetic when asked what they want to be: "I don't know. What's for dinner?" One mom told me that, in hindsight, she wished she had had more conversations with her daughter about her future. Her girl spent much of her twenties dazed and confused, dabbling in a little of everything but always searching for something more. She moved from service job to service job, from city to city, and from relationship to relationship, never seeming to find her place. Although parents cannot predict (or control) the futures of their daughters' lives, they can talk about those futures and trust that those talks will land for their teen girls later in their lives.

Another mom told me, "I worry so much that she is making decisions today that will have severe ramifications and consequences for her future, such as eating poorly, getting distracted from her talents, giving up without asking for help first, believing that she can learn something in five minutes without putting in effort."

Many parents I speak with are united in what they want for their daughters: health and happiness, confidence and significance. How do you prepare them to make that happen for themselves in the twenty-first century? It begins with a puzzle.

Pieces of the Puzzle

Life is a puzzle made up of an assortment of different-coloured and different-shaped pieces. Each piece of the puzzle is distinct in its own way—no two pieces are alike—and yet all of the pieces are necessary for the completion of the puzzle. In life, just like with a puzzle, we don't always see how the pieces will fit. Some days it seems they won't fit at all, and our efforts to put the puzzle together seem futile. Sometimes we attempt to force pieces to fit into specific spaces, but we are unsuccessful. Other times, the pieces do fit perfectly, eventually bringing meaning and clarity. I call this the "click experience," when all the pieces fit together and life makes sense.

For a teen girl, this "click experience" may mean feeling happy and energized, having good friends, stepping into independence, completing her homework, earning high grades, and feeling proud of her progress. The lesson to offer girls when you talk about the future and her limitless possibilities is this: Your puzzle will take time to put together, piece by piece and section by section, but keep trying. Keep working on the various pieces until you see the whole picture. The "click" only comes when you try, take chances, make choices, and persist.

I have thought long and hard about how parents can prepare girls for the puzzle of life. You know that the modern world—so different from what it was only a few decades ago—will require her to be tech savvy and multimedia-fluent, analytical, communicative, and collaborative. She will need to be curious and reflective, open-minded and flexible, and challenged as much as she is inspired. But there are less obvious areas of strength that you can help her to discover and develop. After speaking with girls about what matters most to them about their future, I want to explore with you the areas of bravery, imagination, passion, and making a difference.

Be Brave, Bold, and a Little Bit Badass

"Some people worry about our federal deficit but I . . . I worry about our bravery deficit." No words could have resonated more deeply with me than those of Reshma Saujani in her world-renowned TED Talk, "Teach Girls Bravery, Not Perfection."[1]

I see the fear in the faces of some of the girls I work with when I suggest they ask a teacher for an assignment extension or tell someone they are "just not that interested" in them. Some girls are afraid of doing something for the first time, taking a risk outside of their comfort zone, being uncomfortable, changing, making a mistake, or, worse, failing. They simply aren't brave—yet!

Bravery is an essential piece of a teen girl's life puzzle. Being brave and courageous, strong and bold isn't simply the absence of fear but the ability to go for what she wants without worrying too much about the outcome. Bravery is confidence, and girls need more confidence. Many girls I work with are, in fact, brave, and occasionally a little bit badass. They take risks, learn something new, decide to be different, and choose to be themselves. They speak up against sexual violations. They speak up for someone who is being bullied or mistreated. They try out for a team even if they've never played before, even though the other girls are clearly more advanced. They are brave when they decide their gender doesn't feel right and they want to transition; they ask to use the other gender's bathroom at school and join the boys' physical education class. They are brave when they have to confront a teacher who accused them of cheating on a math test to explain that they didn't and the accusation was wrong and hurtful.

Interestingly, girls can be insanely brave in one area—like playing competitive sports—and yet flooded with trepidation in another area, unable to find their words in a classroom discussion, for example. Bravery doesn't always cross over all life areas. The best example of this is my friend's daughter Ajmin. If you saw her slight frame and shy demeanour, you would never guess that she radiates on the dance stage and is the first to raise her hand in class, putting her peers to shame. So I was surprised when I heard she was petrified to give her speech on inspiring women to her class. "How is this possible?" I wondered. Turns out this girl is the definition of brave. Her mother told me how she had to talk Ajmin through her worries about forgetting her words, her fear of judgment from the other kids, and feeling sick to her stomach. Not only did Ajmin win her classroom competition, but she went on to deliver a kick-ass speech to the entire school—and later to the school district—without a hint of fear, and full of confidence and passion. How did she do? She won first place. Mom later proclaimed, "My girl was on fire—she nailed it!" Bravery is doing it anyway, in spite of fear.

When I asked girls about what bravery means to them, they told me things like "Being brave is stepping out of your comfort zone," and "Standing up for what you believe in, even when nobody else is standing beside you." A few girls gave me examples of bravery, such as "speaking your truth" and "showing up to school when you just don't want to be there (ever)." Many of them talked about ensuring their voices were heard and going to social events that made them feel anxious.

Girls said that parents tend to squash their bravery when they get frustrated with them for not being braver, or discourage them with phrases like "I don't think that's a good idea," or when they simply don't encourage them to try. They also told me that parents can help nurture their bravery by reminding them of the rewards of being brave, such as feeling proud of themselves and simply knowing that they are growing. As you continue to have discussions around bravery with your daughter, ask her to articulate her ideas for how she can be brave, starting as small as she needs to. Here are some ideas for how to think about bravery with your teen:

- Giving her opinion and being able to justify it, or telling her teacher not to make fun of her in front of others

- Asking in a clear, confident, concise way for a job, a discount, or help ("I have a problem and I need to talk it out with you")

- Asking without apologizing ("I am sorry but . . ."), explaining ("The reason I'm asking is . . ."), or giving someone an out ("It's totally okay if you can't . . .")

- Saying yes to an offer or an invitation, even though she has no idea how that invitation may play out

- Going for a job interview or telling her boss she can no longer work late on weeknights

- Starting up a club at school to promote inclusivity or deciding not to participate in a field trip to the aquarium because she is an animal rights activist

One idea I use with girls is to create a bravery list. Together we think of examples of what bravery could mean to her. That could be applying for a volunteering position, texting someone she likes, telling a friend she wants to end the relationship, or giving a presentation at her local community centre. Prompts I use include asking her to think of a new challenge, create a change, make a different choice, or take a chance. Whatever she comes up with, help her list the acts of bravery in ascending order from easiest (to her) to most difficult (to her). Starting easy is a smart strategy to help her get a "quick win" and the motivation to try the next, even harder act. As she moves through each example of bravery, affirm what she is doing, whether that is taking a chance, being uncomfortable, or busting through her bravery hesitations. Whatever bravery means to your teen daughter, gently help her make her ideas about bravery tangible so that one day it will be a surplus in her, not a deficit.

Be Imaginative

There is no greater power or piece of the puzzle for girls than imagination: Let her know that she can use her mind as a creative resource when it comes to figuring out what she wants her future to look like. Daring to imagine new possibilities—or even what does not exist—takes tremendous self-belief, passion, and hope. When girls know that their future begins with inquiry and their ability to dare to imagine, they start to picture what they really want. Then they can get to work. "Why wait?" I ask them. "Start now!" I encourage them.

Imagining can generate positive emotions and energy, confidence about her choices, and the excitement that comes with the practice of designing her dreams. And yes, this can start with a Pinterest board.

Once girls have a mental visual and can picture themselves in the future, they can (and should) work backwards, taking small steps toward creating what they can now see. Some girls imagine they will be teachers, and they see themselves in a classroom, delivering their lessons to students. This ignites in them an idea: Why not volunteer at their former elementary school to ensure this is what they really want to do? Other girls may opt to imagine travelling the world and having adventures. They can start to plan their trips by doing research and using Google Maps or Google Earth to choose their potential destinations.

One of my clients, Sakiko, used her incredible imagination to create a career for herself. One spring day, she showed up to our session with a beautiful floral dress. I asked her where she bought it, and with just a hint of pride she told me, "I made it." "You made this!" I exclaimed. "I would buy this from a store—it is fantastic." This catapulted us into a conversation about her passion for sewing, her love of fashion, and her dream to one day live in New York or London as a fashion designer. What was fantastic was that Sakiko was already imagining how she wanted her life to be and putting into practice the expression "You have to see it to be it." She was practising the skills she would need to make this dream her reality. Imagining led her to action. Action will lead her to succeed. I tell every girl to have at least one business idea in her back pocket and to slowly work on it. Why? Because when girls know that they have the skills to build their own businesses, that they have the potential to earn money and support themselves, they give themselves power and security.

You can help your teen girl to be open-minded and flexible, precursors for imagination, by encouraging her to spend time with people who exhibit those traits. At the same time, she retains the consistency and stability of you as her sounding board. Work hard to avoid any hint of negativity or doubt. Phrases such as "You'll have a tough road ahead of you" or "Are you sure that's what you want your life to be?" can indicate a lack of support when it comes to her exploring new activities like pottery, archery, badminton, or a social club.

Talk to your teen girl about the benefits and possibilities of using imagination. Tell her that although imagining the future may feel scary, it can also be exciting and exactly the kind of stimulation her brain needs. Perhaps you can share how you imagined where you wanted to live or how you wanted to cultivate your family life or what kind of job you wanted to find or even create. Or you can try asking her specific questions to get her imagining her future:

- What do you look like?

- What are your hobbies?

- What is making you feel happy and sparkle?

- Where will you live?

- What does your day in your imagined future look like?

- How do you spend your weekends in your imagined future?

- Are you working for someone or for yourself, with others or by yourself?

- Do you travel, and if so, what are your destinations?

GOT FIFTEEN?

Girls get out of life what they put into it. That is why I invented "Got fifteen?" What if we taught girls to take fifteen minutes each day to develop a skill or a talent, whether that is learning how to cook, code, or speak a new language? Fifteen minutes is enough time to get started— and short enough not to be off-putting—and yet it can be the catalyst for momentum. Fifteen minutes each day of anything is long enough to notice some change after a few weeks. Besides learning a new skill, girls can take fifteen minutes to learn about a person or place, current event, or social issue. Or fifteen minutes to consider her day, her challenges and successes, what she's grateful for or looking forward to. Finally, what about taking fifteen minutes to ask herself some specific questions about her future, such as "Where will I be one year, five years, and ten years from now?" Taken consistently and intentionally, fifteen minutes may be just enough to instill in her the value of imagination.

Be Passionate

Living a life of passion and purpose is one of the secrets to happiness, and another valuable piece of her puzzle. An impassioned life encompasses what a girl loves to do, what she wants to improve at, what she cares most about, and what the world needs. When girls find a cause or a calling, when they can give back, they can also challenge the status quo and create change. They can self-advocate or advocate for others. They can step into the light or step up to the plate, and they can bring voices to the voiceless and hope to the hopeless—in essence they have power. You can encourage the power of her passion. Here are some ways to do this:

- Ask her to think about what she likes doing and what she feels most passionate about right now. She doesn't need the corresponding talent for it.

- Find ways (within your means) to follow and support her in her passion, whether this means providing ideas about a new interest, or offering a ride, materials, or equipment.

- Suggest activities she hasn't tried but might become passionate about. Many young girls tell me they discovered a love for fashion or computer coding by taking a small step out of their comfort zone.

Girls love the idea of using their passion for purpose, and they are inspired and nurtured by finding other girls who share their passions. These shared passions result in invigorating conversations and help them gain new ideas and insights into their pursuits. One girl told me that she feels "so happy to make other girls confident by sharing my stories of how I used to struggle with low self-esteem." Julie told me that she felt she had inspired others; she has dyslexia, and even though she will always struggle with reading, she still reads to younger students to motivate them to stay determined. Berkley, whose passion is photography, told me that she hopes to teach at her local community centre.

Unfortunately, many girls are hindered by busy lives when it comes to sharing their passions consistently—they are often too busy with school work and after-school activities. As well, some parents question the value of those passions if they can't see them having an impact on their daughter's future life and career. My sense is that girls need to seek passion outside the day to day of school and other activities; it can help to activate their self-worth and sense of power in the world. And that's why I encourage parents to support their girls in their passion as much as they possibly can.

Teen girls who follow their passions and give back to the world become women who know how to give back. These girls become our leaders and luminaries. Consider Hillary Clinton and Emma Watson; champions and advocates such as Malala Yousafzai, Kheris Rogers, and Emma González; innovators and creators like Margaret Atwood and J.K. Rowling; influencers like Shonda Rhimes and Cardi B; comedians similar to Ali Wong or Tiffany Haddish; heroes such as Aly Raisman and Nancy Pelosi; and powerhouses such as Venus Williams, Jane Goodall, Viola Desmond, and Gloria Steinem.

These women—and others like them—push boundaries and borders, defy stereotypes and social expectations, challenge limiting beliefs, break through glass ceilings, and become amazing examples of what confidence and strength can look like. A teen girl should set and steer her own course, without feeling the need to follow others or those who have blazed the trail before her. She can be her own trailblazer, starting today, and with her unique contribution as her own kind of difference maker.

Be a Difference Maker

The last piece of your teen girl's life puzzle is about contribution and giving back. The girls I talk with often think of being a difference maker in extremes: a leader, an initiator, a developer, a CEO of a Fortune 500 company, a foundation organizer, or a celebrity. They conclude, "That can't be me." They believe you have to be a "somebody" to have an impact. Girls may think they have to have money to give to others. Girls may feel they have nothing to offer. So they do nothing and trust someone else will do something instead. But the responsibility of difference making belongs to all of us, and teen girls are no exception. They can start thinking about their impact by exploring the small steps they can take rather than focusing on what they can't do. Moreover, they can start now.

Rethinking and redefining how to make a difference is the beginning. I like this idea by artist and poet Cleo Wade: "Start by doing what you can with what you've got, where you are, and in your own way."[2] In other words, it doesn't matter what's happening in your life—you can always do something. In the teen years, girls are developmentally self-centred. Yet we can nudge them to see (and act) outside of themselves, not only because we want them to look up from their screens and join the world, but because doing good feels good.

There are so many ways to give back every day, and you can help her actively look for opportunities. Sometimes these ways can be planned—like donating money monthly to a cause or a non-profit organization or giving her time to help or teach. Sometimes her contributions will be more random and spontaneous: giving her change to a homeless person perched outside of the grocery store or providing directions to a lost tourist.

Girls who give back tell me they love the feeling they get—the feeling that they matter and are helping. Contributing to society in big and small ways instills empathy in our girls. It also jolts them out of their "problems" and offers a greater perspective. Teens are easily consumed with their own misery and frustration. Perhaps her lacrosse coach benched her, or a friend is being super-competitive. By spending an afternoon at the animal shelter, for example, she forgets her woes and shifts to thinking about adopting a rescue dog and learning how to care for another. She learns to break out of her rumination and create positive change, not to mention positive energy. She learns to think of others. She learns there's so much more than her small world. Energy begets energy, and there is energy in helping, making someone smile, or seeing that your decision to offer your time or talent is improving the life of someone else. Once your teen girl sees and feels this energy, she will likely want to continue.

Personal Best—Not Perfection

When you tell a teen girl to be more disciplined, all she hears (despite your best intentions) is that she can't sleep in on Saturday morning and will have to do homework from morning until night. What she hears is that you are demanding more from her—more rules, more telling her what she can and cannot do—and that she will have less freedom and downtime. What if you could convey that discipline is not about subtraction but addition? A daily habit of discipline will help her as she imagines her future. This kind of discipline is about embracing a growth mindset—a belief that effort yields progress and expansion. I want to emphasize here that this habit of discipline is not about making your teen girl perfect or encouraging perfectionism in her. What I am suggesting is that you teach your teen girl to strive for her personal best and avoid complacency.

Personal best is a concept that is often new to teen girls. Striving for a personal best means trying to achieve a personal standard of excellence that matters exclusively to her. Her best is her daily dedication and commitment to ongoing growth and improvement, whether this is in the area of her personality (she'd like to be a better listener or a less selfish person), her schooling (she wants to spend more time studying to get better exam marks), or her friendships (she wants to be more inclusive so she can better understand diversity). This does not mean that you or the world will not occasionally demand more from her, but it does mean you should encourage her to be better and even best—her best. After all, if we can inspire her to approach each day with the goal to be a bit better than yesterday, she will embody the idea that she designs her day and, by extension, her destiny. This begins with her belief that she can be in charge of herself.

In *Girl, Stop Apologizing*, Rachel Hollis addresses the necessity for self-belief. "It means that you're going to have to lead yourself well," she writes. "It means that you're going to have to treat yourself with kindness but challenge yourself to become better! There are a lot of things you are going to have to do. None of them are easy, but all of them are simple. The easiest way, the fastest way, to get where you want to go is to not quit on yourself."[3] If your teen girl practises daily who she wants to be and pushes herself in a positive way, she will learn an essential life lesson: you get out of life what you put into it. If she can define success and what realistic means to her, she is on her way to her "best self." In the words of four-time Olympian Heather Moyse, "Imagine if you knew you were unstoppable. Unconquerable. Where would you end up?"[4] We need girls to hear this message—you are unstoppable.

To champion your teen girl toward becoming her "best self" as she learns to adult (yes, it is now a verb), encourage her to put the necessary time and effort into designing her dreams with a full, and not fearful, heart. You can do this by helping her with her puzzle.

LAUREN

Although there is always stress and worry in the back of my mind, the main feeling I have for the future is excitement. I'm excited to see where I will end up. Will I end up where I expect myself to be? Or will I be somewhere totally different? I'm excited to see the results of my hard work leading to the future, as well as the unexpected and the challenges awaiting me. I really, really want to become a happy, independent, and successful person in the future. I do want to be able to earn enough money to maintain a certain quality of life. Of course, I need to balance the outcome with the process. I see a hard-working and independent woman and I also see myself, if we look really far into the future, as one that enjoys travelling around the world, discovering new and different cultures and foods, and who feels balanced. The advice I would give to my younger self is: really enjoy and appreciate every moment (whether as a child or teen), because time passes by so quickly.

When we view our teen girl's life as a puzzle and help her work on each piece, we are preparing her for the twenty-first century. Consequently, she is better able to internalize two key concepts: life doesn't always make sense, and growth requires effort. There will be moments when her puzzle pieces are out of place. She may feel she has chosen wrong, gone the wrong way, or that she is wrong. She will wonder, "How will I ever make it through and find my way? How will I sort this out?" She will want to give up, give in. You can guide her to examine the pieces that make up her life, turning them this way and that to figure out where and how they fit into the big picture. This helps her to get closer to the right fit and to be ready for the "click experience." It always comes. She has all the pieces, but they may need rearranging. Life doesn't always make sense, but we can teach girls to stay the course until all the pieces fit.

How Parents HELP Growth

- Talking about the future to help her feel excited, not afraid
- Listening to and supporting her ideas and dreams, no matter how unrealistic
- Emphasizing her character over status and achievement
- Noticing who she is and who she is becoming
- Exploring what bravery means to her and all the different ways she can be brave
- Encouraging her to be brave—to take a risk, a chance, a challenge, to make a choice, and to create change
- Daring her to imagine—and then daring her to imagine bigger
- Helping her define her personal best

How Parents HINDER Growth

- Avoiding talking about her future at all
- Overwhelming her by telling her that life is hard and she'll need to work hard to survive
- Threatening her with phrases like "In the real world, you'd never get away with that," or "You are going to have to start doing more on your own—how will you ever have a job?"
- Discouraging her when she tries to be brave
- Squashing any version of her imagined future self
- Telling her she is selfish
- Demanding or insinuating that she be perfect

CONCLUSION

IT'S 5 A.M. I am sitting in the same local coffee shop where I began writing this book. My pencils are sharpened, and, once again, my brightly coloured Crayolas are spread across the table. My notebook is turned to the last blank page. Now, things are different. I am ready to write, but this time I am at the conclusion. I can't believe it. What's more surprising to me is that I am procrastinating, something this former perfectionist never does. Why am I delaying the finish? It is because I don't want this journey to end. Yet here we are. Once again, I have a problem: What is there left to say? What else can I offer you? Do you feel ready to try a new approach and some new ideas with your teen girl?

Suddenly, inspiration strikes: I will end in a similar way to how I began—with what I am wondering, worrying, and wishing. But I want to shift focus. Instead of telling you what I'm worrying about, wondering about, and wishing for teen girls, I want to concentrate on what I wonder about, worry about, and wish for the parents who are supporting them.

I wonder if you feel equipped and empowered to raise your teen after reading this book.

I worry that you may not feel you can do it, especially as your teen girl pushes you away in the natural course of her development.

And I wish . . . I wish for every parent to hear this message: *you can do this.*

Is it easy? No way. Is it quick? Absolutely not. You will need to invest time. You will need to be patient and persistent as you learn new ways to connect with her and new approaches that work for both of you. All parents feel overwhelmed every now and again: underqualified, unappreciated, and undervalued. I am here to tell you to take it one step at a time and one day at a time, to push through the toughest of days even though it's hard, and especially when it gets uncomfortable. Press on even though every part of you wants to give up. Why? Because no matter what, your teen girl needs you—your love, your time, your interest. My hope is that as you settle in to your new role as a periphery parent, you can help her to become rooted, resilient, and ready.

This world can seem like a big and scary place. This is especially true for a young, impressionable teenage girl who is just trying to make sense of her world, never mind the wider world. We live in tumultuous times of change and uncertainty, times that are filled with implicit contradictions. This is the post-truth era of fake news and fake facts. The world is unfair and unjust, busy, fast-paced, and incredibly overstimulating. There are massive divisions between political, social, economic, environmental, and spiritual ideologies. The world can seem so cruel and tough and full of "isms" (racism, sexism, ageism), not to mention homophobia and xenophobia. We are plagued by crime, violence, terrorism, and wars.

Even so, I am going to ask you to dare to imagine the world not as it is but as we wish it to be for our girls. I dare you to imagine a girl who can look at this world and be fierce, fearless, strong, and brave, who lives her life without fear, hesitation, or apology, and who can get up every morning and believe in herself. I dare you to imagine that she cares not about what others think of her but about what she thinks of herself, and that she is passionate about what her contribution will be. I am going to ask you to imagine that world and then work with her to create it. This is supporting her in becoming.

Becoming

As your teen girl is becoming, I encourage you to help her take the time to consider what she wants more and less of. If you help her focus on what she wants less of—such as doubting herself, negative thinking, fear of failure, procrastination, perfectionism, worry, comparison, fear of disappointing others, self-neglect, and being a people pleaser—you will help her focus on what she wants more of. This can include believing in herself, positive thinking, boldness, wonder, honouring herself, self-care, and helping others where she can. She doesn't have to be perfect, popular, or polished. She doesn't have to push herself too hard or stress about pleasing others. She doesn't need to sculpt her body, or increase the number of followers on her social media accounts or the marks on her report card. She doesn't have to wear a mask or be afraid of judgment. She doesn't need to beat herself up or tear herself down, and nor should she fear being "too assertive" or "too confident." In fact, she needs to bring bossy back.

What your teen girl does need is to be open to learning, growing, and progressing. She does need to be herself, show up for herself, and give herself permission to fall, to be messy, wild, crazy, and free. She doesn't need to make sure she has life all figured out. But she does have to be willing to try to figure out its meaning; more specifically, she needs to figure out her meaning so that she can be rooted, resilient, and ready, and the very best she can be.

I love Kathryn Hahn's words in *My Wish for You*, written for her daughter, Mae. "I want young girls and women to feel empowered, inspired, free to be themselves. I want everyone to find joy in the 'little' things. It's okay to act silly; it's okay to feel sad. It's important to be brave, but it's okay to be scared. Be curious. Be strong. Be vulnerable. I want girls to live life on their own terms. To never be afraid of loving oneself—flaws and all—in a world that demands perfection."[1]

Girls have more choices and more challenges than ever before. This brings them overwhelming stress and anxiety that coincides with opportunity. Teenage girls desperately need our unconditional and unwavering help. If she loses her way, she can find her way back—with your care and compassion. If she gives in to the pressures of social media, relationships, or sex, or wants to give up, she can develop the resilience to avoid giving in next time—with your guidance. If she doesn't feel ready for what's next, she can trust that waiting is valuable and that she will gain clarity—with your encouragement and support.

As you adjust to being a periphery parent, you can help her to know who she is, to love her body and think beyond her appearance, to promote positive mental health. You can help her to be intentional with her social media use, guide her to cultivate healthy relationships, prepare her to withstand peer pressure, talk about ways to safely explore sex, and work with her as she gets ready for the future.

I want to end this book with my audacious hopes about who your teen girl is, who she is becoming, and how you are helping her do so with your presence and efforts.

She is strong enough to keep her heart and mind open to new ideas, and to embrace change.

She listens to and trusts her heart and mind above all other voices.

She is kind, loving, gentle, and compassionate with herself and with others as she builds diverse and inclusive communities.

She knows her real measurements have nothing to do with a scale, numbers, or statistics, and that her true self-worth has everything to do with nurturing her qualities and finding her sparkle.

She is inspired and inspiring, empowered and empowering, motivated and motivating, just by being herself.

She takes chances and is daring—taking small steps out of her comfort zone, risking failure, mistakes, and imperfection—knowing the struggle is how she grows into greatness.

She imagines and dreams, and then hustles with grit and determination, ignoring those who tell her she has limitations.

She sees every setback and obstacle as an opportunity, and every ending as a new beginning.

She welcomes the unexpected twists and turns of her journey.

She realizes daily that she is the only one she has been waiting for.

She is rooted in knowing who she is, resilient in knowing how to bounce back, and ready to design her dreams.

ACKNOWLEDGEMENTS

I USED TO PRIDE myself on my independence and self-reliance. I believed I could "do" life alone and be a better person for this choice. I don't think that could have been further from the truth. This book is proof of the fact that we all need help, and I am no exception.

Yes, I wrote *Rooted, Resilient, and Ready*, and I worked diligently every day to create a book that was real, raw, authentic, and heartfelt, and would be accessible to those who need help and hope in raising a teenage girl. I devoted my time, my creativity, my determination, and my perseverance. So did many, many other amazing and talented people.

I begin by thanking the girls I journey alongside every day, and who contributed to this book in various ways by sharing their ideas and their voices. They let me into their lives, their worlds, and boldly shared with me what it's like to be a teenage girl today. I sincerely appreciate their trust in me, as well as their candour, the inner beauty they allowed me to see, and the unique details in the stories they proffered me—details I never would have thought about on my own. These girls inspired me to see them as they are and challenged me to understand their experiences from the inside out. I am so thankful for them and eternally proud of them.

Next, I want to thank all the adults—moms, dads, principals, teachers, therapists, mentors, caregivers, and friends—who took time out of their busy schedules to share with me how they experience teen girls. They spoke to me about their worries and their concerns, and about their hope and optimism for future generations. I learned an incredible amount by listening to what they wanted to share, and I garnered their insights and wisdom.

I am thankful to you—the readers who are so dedicated to growing girls to be happy, healthy, and whole, and to preparing them for what life brings. I know girls are in good hands because they have you to lead and shape them.

I must thank everyone at LifeTree Media: Maggie Langrick, my fearless publisher; Sarah Brohman, my talented editor; and Setareh Ashrafologhalai, my dedicated designer. Also, I feel so privileged to once again work with the team at ZG Communications: Zoe Grams and Ariel Hudnell. Your belief in me has helped me to further believe in myself. Thank you so much for your expertise, experience, honesty, and integrity, and for being willing to be part of my vision to influence girls and those who raise them and to make a difference in how teen girls grow up.

To my family and friends—thank you for being who you are and for encouraging me along the way. A special thanks to Brittany Manulak for her last-minute editing support.

To Kelvin, my partner and forever family, who pushes me to be better every single day, and who supports me like nobody ever has and nobody ever could. I am so grateful we get to design our lives together, just as we dreamed.

Finally, to those of you who feel, as I once did, that you are better off alone, I have a request: take the chance on finding others who love you for who you are, who bring out the best in you, who encourage you to grow into the greatest image you hold for yourself, and who believe you will do great things. The truth is we need each other— we are stronger, bolder, and better together. Trust me on this one.

NOTES

Introduction

1. Larry D. Rosen, "Welcome to the iGeneration!" *Psychology Today*, March 27, 2010, https://www.psychologytoday.com/ca/blog/ rewired-the-psychology-technology/201003/welcome-the-igeneration.

2. Karen Wallace, "Teens Spend a 'Mind-Boggling' 9 Hours a Day Using Media, Report Says," CNN, November 3, 2015, https://www.cnn.com/2015/11/03/ health/teens-tweens-media-screen-use-report/index.html.

3. Zoe Williams, "Early Puberty: Why Are Kids Growing Up Faster?," *The Guardian*, October 25, 2012, https://www.theguardian.com/society/2012/oct/25/ early-puberty-growing-up-faster.

4. Diane E. Levin and Jean Kilbourne, *So Sexy So Soon: The New Sexualized Childhood and What Parents Can Do to Protect Their Kids* (New York: Ballantine Books, 2008).

5. Louann Brizendine, *The Female Brain* (New York: Harmony, 2006), 8.

6. Rachel Carlyle, "Bringing Up Baby: Are You a Tiger Mum or a Helicopter Dad?," *Express*, October 5, 2014, https://www.express.co.uk/life-style/life/518377/ Different-parenting-techniques.

7. Shimi Kang, *The Dolphin Way* (Toronto: Viking, 2014).

8. Inge Bretherton, "The Origins of Attachment Theory: John Bowlby and Mary Ainsworth," *Developmental Psychology* 28, no. 5 (September 1992): 759–75.

Chapter 1

1. David G. Meyers and C. Nathan DeWall, *Psychology*, 11th ed. (New York: Worth Publishers, 2015), 204.
2. Robin Nixon, "Adolescent Angst: 5 Facts About the Teen Brain," *LiveScience*, July 8, 2012, https://www.livescience.com/21461-teen-brain-adolescence-facts.html.
3. Emily Esfahani Smith, "Social Connection Makes a Better Brain," *The Atlantic*, October 29, 2013, https://www.theatlantic.com/health/archive/2013/10/social-connection-makes-a-better-brain/280934/.
4. Cameron Russell, "Looks Aren't Everything. Believe Me, I'm a Model," filmed October 2012 in Washington, DC, TED video, 9:23, https://www.ted.com/talks/cameron_russell_looks_aren_t_everything_believe_me_i_m_a_model?language=en.
5. Jesse Singal, "When Children Say They're Trans," *The Atlantic*, July/August 2018, https://www.theatlantic.com/magazine/archive/2018/07/when-a-child-says-shes-trans/561749/.
6. Rachel Ehmke, "How Using Social Media Affects Teenagers," Child Mind Institute, accessed August 2018, https://childmind.org/article/how-using-social-media-affects-teenagers/.
7. Karen Jensen, *Three Brains: How the Heart, Brain, and Gut Influence Mental Health and Identity* (Coquitlam, Mind Publishing, 2016), 97.
8. Rachel Simmons, *Enough as She Is: How to Help Girls Move Beyond Impossible Standards of Success to Live Healthy, Happy, and Fulfilling Lives* (New York: HarperCollins, 2018), xii.

Chapter 2

1. Louann Brizendine, *The Female Brain* (New York: Harmony, 2006), 31.
2. Ginny Jones, "How to Improve Teen Body Image," More-Love.org, March 29, 2018, https://more-love.org/2018/03/29/how-to-improve-teen-body-image/.
3. Emily Nagoski, *Come as You Are: The Surprising New Science That Will Transform Your Sex Life* (New York: Simon & Schuster, 2015), 165.
4. Amy Cuddy, "Your Body Language May Shape Who You Are," filmed June 2012 in Edinburgh, Scotland, TED video, 20:48, https://www.ted.com/talks/amy_cuddy_your_body_language_shapes_who_you_are?language=en.
5. "Sleep Drive and Your Body Clock," National Sleep Foundation, accessed September 2018, https://www.sleepfoundation.org/articles/sleep-drive-and-your-body-clock.
6. Steve Biddulph, *10 Things Girls Need Most: To Grow Up Strong and Free* (London: Harper Thorsons, 2017), 100.
7. John Mackey, Alona Pulde, and Matthew Lederman, *The Whole Foods Diet: The Lifesaving Plan for Health and Longevity* (Boston: Grand Central L&S, 2017), 11.

8. Jensen, *Three Brains*, 97.
9. Alexandra Sifferelin, "Feel Good Foods" in "100 Most Healing Foods," ed., Edward Felsenthal, special issue, *Time*, June 29, 2018, 5.
10. Richard Bailey, "Do Sports and Other Physical Activities Build Self-Esteem?," *Psychology Today*, August 7, 2014, https://www.psychologytoday.com/gb/blog/smart-moves/201408/do-sports-and-other-physical-activities-build-self-esteem.
11. Deborah MacNamara, *Rest Play Grow: Making Sense of Preschoolers (or Anyone Who Acts Like One)* (Vancouver: Aona Books, 2016), 53.
12. Lawrence Robinson, Melinda Smith, and Jeanne Segal, "Laughter Is the Best Medicine," HelpGuide.org, last updated June 2019, https://www.helpguide.org/articles/mental-health/laughter-is-the-best-medicine.htm.
13. "Body Image & Eating Disorders," National Eating Disorders Association, accessed November 2018, https://www.nationaleatingdisorders.org/body-image-eating-disorders.
14. Maria Makino, Koji Tsuboi, and Lorraine Dennerstein, "Prevalence of Eating Disorders: A Comparison of Western and Non-Western Countries," *MedGenMed* 6, no. 3 (September 27, 2004): 49, https://www.ncbi.nlm.nih.gov/pmc/articles/PMC1435625/.
15. Greta Gleissner, "Social Media and Its Effect on Eating Disorders," HuffPost, May 10, 2017, https://www.huffpost.com/entry/social-media-and-its-effect-on-eating-disorders_b_591343bce4b0e3bb894d5caa.
16. Eric W. Dolan, "Study Suggests Brain Reward Response Plays an Important Role in Anorexia Nervosa," PsyPost, November 17, 2018, https://www.psypost.org/2018/11/study-suggests-brain-reward-response-plays-an-important-role-in-anorexia-nervosa-52550.

Chapter 3

1. Colin Perkel, "Teen Girls Twice as Likely as Boys to Report Poor Mental Health: Study," HuffPost, July 25, 2018, https://www.huffingtonpost.ca/2018/07/25/teen-mental-health-study_a_23489469/.
2. Jensen, *Three Brains*, 119.
3. "Fast Facts About Mental Illness," Canadian Mental Health Association, accessed December 2018, https://cmha.ca/about-cmha/fast-facts-about-mental-illness.
4. Lisa Damour, *Under Pressure: Confronting the Epidemic of Stress and Anxiety in Girls* (New York: Ballantine Books, 2019), 4.
5. Lawrence Shapiro, *Stopping the Pain: A Workbook for Teens Who Cut and Self-Injure* (Oakland: Instant Help Books, 2018), 21.
6. Patti Neighmond, "More and More, Young Women Are Being Diagnosed with ADHD," NPR, June 9, 2014, https://www.npr.org/sections/health-shots/2014/

06/09/319208317/more-and-more-young-women-are-being-diagnosed-with-adhd.

7. "Bipolar Disorder," Teen Mental Health Organization, accessed December 2018, http://teenmentalhealth.org/learn/mental-disorders/bipolar-disorder/.

Chapter 4

1. Sarah-Jayne Blakemore, *Inventing Ourselves: The Secret Life of the Teenage Brain* (New York: Public Affairs, 2018), 7.
2. Eric Jensen and Carole Snider, *Turnaround Tools for the Teenage Brain: Helping Underperforming Students Become Lifelong Learners* (San Francisco: John Wiley and Sons/Jossey-Bass, 2013), 22.
3. Jean M. Twenge, "Have Smartphones Destroyed a Generation?," *The Atlantic*, September 2017, https://www.theatlantic.com/magazine/archive/2017/09/has-the-smartphone-destroyed-a-generation/534198/.
4. Jinjing Jiang, "How Teens and Parents Navigate Screen Time and Device Distractions," Pew Research Center, August 22, 2018, http://www.pewinternet.org/2018/08/22/how-teens-and-parents-navigate-screen-time-and-device-distractions/.
5. Simmons, *Enough as She Is*, 29.
6. Sharon Jayson, "Survey: Young People Who Use Social Media Seek Fame," *USA Today*, April 18, 2013, https://www.usatoday.com/story/news/nation/2013/04/18/social-media-tweens-fame/2091199/.
7. Joe Rogan, "The Ethics of Becoming an Instagram Model, with Gabrielle Reece," YouTube, April 3, 2019, 14:35, https://www.youtube.com/watch?v=Naz_DWHgOeA.

Chapter 5

1. Smith, "Social Connection Makes a Better Brain."
2. Michelle Anthony and Reyna Lindert, *Little Girls Can Be Mean: Four Steps to Bully-Proof Girls in the Early Grades* (New York: St. Martin's Griffin, 2010), 14.
3. Katie Hurley, *No More Mean Girls: The Secret to Raising Strong, Confident, and Compassionate Girls* (New York: TarcherPerigee, 2018), 149.
4. Brizendine, *The Female Brain*.

Chapter 6

1. Robin Nixon, "Adolescent Angst: 5 Facts About the Teen Brain."
2. "Teens and E-cigarettes," National Institute on Drug Abuse, last updated February 2016, https://www.drugabuse.gov/related-topics/trends-statistics/infographics/teens-e-cigarettes.

3. Elana Pearl Ben-Joseph, "Smoking," TeensHealth, last updated June 2016, https://kidshealth.org/en/teens/smoking.html.

4. Ibid.

5. Steven Dowshen, "Alcohol," TeensHealth, last updated September 2016, https://kidshealth.org/en/teens/alcohol.html?WT.ac=ctg#catalcohol.

6. Steven Dowshen, "Drugs: What to Know," TeensHealth, last updated May 2018, https://kidshealth.org/en/teens/know-about-drugs.html?WT.ac=ctg#catdrugs.

7. Lawrence Robinson, Melinda Smith, and Jeanne Segal, "Drug Abuse and Addiction," HelpGuide, last updated June 2019, https://www.helpguide.org/articles/addictions/drug-abuse-and-addiction.htm.

8. Melinda Gates, *The Moment of Lift: How Empowering Women Changes the World* (New York: Flatiron Books, 2019), 2.

Chapter 7

1. Levin and Kilbourne, *So Sexy So Soon*, 8.

2. Melissa Atkins Wardy, *Redefining Girly: How Parents Can Fight the Stereotyping and Sexualization of Girlhood, from Birth to Tween* (Chicago: Chicago Review Press, Inc., 2014), 7.

3. Eileen Zurbriggen et al., "Sexualization of Girls is Linked to Common Mental Health Problems in Girls and Women—Eating Disorders, Low Self-Esteem, and Depression; An APA Task Force Reports," American Psychological Association, February 19, 2007, https://www.apa.org/news/press/releases/2007/02/sexualization.

4. Liz Dwyer, "Girls Get Catcalled at a Younger Age Than You Might Think," Take Part, June 1, 2015, http://www.takepart.com/article/2015/06/01/girls-get-catcalled-younger-age-than-you-think.

5. Daniel J. DeNoon, "When Do U.S. Youths Start Oral Sex, Intercourse?," WebMD, August 16, 2012, https://www.webmd.com/sex-relationships/news/20120816/when-do-us-youths-start-oral-sex-intercourse#1.

6. Kendall, "What's the Average Age That Girls Have Sex for the First Time?," Planned Parenthood, August 8, 2011, https://www.plannedparenthood.org/learn/teens/ask-experts/what-e2-80-99s-the-average-age-that-girls-have-sex-for-the-first-time.

7. "Facts about Girls in Canada," Canadian Association for the Advancement of Women and Sport and Physical Activity, January 10, 2016, https://www.caaws.ca/facts-about-girls-in-canada/.

8. Peggy Orenstein, *Girls & Sex: Navigating the Complicated New Landscape* (New York: Harper, 2016), 2.

9. "Preventing STDs and Pregnancy," Planned Parenthood, accessed February 2019, https://www.plannedparenthood.org/learn/teens/preventing-pregnancy-stds.

10. "Condom Facts Sheet in Brief," CDC Centers for Disease Control and Prevention, last updated March 5, 2013, https://www.cdc.gov/condomeffectiveness/brief.html.

11. "11 Facts About Sexting," DoSomething.org, accessed March 2019, https://www.dosomething.org/us/facts/11-facts-about-sexting.

12. Orenstein, *Girls & Sex*, 22.

13. "11 Facts About Sexting," DoSomething.org.

14. "The Facts About Barriers Girls Face," Canadian Women's Foundation, accessed August 2016, https://canadianwomen.org/facts-about-girls.

15. Jennifer Ashton, "What to Do If You Are the Victim of a Rape or Sexual Assault," JenniferAshtonMD.com, accessed April 2019, https://jenniferashtonmd.com/what-to-do-if-you-are-the-victim-of-a-rape-or-sexual-assault/.

16. Pamela Falk, "Human Trafficking of Girls in Particular 'on the Rise,' United Nations warns," CBC News, January 30, 2019, https://www.cbsnews.com/news/human-trafficking-girls-un-report-sexual-exploitation-primary-motivation/.

17. Angelyn Bayless and Dominique Roe-Sepowitz, "Teen Sex Trafficking," Arizona State University School of Social Work, http://endsextrafficking.az.gov/sites/default/files/asuteensextraffickingawareness.pdf.

Chapter 8

1. Reshma Saujani, "Teach Girls Bravery, Not Perfection," filmed February 2016 in Vancouver, BC, TED video, 12:32, https://www.ted.com/talks/reshma_saujani_teach_girls_bravery_not_perfection?language=en.

2. Cleo Wade, "Want to Change the World? Start by Being Brave Enough to Care," filmed November 2017 in New Orleans, Louisiana, TED video, 10:54, https://www.ted.com/talks/cleo_wade_want_to_change_the_world_start_by_being_brave_enough_to_care?language=en.

3. Rachel Hollis, *Girl, Stop Apologizing: A Shame-Free Plan for Embracing and Achieving Your Goals* (New York: HarperCollins Leadership, 2019), 209.

4. Heather Moyse, *Redefining "Realistic": Shift Your Perspective. Seize Your Potential. Own Your Story.* (Toronto: Red Roots Publishing, 2017), 5.

Conclusion

1. Kathryn Hahn and Brigette Barrager, *My Wish for You* (New York: Orchard Books, 2018).

BIBLIOGRAPHY

Anthony, Michelle, and Reyna Lindert. *Little Girls Can Be Mean: Four Steps to Bully-Proof Girls in the Early Grades*. New York: St. Martin's Griffin, 2010.

Biddulph, Steve. *10 Things Girls Need Most: To Grow Up Strong and Free*. London: Harper Thorsons, 2017.

Blakemore, Sarah-Jayne. *Inventing Ourselves: The Secret Life of the Teenage Brain*. New York: Public Affairs, 2018.

Boachie, Ahmed, and Karin Jasper. *A Parent's Guide to Defeating Eating Disorders: Spotting the Stealth Bomber and Other Symbolic Approaches*. London: Jessica Kingsley Publishers, 2011.

Brizendine, Louann. *The Female Brain*. New York: Harmony, 2006.

Damour, Lisa. *Under Pressure: Confronting the Epidemic of Stress and Anxiety in Girls*. New York: Ballantine Books, 2019.

David J. Miklowitz. *The Bipolar Disorder Survival Guide: What You and Your Family Need to Know*. New York: Guilford, 2011.

Feinstein, Sheryl. *Parenting the Teenage Brain: Understanding a Work in Progress*. Lanham, MD: R&L Education, 2017.

Forgan, James W., and Mary Anne Richey. *Raising Girls With ADHD: Secrets for Parenting Healthy, Happy Daughters*. Waco: Prufrock Press, 2014.

Gates, Melinda. *The Moment of Lift: How Empowering Women Changes the World*. New York: Flatiron Books, 2019.

Hahn, Kathryn, and Brigette Barrager. *My Wish for You*. New York: Orchard Books, 2018.

Hollis, Rachel. *Girl, Stop Apologizing: A Shame-Free Plan for Embracing and Achieving Your Goals*. New York: HarperCollins Leadership, 2019.

Howes, Lewis. *The Mask of Masculinity: How Men Can Embrace Vulnerability, Create Strong Relationships, and Live Their Fullest Lives*. New York: Rodale, 2017.

Hurley, Katie. *No More Mean Girls: The Secret to Raising Strong, Confident, and Compassionate Girls*. New York: TarcherPerigee, 2018.

Jennings, Jazz. *Being Jazz: My Life as a (Transgender) Teen*. New York: Penguin Random House, 2016.

Jensen, Eric, and Carole Snider. *Turnaround Tools for the Teenage Brain: Helping Underperforming Students Become Lifelong Learners*. San Francisco: John Wiley and Sons/Jossey-Bass, 2013.

Jensen, Karen. *Three Brains: How the Heart, Brain, and Gut Influence Mental Health and Identity*. Coquitlam: Mind Publishing, 2016.

Kambolis, Michele. *Generation Stressed: Play-Based Tools to Help Your Child Overcome Anxiety*. Vancouver: LifeTree Media, 2014.

Kampakis, Kari. *10 Ultimate Truths Girls Should Know*. Nashville: Thomas Nelson, 2014.

Kang, Shimi. *The Dolphin Way: A Parent's Guide to Raising Happy, Healthy, and Motivated Kids—Without Turning into a Tiger*. Toronto: Viking, 2014.

Lahey, Jessica. *The Gift of Failure: How the Best Parents Learn to Let Go So Their Kids Can Succeed*. New York: HarperCollins, 2015.

Levin, Diane E., and Jean Kilbourne. *So Sexy So Soon: The New Sexualized Childhood and What Parents Can Do to Protect Their Kids*. New York: Ballantine, 2008.

Mackey, John, Alona Pulde, and Matthew Lederman. *The Whole Foods Diet: The Lifesaving Plan for Health and Longevity*. Boston: Grand Central L&S, 2017.

MacNamara, Deborah. *Rest Play Grow: Making Sense of Preschoolers (or Anyone Who Acts Like One)*. Vancouver: Aona Books, 2016.

Miklowitz, David J. *The Bipolar Disorder Survival Guide: What You and Your Family Need to Know*. New York: Guilford Press, 2019.

Moyse, Heather. *Redefining "Realistic": Shift Your Perspective. Seize Your Potential. Own Your Story*. Toronto: Red Roots Publishing, 2017.

Muhlheim, Lauren. *When Your Teen Has an Eating Disorder: Practical Strategies to Help Your Teen Recover from Anorexia, Bulimia, and Binge Eating*. Oakland: New Harbinger Publications, 2018.

Nagoski, Emily. *Come as You Are: The Surprising New Science That Will Transform Your Sex Life*. New York: Simon & Schuster, 2015.

Obama, Michelle. *Becoming*. New York: Crown, 2018.

Orenstein, Peggy. *Girls & Sex: Navigating the Complicated New Landscape*. New York: Harper, 2016.

Parker, Kate T., *Strong is the New Pretty: A Celebration of Girls Being Themselves*. New York: Workman, 2017.

Rubin, Gretchen. *The Happiness Project*. Toronto: HarperCollins, 2012.

Sandberg, Sheryl, and Adam Grant. *Option B: Facing Adversity, Building Resilience, and Finding Joy*. Toronto: Knopf, 2017.

Saujani, Reshma. *Brave, Not Perfect: Fear Less, Fail More, and Live Bolder*. New York: Currency, 2019.

Schab, Lisa M. *Beyond the Blues: A Workbook to Help Teens Overcome Depression*. Oakland: Instant Help Books, 2008.

———. *The Anxiety Workbook for Teens: Activities to Help You Deal with Anxiety and Worry*. Oakland: Instant Help Books, 2008.

Shapiro, Lawrence E. *Stopping the Pain: A Workbook for Teens Who Cut and Self-Injure*. Oakland, Instant Help Books, 2008.

Simmons, Rachel. *Enough as She Is: How to Help Girls Move Beyond Impossible Standards of Success to Live Healthy, Happy, and Fulfilling Lives*. New York: HarperCollins, 2018.

Taylor, Julia V. and Melissa Atkins Wardy. *The Body Image Workbook for Teens: Activities to Help Girls Develop a Healthy Body Image in an Image-Obsessed World*. Oakland: Instant Help Books, 2014.

Toner, Jacqueline B. and Claire A. B. Freeland. *Depression: A Teen's Survival Guide to Survive and Thrive*. Washington: Magination Press, 2016.

Twenge, Jean M. *iGen: Why Today's Super-Connected Kids Are Growing Up Less Rebellious, More Tolerant, Less Happy—and Completely Unprepared for Adulthood—and What That Means for the Rest of Us*. New York: Atria, 2017.

Van Dijk, Sheri, and Karma Guindon. *The Bipolar Workbook for Teens: DBT Skills to Help You Control Mood Swings*. Oakland: Instant Help Books, 2010.

Wardy, Melissa Atkins. *Redefining Girly: How Parents Can Fight the Stereotyping and Sexualization of Girlhood, from Birth to Tween*. Chicago: Chicago Review Press, 2014.

RECOMMENDED RESOURCES

Websites

www.AboutOurKids.org

www.Ahaparenting.com

www.anxiety.bc

www.anxietycanada.com

www.backfit.com (for more information about Dr. Marissa Bentham, whom I interviewed during my research for this book)

www.borntoshinekids.com

www.brainscape.com

www.copingskills4kids.net

www.emindful.com

www.gday.world

www.giddyyoyo.com

www.girlexpocanada.com

www.girlshealth.org

www.Glowellness.com (for more information about Dr. Adrienne Chan, whom I interviewed during my research for this book)

www.graciesgals.com

www.hopscotchgirls.com

www.inspiration.com

www.juliakristina.com (for more information about Julia Kristina Mah, whom I interviewed during my research for this book)

www.kidshealth.org

www.kidspeak.com

www.kimdeon.com (for more information about Kim D'Eon, whom I interviewed during my research for this book)

www.lexasperspective.ca (for more information about Lexa Bergen, whom I interviewed during my research for this book)

www.parentingteens.com

www.peakexperiencecounselling.com (for more information about Tiffani Van Buckley, whom I interviewed during my research for this book)

www.plannedparenthood.org

www.self-compassion.org

www.solegirls.org

www.teenmentalhealth.org

www.thework.com

Smartphone Applications

Audible

Breathe

Buddhify (meditation)

Calm

FamiSafe (screen time)

GoCam

iKeyMonitor

Instagram

iProcrastinate

Life360FamilyCircle

MindShift (anxiety)

mSpy

PhoneSheriff

Qustodio

RecoEmo

Rise Up

Simply Being (meditation)

Snapchat

SnoreLab

Spyzie

VSCO

TED Talks

"10 Ways to Have a Better Conversation," Celeste Headlee

"The Art of Asking," Amanda Palmer

"Do Schools Kill Creativity?," Ken Robinson

"Every Kid Needs a Champion," Rita Pierson

"For Parents, Happiness is a Very High Bar," Jennifer Senior

"The Importance of Raising an Emotionally Intelligent Child," Erika Brodnock

"Looks Aren't Everything. Believe Me, I'm a Model," Cameron Russell

"Kids Need Structure," Colin Powell

"My Year of Saying Yes to Everything," Shonda Rhimes

"Never, Ever Give Up," Diana Nyad

"The Paradox of Choice," Barry Schwartz

"Parenting in the Modern World," Kyle Seaman

"The Power of Vulnerability," Brené Brown

"The Puzzle of Motivation," Dan Pink

"Quit Social Media," Dr. Cal Newport

"Settle Down, Pay Attention, Say Thank You: A How-To," Kristen Race

"Teach Every Child About Food," Jamie Oliver

"Teach Girls Bravery, Not Perfection," Reshma Saujani

"The Surprising Science of Happiness," Dan Gilbert

"Want to Change the World? Start by Being Brave Enough to Care," Cleo Wade

"Want to Help Someone? Shut Up and Listen," Ernesto Sirolli

"Why We Laugh," Sophie Scott

"Your Body Language May Shape Who You Are," Amy Cuddy

"Your Elusive Creative Genius," Elizabeth Gilbert

INDEX